Robert E. Lee

ROBERT E. LEE

A Life Portrait

by David J. Eicher

∞

Foreword by Robert E. Lee IV

∞

Introduction by Gary W. Gallagher

Guilford, Connecticut

An imprint of The Rowman & Littlefield Publishing Group, Inc.
4501 Forbes Blvd., Ste. 200
Lanham, MD 20706
www.rowman.com

Distributed by NATIONAL BOOK NETWORK

Frontispiece: An exceptionally crisp copy of the full-length Vannerson pose measures 8¼ ×
11 and was signed by Robert E. Lee. On the verso of this copy Edward D. Valentine wrote,
"sent through blockade to Berlin in modelling a statuette for a bazaar in Liverpool, E.V.
Valentine." *The Valentine Museum, Richmond.*

British Library Cataloguing in Publication Information available

Library of Congress Cataloging-in-Publication Data available

ISBN 978-1-4930-4808-3 (paper: alk. paper)
ISBN 978-1-4616-2506-3 (electronic)

∞™ The paper used in this publication meets the minimum requirements of American
National Standard for Information Sciences—Permanence of Paper for Printed Library
Materials, ANSI/NISO Z39.48-1992.

For my father, a hero in the most modern sense.

———— ∞ ————

Contents

A variant of E. B. D. Julio's famous portrait *The Last Meeting of Lee and Jackson* resides in this colored engraving by Frederick Halpin, accomplished in New York in 1872. Published widely throughout the early period of Lee memorialization, the image recalls one of the high moments of promise for the young Confederacy, when Stonewall was alive and the Army of Northern Virginia, at Chancellorsville, seemed invincible.

Anne S. K. Brown Military Collection, Brown University

Acknowledgments

For reading the manuscript and offering many helpful suggestions, I thank my father John Eicher and friend Gary Gallagher of Penn State University. I thank Gary as well for his generous support in composing an introduction for this volume. His immense knowledge of Civil War history is a treasure. Many thanks to my editor, Michael Emmerich, for his sage guidance through the publishing process. I thank Robert E. Lee IV, General Lee's great-grandson, for contributing the foreword for this volume. As always, I owe deep gratitude to my wife Lynda and son Chris for their enduring support.

For help in obtaining images, I thank Jerry Bloomer, R. W. Norton Art Gallery, Shreveport, La.; Cathy Bogus, National Archives and Records Administration, Bethesda, Maryland; Mary Ellen Brooks, Hargrett Library, University of Georgia, Athens; Julie Cline, Washington and Lee University, Lexington, Va.; Jim Eber, Louis A. Warren Lincoln Library, Fort Wayne, Ind.; Peter Harrington, Anne S. K. Brown Military Collection, Brown University, Providence, R.I.; Corrine P. Hudgins, Museum of the Confederacy, Richmond, Va.; Judith S. Hynson, Jesse Ball duPont Memorial Library, Stratford Hall Plantation, Stratford, Va.; Robert C. Peniston, Washington and Lee University, Lexington, Va.; AnnMarie F. Price, Virginia Historical Society, Richmond, Va.; Teresa E. Roane, Valentine Museum, Richmond, Va.; C. Vaughn Stanley, James G. Leyburn Library, Washington and Lee University, Lexington, Va.; Guy R. Swanson, Eleanor S. Brockenbrough Library, Museum of the Confederacy, Richmond, Va.; Daryl Watson, Galena Historical Museum, Galena, Ill.; and Ron Wilson, Appomattox Court House National Historical Park, Appomattox, Va.

Foreword

It is with great interest that I welcome a modern and comprehensive volume of the photographs and principal portraits and engravings of Robert E. Lee. It has been nearly fifty years since the appearance of the last definitive picture collection of General Lee. Many of the images in this book are familiar, yet others seem fresh to me as they will to the majority of those who follow Civil War history. The many scenes etched into history are present: the last meeting of Lee and Jackson at Chancellorsville, seated in conference on cracker boxes; the famous "lineup" of Confederate general officers wherein everyone appears equal in height except General Lee, who edges out the others by an inch or two; the poignant sketch of commander Lee riding away from the McLean House at Appomattox; and the many crisp wartime photographs in which the General's face and beard age and gray notably in proportion to the awesome weight of his duties with the beloved Army of Northern Virginia.

Yet there are also many images unrelated to those four years of war and strife. The William E. West Portrait showing Lee in his lieutenant's dress uniform is one of the most striking of Lee images. It is also the first, having been painted in 1838. The first image from the life of Robert E. Lee was a daguerreotype made about 1845, which shows the great officer just prior to the Mexican War with Rooney, aged 8. Perhaps the most celebrated postwar image is that taken in Lexington in the autumn of 1866 by Michael Miley, showing the General seated on Traveller. Two of the truly great color portraits of the General are certainly those by John Adams Elder and Theodore Pine.

Dave Eicher has made an exhaustive effort to collect and present the Lee images in this book. He offers a significant text relating to the General's life, including numerous important quotations from letters and other archival sources that tell much of the Lee story in the words of the participants themselves. The fascination with General Lee seems as strong as ever, as the day when Douglas Southall Freeman's mammoth biography first hit the stores — indeed, as strong as the days of the war itself, when the General was idolized by his soldiers and came to represent, well before the war was over, the strength and unity of the Confederacy itself.

After the surrender at Appomattox, General Lee took the presidency of Washington College and settled in Lexington, Virginia, where he lived the remainder of his life. Demonstrating his compassion for students and a genuine desire to educate the next generation, Lee made perhaps his greatest contribution to society in these final five years of his life. The great commander breathed his last on 12 October 1870, and is buried in Lee Chapel at what is now Washington and Lee University.

With productions such as Ken Burns's *The Civil War* on Public Television and the motion picture *Gettysburg*, a whole new generation is coming to grips with the life and legend of Robert Edward Lee. I am truly glad that Dave Eicher's book, which brings together all of the important images of the General and offers a valuable glimpse of Lee the man and Lee the commander, has arrived to help celebrate my great-grandfather's life.

ROBERT E. LEE IV
McLean, Virginia

Preface

Years ago I never would have imagined writing a volume on Robert E. Lee. Such a vast array of literature has emerged focused on the military hero of the South that production of yet another volume might have seemed superfluous. The legendary attributes of General Lee seemed so well-known, the stories of his Civil War exploits so thoroughly ingrained in the American mind. And besides, I am the descendant of a Union private soldier who fought under Grant and Sherman in the western theater and my first interests, on becoming a Civil War enthusiast, lay with Federal strategy in Mississippi, Tennessee, and Georgia.

Then I delved more deeply into the Lee literature. The more I read about Robert E. Lee, the more captivating the reality behind the myth became. When an editor pitched me the idea of doing a modern photographic biography of Lee, it seemed a natural. The last definitive volume of Lee photographs, portraits, and engravings was published more than fifty years ago. *The Face of Robert E. Lee in Life and Legend* by Roy Meredith, published by Charles Scribner's Sons in 1947, stands today as an important reference item in the collections focused on Lee and the Lee family. Yet it is not only hard to obtain but seriously outdated in some respects and in need of great expansion. Of this book, T. Michael Parrish wrote in "The R.E. Lee 200," a 1996 bibliography of Lee publications: "Still the prime reference on Lee in portraiture and photographs, begging to be revised and greatly expanded." The Civil War Centennial years saw the publication of Philip Van Doren Stern's *Robert E. Lee: The Man and the Soldier*, a book including myriad Lee illustrations and photographs and a general text following Lee's life, published by McGraw-Hill in 1963. This work has also long been out of print (even in a Bonanza reprint edition), and the generally unreliable nature of the text and lack of specific data with the illustrations leaves it unsatisfactory for serious Lee students.

Thus, the reason behind *Robert E. Lee: A Life Portrait*. I have scoured the dozen major institutional collections that hold significant Lee material, turning up what I hope to be the now-definitive collection of photographs, important paintings, and important engravings of Lee. The working number now expands to seventy-one photographs, thirty-three paintings, and sixty-five engravings, for a total of 169 images of the General. I have also added 206 photographs, paintings, and engravings of places significant to Lee's life — Mexican War and Civil War battlefields, structures associated with his career, his relatives and companions in arms, and even a small number of relics and statuary of Lee, although I am not attempting to be inclusive with this material. Many of the images of battlefield areas are contemporary with the Civil War period; others are modern, taken by me on battlefield trips. This treatment presents 375 images altogether, twenty-eight reproduced in color.

The captions provide the relevant material of interest for the images. The text, amounting to some 48,000 words, is not meant to provide a systematic biography of Lee. Instead, I have offered a set of enjoyable vignettes reflecting important moments in Lee's life, supported as much as possible by quotations from primary source materials. The gulf between reality and legend in Lee's legacy is wide—by quoting reliable firsthand sources, I have attempted to focus squarely on the contemporary truth. I have also accented the Civil War years, as have most writers, these being the climactic ones in Lee's life. For a systematic biography of Lee, I suggest several works above all others. First, Douglas Southall Freeman's magisterial *R. E. Lee: A Biography* (Scribner's, 1934–1935) is unparalleled in scope and coverage, although it runs nearly 2,400 pages long. For a briefer, modern biography with excellent attributes, consult *Robert E. Lee: A Biography* by Emory M. Thomas (Norton, 1995). For coverage of the wartime strategy of Lee, read Douglas Southall Freeman's *Lee's Lieutenants: A Study in Command* (Scribner's, 1942–1944). An outstanding volume of source documents and original writings on Lee may be found in *Lee the Soldier*, edited by Gary W. Gallagher (University of Nebraska Press, 1996). Students of the Civil War period cannot be without *The Wartime Papers of R. E. Lee*, edited by Clifford Dowdey and Louis H. Manarin (Little, Brown, 1961) and *Lee's Dispatches: Unpublished Letters of General Robert E. Lee, C.S.A., to Jefferson Davis*, edited by Douglas Southall Freeman (Putnam's, 1915: reprint, 1994). Other important Lee letters appear in *Recollections and Letters of General Robert E. Lee* by Robert E. Lee, Jr. (Doubleday, Page, & Co., 1904). A recent, worshipful volume containing superb thoughts about the General exists in *Reflections on Lee: A Historian's Assessment* by Charles P. Roland (Stackpole Books, 1995).

Four recent, sharply analytical works merit close examination by Lee students. They are *God and General Longstreet* by Thomas L. Connelly and Barbara Bellows (Louisiana State University Press, 1982), *Ghosts of the Confederacy* by Gaines M. Foster (Oxford University Press, 1987), *Lee*

Considered: General Robert E. Lee and Civil War History by Alan T. Nolan (University of North Carolina Press, 1991), and *The Marble Man: Robert E. Lee and His Image in American Society* by Thomas L. Connelly (Alfred A. Knopf, 1977: reprint, 1991).

Although much of the Lee story has been embellished by writers even during Lee's lifetime (and particularly in the 1870s following his death), the sterling personality, great accomplishments, high moral courage, and admirable character of this soldier remain standing after the mythology is stripped away. I hope that by assembling the most important imagery of Robert E. Lee, this volume will add something of lasting value to the mountain of Lee literature.

DAVID J. EICHER
Waukesha, Wisconsin

This outstanding photograph was made by Michael Miley about 10 January 1870 and was one of the last images taken of the fabled commander.

Virginia Historical Society, Richmond

Introduction

Late in the nineteenth century a former chaplain in William Tecumseh Sherman's Army of the Tennessee ruminated about Robert E. Lee's stature during the Civil War. "General Lee, of all the Confederate leaders," observed George W. Pepper in his memoir *Under Three Flags* (1899), "held and deserved the foremost place, and commanded more entirely the confidence and approbation of the Southern people." Describing Lee as "the pillar and center of the Rebellion," Pepper added that the general "always displayed, whenever the opportunity offered, high professional ability." Pepper considered it "one of the wonders and mysteries of the age" that "a man of such brilliant talents, of sagacity, of address, of honor, and of an illustrious Revolutionary ancestry, should find a conscientious reason in the doctrine of State rights to engage in a desperate conspiracy against the Union evoked by the sword of Washington."

Pepper's assessment echoed that of many other Northerners who by the early twentieth century praised Lee's generalship and character while lamenting that he had turned his formidable talents to the task of undoing the Union. In admiring Lee as a soldier and private man, these Northerners joined the overwhelming majority of white Southerners. Pepper correctly described Lee as the Confederate people's great military hero during the war, a man who came to embody the Confederacy for untold thousands of Southerners. A handful of Confederates and some Northern officers (including Ulysses S. Grant) insisted, while the fighting still raged, that Lee's reputation was inflated, a view also expressed later by several historians. But the strong consensus during Lee's lifetime and in the nearly thirteen decades since his death has been that he deserves a place in the front rank of American military leaders.

Writings from the war and postwar years highlight Lee's towering reputation in the South as a Christian gentleman of extraordinary martial skill. South Carolinian John Bratton, who commanded a brigade under Lee, offered typical comments about his chief in August 1864. "Distance does not lend enchantment to the old fellows greatness I assure you," Bratton wrote his wife. "The nearer he comes the higher he looms up. It is plain, simple, unaffected greatness." Bratton concluded that "It is just as natural and easy for him to be great as it is for me to be ordinary, and there is probably less affectation about it." A private in A. P. Hill's Third Corps expressed similar faith in Lee to his father, who had expressed doubts about the outcome of the war: "We will have a fine time after the war [and] you must cheer up," wrote Thomas Walker Gilmer in September 1864. "Old Bobie Lee will take care of the cuntry [sic]."

After the war, Lost Cause writers began with a Lee who already was a hero to white Southerners and turned him into an unblemished icon who never erred on the battlefield nor in his personal life. Jubal A. Early, a corps commander in the Army of Northern Virginia during the second half of 1864, stood out as the most visible and influential of the Lost Cause authors. Early praised Lee's pure character and, stressing Confederate disadvantages in manpower and material goods, rhapsodized about what the Army of Northern Virginia had accomplished against the odds. Countless other writers and orators followed Early's example, among them Archer Anderson, who spoke on 29 May 1890, at the unveiling of the monumental equestrian statue of Lee in Richmond. Anderson hoped the monument would "stand as a memorial of personal honor that never brooked a stain, of knightly valor without thought of self, of far-reaching military genius unspoiled by ambition, of heroic constancy from which no cloud of misfortune could ever hide the path of duty!" Let it stand as well, Anderson told the large crowd of listeners, "as a great public act of thanksgiving and praise, for that it pleased Almighty God to bestow upon these Southern states a man so formed to reflect His attributes of power, majesty, and goodness!"

Few historians invoked such obvious religious imagery in writing about Lee, but many reached conclusions about his generalship and character essentially in agreement with those of the Lost Cause school. The most nearly definitive biographical study remains Douglas Southall Freeman's *R. E. Lee: A Biography* (1934–1935), which won a Pulitzer Prize and set a standard against which all other lives of the General would be measured. Freeman saw Lee as an uncomplicated man and brilliant commander whose polestars were Christian humility and duty. It is a measure of the degree to which Lee had been idolized that Freeman, signing his foreword in August 1934, noted that some readers might be put off because his biography failed specifically "to answer some of Lee's detractors." Among more recent works that sustain the traditional view of Lee as an admirable man and warrior, Clifford Dowdey's *Lee* (1965) and Charles P. Roland's *Reflections on Lee: A Historian's Assessment* (1995) stand out as especially useful. Emory M. Thomas's nuanced interpretation in *Robert E.*

Lee: A Biography (1995) also finds much to admire in Lee's personality but questions many elements of his military performance.

The less enthusiastic tradition of writings about Lee began with Northern authors upset with his decision to fight against the Union, continued through postwar accounts by Frederick Douglass and others who believed the ex-rebel leader received too much praise from above the Potomac River, and extended to the present in the form of works critical of Lee's generalship. In the last category, J. F. C. Fuller's *Grant and Lee: A Study in Personality and Generalship* (1933), Thomas L. Connelly's *The Marble Man: Robert E. Lee and His Image in American Society* (1977), and Alan T. Nolan's *Lee Considered: General Robert E. Lee and Civil War History* (1991) have been most influential. These three books offer a variety of criticisms but agree that as a Confederate general Lee accorded too little attention to events outside Virginia, took the strategic and tactical offensive too often, and wasted precious Southern manpower at a such a rate that the Confederacy was bled white well before the end of the war.

Few historians have questioned Lee's character with the same vigor that Fuller, Connelly, Nolan, and others have employed in criticizing his generalship. Except for Connelly, most have taken pains to offer positive assessments of Lee as a person. For example, Nolan asserted that be believed "Robert E. Lee was a great man —able, intelligent, well-motivated and moral, and much beloved by his army." Fuller similarly discussed at length Lee's Christianity, humility, tactfulness, and sense of duty, concluding that some of the more attractive elements of his personality hindered his performance as a general because, among other things, they rendered him unable to deal harshly with wayward subordinates.

How does the written record concerning Lee compare to the pictorial record so ably compiled by Dave Eicher? Readers will find little among the photographs, engravings, and sketches to suggest anything but a heroic soldier and admirable man. The portraits, whether photographic or on canvas, show a handsome and impressive man whose Confederate service clearly hastened the onset of physical decline. The Minnis and Cowell photograph from 1863 captures the General at the peak of his powers, a striking figure, booted and spurred and wearing his sword and field glasses, who looked the part of the Confederacy's hope and idol. The series of studies taken in Richmond by Mathew Brady following Appomattox caught a determined, almost defiant expression on Lee's face. This is especially true of Brady's grouping with Lee seated between Custis Lee on his right and Walter Taylor on his left, wherein the general looks directly at the camera. Theodore Pine's portrait, finished in 1904 and based closely on the Vannerson full-length photographic view from thirty years earlier, conveys the dignity and sense of duty so many authors have emphasized. Even the late photographs, some of which undeniably capture Lee's physical discomfort, leave no doubt about why so many people found Lee to be an imposing figure.

Several themes emerge from the paintings and prints of Lee. Works such as L. M. D. Guillaume's striking *Gen. Robert E. Lee at the Battle of Chancellorsville, Va.* highlight the general's battlefield triumphs. Everett B. D. Julio's *The Last Meeting of Lee and Jackson*, the quintessential Lost Cause image, places the army chief and his greatest lieutenant together on the field at Chancellorsville just before Jackson began his famous flank march. Julio made Lee clearly the dominant figure in his composition, which as an engraving hung in countless Southern homes after the war and enabled former Confederates to recall their heroes at a moment of supreme military success. In prints depicting groups of famous Confederates, notably the widely disseminated *Lee and His Generals* (A. B. Graham Company, 1907) and *Jefferson Davis and His Generals* (Dr. J. Olney Banning and Son, 1890), the arrangement of figures usually confirms Lee's position as the preeminent Southern leader. Still other prints show Lee's more contemplative side, a genre that includes several representations of Lee at the grave of Stonewall Jackson.

Among the images reprinted in *Robert E. Lee: A Life Portrait*, only the *Harper's Weekly* woodcut of Grant whipping Lee in June 1864 could be considered a negative treatment. A few other wartime cartoons from the Northern illustrated press took a similarly hostile stance toward Lee, but the overwhelming majority of the illustrative record presents a far more positive view.

Whatever readers think about Robert E. Lee, they should be grateful that Dave Eicher put together this book. A turn through its pages underscores how photographs and artworks have assisted the printed word in shaping the ways in which Americans interpret Robert E. Lee.

GARY W. GALLAGHER
Penn State University

CHAPTER ONE

The Uneven Start of a Legend

HEN HE ENTERED THE WORLD, ROBERT EDWARD Lee had all the potential for greatness. Born at "Stratford" in Westmoreland County, Virginia, on 19 January 1807, Lee was the son of a hero of the Revolutionary War, a major general in the regular army, and a former governor of Virginia and U.S. congressman. Henry "Light-Horse Harry" Lee (1756–1818) had also become famous for eulogizing his old commander and close friend George Washington by drawing resolutions for John Marshall that contained the phrase, "first in war, first in peace, and first in the hearts of his countrymen." Lee repeated the phrase in a speech at Philadelphia on 26 December 1799, marking the high point of his career. By the time of Lee's birth, his father's star was already rapidly declining, for reasons that will be discussed.

Light-Horse Harry's first wife Matilda Lee (1763–1790) was his cousin and inherited the magnificent estate at Stratford. On 18 June 1793 he married Anne Hill Carter (1773–1829) of the wealthy family that lived on the James River at "Shirley." (The spelling of Anne's name is often given as "Ann," but I am using as an authority for the spelling Anne handwritten documents I have inspected by Lee family members including Robert E. Lee.) The fifth child of this second union of Light-Horse Harry's would rise from his Virginia upbringing to become one of the greatest heroes of world history. The story of Lee's life is steeped in irony, in apparent contradiction, and of course in grandeur.

Henry "Light-Horse Harry" Lee (1756–1818), Lee's father, painted about 1850 by William E. West or Ernst Fisher after Gilbert Stuart. A hero of the Revolution and former governor of Virginia, Light-Horse Harry abandoned his family after Lee's birth and drifted, father and son never forging a relationship.

Robert E. Lee IV, McLean, Va.

That he took the path of becoming a soldier probably reflects both admiration for his father (although they never knew each other as adults), Washington, and Lafayette, and the fact that in an extensive family studded with privilege and money, Lee's branch turned out to be the poorest one. In any case, he achieved a sterling record at West Point, placing second in the class of 1829, and performed important engineering duties in a variety of places before the Mexican War. During this conflict Lee served on the staff of Winfield Scott, the war's greatest hero, and was admired by Scott as "the very best soldier I ever saw in the field."[1] During part of the 1850s Lee served as superintendent of West Point. And then the war came.

Although he had been fiercely loyal to the army and the Federal government, in 1861 Lee could not turn against his family and his native state. He declined an unofficial "offer" to head what became the army led by Irvin McDowell at First Bull Run (a com-

A print published in 1886 by Mrs. B. A. Marshall shows the Lee genealogy as a tree with a complex set of branches and is decorated with vignettes of Stratford Hall and Lee Chapel and surrounding buildings at Washington and Lee University.

Library of Congress

mand he probably would not have received, anyway). Instead, Lee accepted command of the Virginia Militia, oversaw military operations in western Virginia and in South Carolina, served as a military advisor to Jefferson Davis, and by a quirk of fate took command of the Army of Northern Virginia when his friend Joe Johnston was wounded at Seven Pines. After saving the Confederate capital from McClellan's invading hordes, Lee became a national hero, though he did not become legendary until later in the war. Despite increasingly ill health, Lee led his great eastern army throughout three years of war until surrendering to Grant at Appomattox in April 1865. During the final year of the struggle Lee and his army had become synonymous with the Confederacy itself—on his surrender, the universal perception was that all was lost. Only a few weeks prior to the war's end did Lee become general-in-chief of all Confederate armies in the field.

Richard Henry Lee (1732–1794), born at Stratford, was Lee's first cousin, twice removed. A continental congressman, he signed the Declaration of Independence, and vigorously opposed adoption of the U.S. Constitution. *Independence National Historical Park, Philadelphia*

After contemplating life as a gentleman farmer, Lee in 1865 accepted the presidency of Washington College in Lexington, Virginia, and settled there with his family for the remaining five years of his life. During this period his magnanimous personality and charitable, level-headed logic guided his important wishes for educating the young people of the South. Once defeated, he preached conciliation and worked to discourage anti-government sentiment during the early postwar years.

The greatest irony of Lee's life is that despite having failed at his most famous endeavor, having in fact been militarily vanquished, he is revered perhaps more than any other American military figure—perhaps more than U. S. Grant, who defeated him. In Civil War circles, he ranks together with Abraham Lincoln as the two most celebrated figures of the period.

Much of this admiration stems from one who apparently stuck to his principles against all odds and made a monstrous effort to achieve the near-impossible. As we will see, part of this perception comes from the 1870s myth-building of Lee as ex-Confederates continued to fight the war on paper. Part of this admiration comes from the viewing of Lee as a representative of old American aristocracy. Indeed, in an age with vastly fewer people in the country and with those in certain circles often intermarrying, Lee has an astonishing set of relatives, especially if one searches long and hard enough. We have seen that his father and mother were from well-known, distinguished Virginia families.

Stratford, one of the most luxurious plantation houses in Virginia, the birthplace of Lee. At age three, Lee was forced to move with his family due to Light-Horse Harry's financial woes. This photograph was made during the 1860s.

National Archives and Records Administration

The connection to Washington solidified, as we will see, when Lee married Mary Anne Randolph Custis (1807–1873), the only daughter of George Washington Parke Custis (1781–1857), grandson of Martha Washington. In 1831, then, Lee became a great-grandson-in-law, by an adoption, of George Washington.

The circle of notable, wealthy, and powerful relatives did not stop there. Charles Lee (1758–1815), Washington's attorney general, was Lee's uncle. Richard Henry Lee (1732–1794), born at Stratford, was a first cousin, twice removed. Remembered chiefly as a signer of the Declaration of Independence, he also served as a continental congressman and subsequently opposed adoption of the U.S. Constitution on a variety of grounds. His brother Francis Lightfoot Lee (1734–1797) also was born at Stratford and signed the Declaration. Richard Lucian Page (1807–1901), a captain in the Confederate navy and a Confederate brigadier general, was Lee's first cousin; Edwin Gray Lee (1836–1870), a Confederate colonel (whose commission as brigadier general was never confirmed), was a first cousin, once removed; Samuel Phillips Lee (1812–1897), an acting Rear Admiral U.S.N., was a third cousin; Confederate Maj.

Gen. Fitzhugh Lee (1835–1905) was a nephew; Fitzhugh's father Sidney Smith Lee (1802–1869) was Lee's brother and became a captain in the Confederate navy; Samuel Cooper (1798–1876), ranking general of the Confederate armies, was a brother-in-law; and two of Lee's sons became Confederate major generals: George Washington Custis Lee (1832–1913) and William Henry Fitzhugh Lee (1837–1891).

More collateral relatives among the Civil War era personalities include Richard Lee Turberville Beale (1819–1893), a Confederate brigadier general, who was a third cousin-in-law, twice removed; Francis Preston Blair, Jr. (1821–1875), a Union major general, a third cousin-in-law; Francis Preston Blair, Sr. (1791–1897), a member of Andrew Jackson's "kitchen cabinet," a third cousin-in-law, once removed; Montgomery Blair (1813–1883), Lincoln's first postmaster general, a third cousin-in-law; George Bibb Crittenden (1812–1880), C.S.A. major general, a fourth cousin; John Jordan Crittenden (1787–1863), the Kentucky politician and U.S. Senator, a fourth cousin-in-law, once removed; Thomas Leonidas Crittenden (1819–1893), Union major general, a fourth cousin; Thomas Turpin Crittenden (1825–1905), Union brigadier general, a fourth cousin-in-law; Jefferson Finis Davis (1808–1889), the Confederate president, a fourth cousin-in-law; William Nelson Pendleton (1809–1883), C.S.A. brigadier general

A view of Alexandria in the early nineteenth century, showing the Lee House on Oronoco Street near center and the Potomac River in the background.
National Archives and Records Administration

and Lee's nominal artillery chief (and who vaguely resembled Lee), was the father of a first cousin-in-law, once removed; George Wythe Randolph (1813–1867), Confederate secretary of war, a fourth cousin-in-law; and Frank Wheaton (1833–1903), Union brevet major general, a nephew-in-law.

More distant relatives yet include presidents Stephen Grover Cleveland, Benjamin Harrison, William Henry Harrison, Thomas Jefferson, James Madison, James Monroe, James Knox Polk, Franklin D. Roosevelt, Theodore Roosevelt, Zachary Taylor, Martin Van Buren, and—hold onto your hats, fans of the Army of Northern Virginia—Ulysses S. Grant. Distant relatives among the Civil War era personalities, including other prominent officers, are John C. Breckinridge, George Davis, William M. Dunn, John B. Floyd, John B. Gordon, John B. Grayson, Wade Hampton, Eppa Hunton, Thomas J. Jackson, Albert Sidney Johnston, Joseph E. Johnston, Robert G. H. Kean, John Love, Christopher Gustavus Memminger, William H. F. Payne, Leonidas Polk, William Preston, James E. Slaughter, Edmund Kirby Smith, James E. B. Stuart, Joseph Pannell Taylor, Richard Taylor, Allen Thomas, Daniel Tyler, John Henry Winder, Robert Crook Wood, Jr., and Robert Crook Wood, Sr.

Other notables with distant connections to Lee include Patrick Henry; John Marshall; and Queen Elizabeth II, Alexandra

In 1811 Lee moved with his parents and five siblings to the final home owned by Light-Horse Harry, at 607 Oronoco Street in Alexandria. Built in 1795, the structure housed Anne Carter Lee and children until 1825, the year Lee went to West Point.

David J. Eicher

Mary Windsor. See Appendices 2 and 3 for descriptions of these relationships.

During the early days, however, virtually all of these relationships were yet to be forged. The General's lineage is usually regarded as what has come to be called the Shropshire Antecedence, English origins traceable back to Reyner de Lega (*ca.* 1200) of Shropshire, England. Variant names for this gentleman included Lee, which descendants adopted, and which means on the lee or protected side of a mountain range or, alternatively, a clearing, or cultivated field, or meadowland. Most sources including the nineteenth-century Lees who worked on genealogy believed that the first American Lee, Richard Lee I (1618–1664), called "The Emigrant" because he came to Virginia, was descended from Reyner de Lega. A recent, prominent historian has suggested an alternative ancestry, however, called the Worcester Antecedence. See Appendix 2 for a description of these lineages.

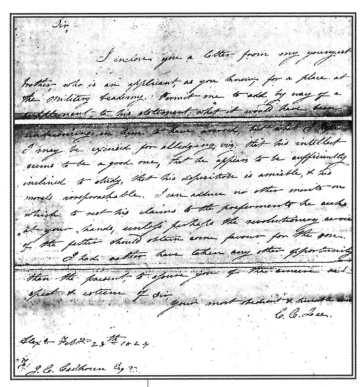

Lee's older brother Charles Carter Lee (1798–1871) wrote Secretary of War John C. Calhoun on 28 February 1824, urging his brother's acceptance as a cadet at West Point. C. C. Lee said of his brother: "His intellect seems to be a good one . . . his disposition is amiable, and his morals irreproachable."

National Archives and Records Administration

Two generations after The Emigrant settled in Virginia came the origins of Stratford. Now one of the most beautifully preserved plantations in Virginia, Stratford (or Stratford Hall) was the brainchild of Thomas Lee (1690–1750), acting colonial governor of Virginia. In the late 1730s he began construction of the massive brick house on part of the 16,000 acres of land under his ownership. Gracefully overlooking the Potomac River, the structure resembles a twin blockhouse with towers consisting of four chimney columns joined by a central great hallway, giving the house an H-shaped layout. The house's spacious and classic architecture and expansive, surrounding gardens and vistas make it a great sensory pleasure.

And so it was when the infant Lee spent his first days in a crib that still rests in the master bedroom. The plantation had passed through the Lee family until Phillip Ludwell Lee's death (1726–1775), when his daughter Matilda, Light-Horse Harry's first wife, inherited the property. Matilda bore four children, Nathaniel Greene Lee (1788–?), Lucy Grymes Lee (1786–1860), Henry Lee IV (1787–1837), nicknamed "Blackhorse Harry," and Philip Ludwell

On 1 April 1824 Lee wrote the Secretary of War John C. Calhoun, accepting his appointment to West Point.

National Archives and Records Administration

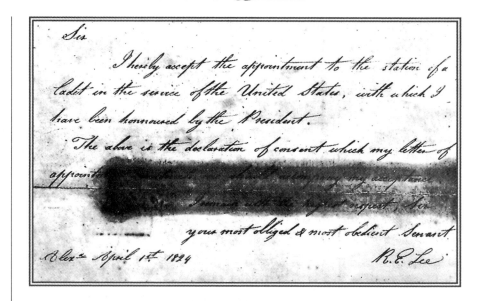

Lee (1789–1794?). On Matilda's death in 1790, Light-Horse Harry received an interest in the plantation.

The tragic story of Light-Horse Harry Lee baffles the mind. How could one fall so far so fast? Light-Horse Harry entered military service less than a month prior to the signing of the Declaration of Independence. On 18 June 1776, Lee became Captain of Company A, Virginia Dragoons, a unit of mounted infantry. This company was attached to and formed part of the First Continental Dragoons on 31 March 1777.

Light-Horse Harry won plaudits from the Continental Congress for his Revolutionary War service, acting as Washington's cavalry chief. By the Act of 7 April 1778, it was "Resolved, whereas Captain Henry Lee, of the Light Dragoons, by the whole tenor of his conduct during the last campaign, has proved himself a brave and prudent officer, rendered essential service to his country, and acquired to himself and the corps he commanded distinguished honor, and, it being the determination of Congress to reward merit, Resolved, that Captain H. Lee be promoted to the rank of major commandant; that he be empowered to augment his present corps by enlistment of two troops of horse, to act as a separate corps."

On 21 October 1780, Lee's battalion was designated Lee's Partisan Corps, and Lee was commissioned lieutenant colonel in the Continental army to rank from 21 October 1780. He served to the close of the war.

With the glories of the Revolution behind him, he experienced a shock in 1790 when his wife Matilda died. Two years later he was inaugurated governor of Virginia and went to live in Richmond. After his marriage to Anne Hill Carter on 18 June 1793, his wife spent much time at Shirley, her ancestral home. Despite this, they had six children, Algernon Sidney Lee (1795–1796), Charles Carter Lee (1798–1871), Ann Kinloch Lee (1800–1864), Sidney Smith Lee (1802–1869), Robert Edward Lee (1807–1870), and Catherine Mildred Lee (1811–1856). While governor, in 1794, Light-Horse Harry headed the army that put down the Whiskey Rebellion. After his tenure as governor, in 1796, the family moved to Stratford, and shortly thereafter their first child died. On 19 July 1798, Light-Horse Harry was commissioned major general in the Regular Army. In 1799 he entered Congress, and the move marked the beginning of the downfall of his fortunes. The U.S. Congress honored Lee by the Act of 24 September 1799. It was "Resolved that the Thanks of Congress be given to Major Lee for the remarkable prudence, address, and bravery displayed in the attack on the enemy's fort and work at Powles' Hook, and that they approve the humanity shewn in circumstances prompting to severity, as honorable to the arms of United States, and correspondent to the noble principles on which they were assumed, and that a gold medal emblematic of this affair be struck under the direction of the Board of Treasury, and presented to Major Lee."

Light-Horse Harry had for some time been plagued by debt and besieged by creditors. His poor financial dealings, ridiculous land speculation investments, spendthrift nature, and other assorted problems brought the family to the brink of financial ruin more than once. Fortunately, Anne Carter Lee's own substantial family money could be brought to bear at certain critical times. But by 1808 and 1809, when the infant Lee lived chiefly in the master bedroom and the adjoining nursery at Stratford, Light-Horse Harry was imprisoned as a debtor, first in the Westmoreland County Jail and later at Spotsylvania Court House, near which fifty-five years later his son would fight a great battle. The family appeared to be falling to pieces. Light-Horse Harry used the time to write *Memoirs of the War in the Southern Department of the United States*, published in 1812.[2] The senior male member of the household at Stratford was now twenty-two-year-old Blackhorse Harry. Anne Carter Lee determined to move from Stratford, and in 1811 the family, Light-Horse Harry having been released, moved to Alexandria, a town of 7,500 steeped in the history of George Washington. Two iron angels graced the fireplace in Stratford's nursery; according to family tradition, the last thing three-year-old Robert E. Lee did before leaving Stratford was to tell his two angel friends "goodbye."

The Lee House at 607 Oronoco Street in Alexandria was the last owned by Light-Horse Harry. Here Robert E. Lee grew up and found a direction in life. It certainly did not come from his father, however. Taking an unpopular stand against the War of 1812, Light-Horse Harry helped to defend a friend's press in Baltimore, the *Federal Republican*, against an angry mob in July 1812. Imprisoned again, he was attacked in jail and suffered severe injuries from which he never fully recovered. Virtually broke and in failing health, Light-Horse Harry retreated to the West Indies for his "health." Several years later, dying, he attempted to return to his family, but expired at "Dungeness," the plantation of his Revolutionary War commander, Nathaniel Greene, at Cumberland Island, Georgia. The date was 25 March 1818. Amazingly, the father never really got to know his youngest son, who was 11 years old when his stranger-father died. The last time Lee had *seen* his father was when he was six. Years later Lee would visit his father's grave, twice in fact, and write letters about it. When in his old age Lee was editing a new edition of his father's memoir, he wrote of Light-Horse Harry's last days. His father "sank rapidly, and his last effort at communication with this world, was to send a message, which, after many attempts, he failed to make comprehensible. . . . [He] thus faded from the world, like the sun from the horizon, in a last lingering radiation of life and love."[3] In 1913 Light-Horse Harry's remains were reunited with those of his son in Lexington, Virginia.

Because Lee's father figure was essentially absent even when he was alive, the younger Lee created a replacement. The shadow of George Washington loomed large over the Lee family at Stratford, due to Light-Horse Harry's connection in the war, and the whole town of Alexandria was infested with the Washington tradition. Besides being the national hero, Washington was a per-

On 21 August 1829 Lee wrote Secretary of War John H. Eaton, accepting his appointment (and subsequent commission) as brevet second lieutenant, U.S.A. in the corps of engineers. "I was born in Westmoreland County in the State of Virginia," he added.

National Archives and Records Administration

sonal hero of Light-Horse Harry's. "The fame and memory of his chief was the fondly-cherished passion to which he clung amid the wreck of his fortunes," wrote George Washington Parke Custis of Light-Horse Harry's later days. "[It was] the hope, which gave warmth to his heart when all else around him seemed cold and desolate."[4] Like father, like son: Lee adopted Washington as a personal hero and incorporated the best Washingtonian ideals into his emerging personality.

Lee's schooling was progressing well. He had spent some time with his cousins at the Carter family school in Fauquier County and he presumably had an active life of sport, riding, swimming, and hunting around Alexandria. About 1820 Lee entered William B. Leary's School on Washington Street. His brother Sidney joined the navy; much older brother Charles returned from Harvard and established a law practice in Washington. Anne Carter Lee was now becoming an invalid, and Lee's sister Ann was frequently ill with nervous disorders. In 1824 the Marquis de Lafayette visited Alexandria and called on the Lee household. About this time Lee decided he wanted to be a soldier. At Benjamin Hallowell's School during the winter of 1824–1825, he impressed his teacher as "a most exemplary student in every respect. He was never behind-time at his studies; never failed in a single recitation; was perfectly observant of the rules and regulations of the institution; was gentlemanly, unobtrusive, and respectful."[5]

The diligent work led to attainment of Lee's goal: an appointment to the U.S. Military Academy at West Point. He secured the appointment in part due to the debt government officials felt toward Light-Horse Harry.[6] He became a cadet on 1 July 1825. The program of studies included mathematics, natural philosophy, drawing, engineering, chemistry and mineralogy, rhetoric and moral philosophy, French, tactics, and artillery. Lee amassed a sterling record, graduating second of forty-six in the class of 1829 and receiving no demerits. As such, he was commissioned brevet second lieutenant, U.S.A. to rank from 1 July 1829, and assigned to the corps of

Following West Point, Bvt. 2d Lt. Lee was ordered to Cockspur Island, Georgia, near Savannah, to help engineer the construction of Fort Pulaski. The project would produce one of the largest brick masonry forts in North America.

David J. Eicher

This sketch by Lee made in 1830 shows Cockspur Island and Fort Pulaski and was based on surveying done on-site in 1829.

National Archives and Records Administration

engineers, the most prestigious arm of the service. After graduating, Lee continued vigorously with his studies, deepening his appreciation of military theory, especially that of the prominent Swiss military educator Antoine H. Jomini. This adherence to a self-study program was unusual at the time.[7] He received his diploma, a two-month furlough, $103.58, and orders to report in August to Cockspur Island, Georgia.

And then came another tragedy. On 26 July 1829 Anne Hill Carter Lee, careworn and exhausted from her family trials, died at Ravensworth, another Lee family home. Staying around Georgetown until October to settle his mother's estate and reassemble the family, Lee set off for coastal Georgia late that month. Arriving in Savannah about 1 November, he began seventeen months of engineering work, helping to supervise what would become Fort Pulaski, one of the premier brick masonry forts in North America. Ironically, the Federal bombardment of Fort Pulaski in 1862 would undo the military usefulness of such forts. But for now, Lee's work on the fort, though forcing habitation in a drab and desolate spot, forged the start of a useful record in the peacetime army.

Before the year was out he would have to endure one more family scandal, that of his half-brother Blackhorse. An adherent to Andrew Jackson, Blackhorse Harry was offered the post of U.S. consul to Morocco. But before he left the United States it became public knowledge that he had had an affair with his wife's sister, producing a child who died at birth. Condemnation was universal and Senate confirmation of his appointment was out of the question. The family seemed discredited, and Lee must have entered the year 1830 wishing for a new family identity of his own.

CHAPTER TWO

A Man's Life in the Army

THE MONOTONOUS WORK OF DESIGNING AND
constructing Fort Pulaski ground on through the year 1830,
except for a hiatus for most of the garrison during the
summer due to the intense heat and increased danger of disease
from mosquitoes. Lee spent time with friends in the Washington
area and acquainted himself with one Mary Randolph Custis
(1807–1873), an eligible young lady who lived with her parents at
"Arlington." The stately mansion, built 1802–1817, offered a commanding overlook of Washington City and the Potomac. Lee
later described it as a house "anyone might see with half an
eye." And its associations with Washington were overpower-
ing. Mary's father George Washington Parke Custis
(1781–1857) was the step-grandson of George Washington. The
grandson of Martha Washington and her first husband, Daniel
Parke Custis, he was raised after Daniel Custis's death by
Martha and George at Mount Vernon. A self-appointed gentleman of leisure and part-time artist and playwright, Custis maintained what amounted to a shrine to his celebrated
step-grandfather throughout Arlington. Washington relics littered
tables and were stored away for occasional show. Custis's wife,
Mary Lee Fitzhugh Custis (1788–1853), maintained the home in an
immaculate manner and doted over young Mary, their only child
to survive infancy.

Originally, the acquaintance between Lee and young Mary

The first portrait of Lee was painted by
William E. West in 1838. The image
shows him in the dress uniform of a
first lieutenant of engineers. For a color
reproduction, see the color photograph
section.

Valentine Museum, Richmond

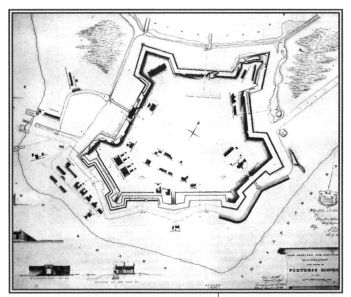

Lee's superior and friend Andrew Talcott drew this map of Fort Monroe, where Lee arrived on 7 May 1831. Seven weeks later Lee married Mary Randolph Custis, and a family was not long in following.

National Archives and Records Administration

Custis developed because their mothers were cousins. Entranced by the young Mary Custis, Lee in 1830 courted her at Arlington and followed her to "Chatham" near Fredericksburg, an estate formerly belonging to Mary's mother's family. The elder Mary Custis was encouraging of Lee's pursuit; her father was skeptical of the twenty-three-year-old army officer. He knew all about the dark past of that branch of the Lee family and wanted a wealthy suitor for his daughter. As Lee spoke eloquent phrases to Mary on the ridge opposite Fredericksburg, he could not have begun to envision that thirty-two years later he would orchestrate a great battle raging over the whole town and landscape below.[1]

Instead, Lee returned by packet boat to Cockspur Island. When he arrived on 11 November, Lee was hardly pleased. "The late gale has destroyed the embankment in several places around the Island, and that across the mouth of the canal has entirely been washed away," he wrote Charles Gratiot, the army's chief engineer. "The wharf from its exposed situation has been so much injured, as I fear to be beyond repair."[2] Progress on rebuilding the fort was slow. "Since my arrival here I have been engaged in repairing the embankments, etc.," he wrote Gratiot on 1 December. "And [I] have succeeded in stopping the water off that half of the Island, where our operations are carried on."[3] Soon thereafter 2d Lt. Joseph K. F. Mansfield arrived at the fort as superintendent. Early in 1831 Mansfield determined that plans for Fort Pulaski would need to be reworked, and this allowed Lee to travel back north. Ordered to Fort Monroe at Old Point Comfort, Virginia, Lee arrived on 7 May.[4]

The construction of Fort Monroe had been underway for 12 years when Lee arrived. It was largely completed, but required the construction of approaches and outworks. Vast physical work on the fort still remained: moving dirt, digging and filling the moat, and adding to the structure itself. Additionally, Lee helped to oversee construction of the "rip-raps" that would become Fort Calhoun and later Fort Wool, by piling uncountable numbers of boulders onto the foundation of this diminutive rock pile a mile out into Hampton Roads. Lee's commanding officer was Bvt. Col. Abram Eustis; his closest friend was Capt. Andrew Talcott.

About the time he arrived at Fort Monroe, Lee had the occasion to spend some time at Arlington, and enjoyed one afternoon of reading a novel of Walter Scott's to Mary and her mother. Seizing the opportunity to confront Mary in the dining room, in front of a fruitcake, Lee asked Mary to marry him, and she said yes.[5] Parke Custis assented, withdrawing his reservations in the face of female solidarity, and the marriage was planned for 30 June.

The families initiated a grandiose set of preparations for the big event, inviting important guests and bridesmaids and the Rev. Reuel Keith. A rainstorm unleashed itself on the hills and valley in view of Arlington and despite this unhappy weather, the marriage proceeded happily inside the house, Lee later writing that "[The minister] had few words to say, though he dwelt upon them as if he had been reading my death warrant, and there was a tremulousness in the hand I felt that made me anxious for him to end."[6] The ceremony had somewhat of a comic overtone because Keith, a tall, thin man, had been drenched on his way to the house. The only replacement clothes to be found were Parke Custis's, and he was a short man "of unequal proportions."[7] Thus, the minister wore a hopelessly ill-fitting suit as he conducted the marriage.

The marriage was of course a key event in Lee's life. During most of their married years the Lees lived with the Custis family in the house at Arlington. As with his father, Lee had married into an influential and wealthy branch of a familiar family and gained entry into an impressive estate because of it. The influence of Arlington would deepen his appreciation of Washington and reverence for the general. Inside this shrine to Washington, his own family would take form. Although Lee would be gone for major portions of the coming years, Mary Custis Lee would bear seven children over the period 1832–1846. In many ways Mary forged a striking contrast to her husband. She was personally careless of her appearance and her housekeeping style was negligent at best. She was destined to become an invalid, stricken with a variety of ailments more severe than those of Lee's mother, primarily rheumatism, arthritis, and

What is almost certainly the first photograph of Lee shows the army officer with his son Rooney about 1845, perhaps in the autumn of that year. This daguerreotype was probably made in New York, possibly at Brady's studio, and shows Lee at age thirty-eight and Rooney at age eight. The original has been lost; fortunately, Michael Miley copied it in Lexington during the late 1860s.

Virginia Historical Society, Richmond

the effects of child-bearing illnesses that would confine her to a wheelchair. She was forgetful and habitually late. But she loved Lee and was devoted to him.

In August 1831 the newlyweds arrived at Fort Monroe and spent the first few days of what turned out to be a three-year residence. Shortly thereafter, Eustis discovered a reported insurrection of slaves taking place in Southampton County, some forty miles from Norfolk. A detachment of several companies of artillery departed only to find that despite the murders of nearly sixty white Virginians, the uprising had fizzled. Lee did not accompany the expedition, which provided the most noteworthy event of the stay at Fort Monroe. Part of the fallout from this scare was to increase the fort's garrison to 680 men.[8]

Late in 1840 Lee inspected Fort Macon near Beaufort, North Carolina, a post in need of repair. Water seeping into the fort had damaged walls and foundations, producing worries in Washington.

Library of Congress

Life at the fort continued with its rather mundane characteristics. The Lees were a happy couple, however, and their new life together was emotionally uplifting for both. One of the new officers at the fort was Joseph Eggleston Johnston, a friend of Lee's from his West Point days and destined to be a close future companion and fellow Confederate general. They spent a fair amount of joyous time together until the Christmas holidays interrupted and the Lees journeyed to Shirley and Arlington. Mary apparently stayed at Arlington after the holidays, and Lee and Johnston formed a close bond back at Fort Monroe.[9] The two officers were kindred spirits in that, unlike many of the fort's officers, they abstained from drinking, smoking, and gambling.

When the weather warmed somewhat, Mary returned to Fort Monroe. Despite her occasional sicknesses and travels away from the fort, Mary gave birth at Fort Monroe to the couple's first baby, a son, on 16 September 1832. George Washington Custis Lee

(1832–1913) was named for his grandfather. He was as an infant called "Boo," and Lee wrote shortly after his birth that "Master Custis is the most darling boy in the world."[10] For the sake of distinguishing him from other family members, the group would come to call him simply Custis.

Having been blessed with Custis's arrival, Lee now found a favorable situation developing professionally. On 19 July 1832, Special Orders No. 62, issued from the Adjutant General's Office, announced the promotion of Lee to second lieutenant, U.S.A., to rank from 1 July 1829, the date of his brevet commission. Additionally, Talcott, who had also gone to Fort Monroe from the fledging Fort Pulaski, was away from the fort much of the time during the next three years. This provided Lee with the opportunity not merely to assist but to supervise the daily operations. Cholera had reduced the available work force in 1832 and slowed the work pace through 1833. As warm weather spread over Virginia in 1834, Lee rode from Arlington to Fort Monroe overland, initiating a more gregarious season of hard work on the

Lee may have inspected Fort Caswell, North Carolina, near the end of 1840. The dikes protecting Caswell and Oak Island, south of Cape Fear, had been damaged by storms in 1835. Such mundane service marked this period of Lee's career.
National Archives and Records Administration

Lee spent much of the period 1841–1846 at Fort Hamilton, New York, at the western end of Long Island. The period was dull and uneventful in military terms and must have left Lee longing for the adventure that followed in the Mexican War.
Library of Congress

remaining construction. This occurred despite facing uncertain appropriations from the Jackson administration, and the pile of stone now called Fort Calhoun, the rip-raps out in Hampton Roads, sank by three inches per year. Constructing the fort seemed, then, impossible. During this period Lee earned as an annual compensation $1,113.40.[11]

In early autumn 1834 Lee was assigned to focus on constructing Fort Calhoun. And then, in November, he was abruptly ordered to report to Washington as assistant to the chief of engineers, Gratiot. Lee did not like office work, and he viewed the situation as temporary. It allowed him to be close to Arlington and focus somewhat more on his family, however, which was about to increase in size again. In this eventful year Lee had traveled to the Great Lakes to formulate a report relating to the dispute between Ohio and Michigan Territory over boundaries. Meanwhile, on 12 July 1835, Mary Custis Lee gave birth at Arlington to the Lees' first daughter, also named Mary Custis Lee (1835–1918). Lee returned in October and went to Ravensworth, where his wife was ill in bed from the effects of childbirth. She was unable to walk until early 1836.[12] Lee's brother and naval officer Sidney Smith Lee, who went by Smith Lee, had been married the previous year. On 19 November his first child was born, a son, Fitzhugh Lee (1835–1905), and Lee had a new nephew. This occurred at "Clermont" in Fairfax County.

Frustration grew in Lee's mind. He was becoming bored with the routine duties of frontier engineering, disliked paperwork, and his friend Talcott had resigned for a more lucrative position as an engineer in civilian life. He wrote Talcott on 2 February 1837: "You ask what are my prospects in the Corps? Bad enough—unless it is increased and something done for us."[13] He wrote this despite his commission as first lieutenant to rank from 21 September 1836, proclaimed in Special Orders No. 46, Adjutant General's Office, 1 November 1836. He had finally fully advanced beyond the grade that had accompanied him out of West Point. In the spring of 1837 would come another addition to the growing Lee family: William Henry Fitzhugh Lee (1837–1891) was born at Arlington on 31 May. He was named for his wife's uncle, William Henry Fitzhugh of Ravensworth. Called "Rooney" to distinguish

On 16 February 1846 Lee wrote directly to the adjutant general of the army, Roger Jones, seeking a resolution of pay difficulties. Lee had been paid twice for the period May–June 1845. The mix-up had caused Lee "more mortification than any other act of my life," he wrote.

National Archives and Records Administration

him from other Fitzhugh Lees, the youngster would, along with his brother Custis, play a pivotal role in this new generation of the Lee family.

About this time the appropriations of Congress again interceded on Lee's behalf. He got his wish to depart the Washington area and get away from office duty in April 1837, when he received orders to head west to St. Louis, Missouri, to oversee construction of a pier to manage water flow on the Mississippi River. Because Mary Custis Lee was still expecting, Gratiot himself went to St. Louis, his native area, to initiate the project. After Rooney's birth, Lee departed along with another engineering officer, Bvt. 2d Lt. Montgomery C. Meigs, fresh from West Point. Meigs became quartermaster general of the U.S. Army during the Civil War. The two went to Pittsburgh, to Louisville, and on to St. Louis, where they arrived on 5 August. "It is the dearest and dirtiest place I was ever in," Lee later wrote.[14] This, after some perilous episodes on the steamer getting to the city, having had to camp in broken-down log cabins at Des Moines among other adventures. For a philosophical aristocrat from Virginia, it was surely an unusual awakening to the lowly life of the frontier middle west. He would stay in St. Louis on duty, interjected by several trips back to Virginia and winters spent back east, until October 1840. Much of the time he lived on a riverboat as the engineering work on dikes and various waterfront improvements progressed. The work he performed was splendid, and on 12 July 1838, General Orders No. 23, Adjutant General's Department, announced his promotion to captain, U.S.A. to rank from 7 July 1838.

For a diversion from the routine in St. Louis, Lee commenced a project to study his family genealogy. Now 31 and with a family of his own, he was old enough to turn his attention backward in time toward his origins. "I believe I once spoke to you on the subject of getting for me the crest, coat of arms, etc., of the Lee family, and which, sure enough, you never did," he wrote Cassius F. Lee, his cousin in Alexandria, on 20 August. "My object in making the request is for the purpose of having a seal cut with the impression of said coat, which I think

On 1 August 1846, about to head south to participate in the Mexican War, Lee created a will. It provided for Mary Custis Lee, named Custis a co-executor on reaching his twenty-first birthday, and asked for special help for daughter Annie due to her debilitating eye injury.

Leyburn Library, Washington and Lee University

Winfield Scott (1786–1866), general-in-chief of the army and hero of the Mexican War, provided a staff assignment for Lee. Later they would part philosophical ways with the dissolution of the Union.

Library of Congress

is due from a man of my large family to his posterity, and which I have thought, perhaps foolishly enough, might as well be right as wrong."[15] The interest in family was also demonstrated by the Lees in the spring of 1838, when they visited Baltimore and the artist William Edward West painted matching portraits of Lee and Mary Custis Lee. The former constitutes the first image of the future general (see the section of color illustrations). Mary told her mother that the portrait of her husband was "a very admirable likeness and fine painting."

Lee departed once again for the west on 25 May 1839, traveling to Staunton, Cincinnati, Louisville, and finally to St. Louis. Mary was pregnant again, and about 1 July he received word that he had a new daughter, Anne Carter Lee (1839–1862), named for Lee's mother and called "Annie." She was born on 18 June at Arlington. In November of the same year Lee wrote a friend, "Do you know how many little Lees there are now? . . . I am sure to be introduced to a new one every Christmas."[16] Meanwhile, dike building, pile driving, earth and rock moving, and foundation planning for the St. Louis pier moved forward at full speed until it was halted abruptly in late August by a lawsuit brought by landowners on the Illinois side of the river. Perilous results loomed over another engineering project. Work instead concentrated on the Des Moines rapids. Gone for some seven months, Lee returned to Arlington as winter approached and met his new daughter. About this time, when Custis was a very young boy, his father

U.S. forces land on the beach opposite Vera Cruz on 10 March 1847, meeting no resistance from the Mexican troops. Here Lee narrowly escaped injury when a nervous picket fired a pistol at him.

Library of Congress

The naval battery participated in the assault on Vera Cruz, visible in the background. Lee's brother, Sidney Smith Lee, manned the gun shown third from the right.
Library of Congress

recorded an incident. One day in the winter, Lee took Custis for a walk in the snow and Custis lagged behind. He looked over his shoulder and saw Custis imitating his every move, placing his feet in Lee's tracks. "When I saw this," he said later, "I said to myself, 'It behooves me to walk very straight, when this fellow is already following in my tracks.'"[17]

Now 33 years old with a family of four children, Lee spent the period January–April 1840 in the Washington area awaiting a decision on further appropriations for engineering projects. He started west again shortly after 24 July, arriving in St. Louis and overseeing adjustments on the dikes and channels through the next three months. Clearly, his thoughts were turned toward the approach of another baby at home. On 4 September he wrote his wife, "Feeling lonesome . . . and out of sorts, I got on a horse and took a ride. On returning through the lower part of the town, I saw a number of little girls all dressed up in their white frocks and pantalets, their hair plaited and tied up with ribbons, running and chasing each other in all directions. . . . it was the prettiest sight I have seen in the West, and perhaps in my life."[18]

Lee returned to Washington on 22 October and awaited an assignment, pending government appropriations for another project. The chief engineer, Col. Joseph G. Totten, sent him on an inspection tour of two forts in coastal North Carolina. He arrived at Beaufort about 7 November and proceeded to nearby Fort Macon, where he drew up a report on the fort's leaky casemates

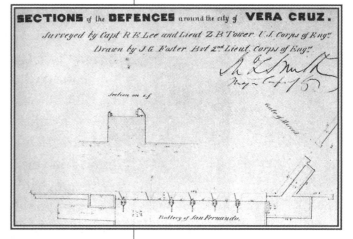

Following the capture of Vera Cruz on 29 March 1847, Lee supervised a survey of the city's defenses, assisted by future Union generals Zealous B. Tower and John G. Foster.
National Archives and Records Administration

At Cerro Gordo on 18 April 1847, Lee first directly encountered the violence of large-scale battle. Wrote Lee: "all their cannon, arms, ammunition, and most of their men fell into our hands. My friend Joe Johnston was wounded."

Library of Congress

and the necessity of a dike to protect part of the fort from flooding. From there the record of his trip is sketchy: supposed to proceed south to Fort Caswell, near the mouth of the Cape Fear River, he may have reached the position but shortly thereafter went home for the holidays. Afterward, rather than returning to North Carolina, he chose to proceed to New York to supervise work on harbor fortifications, and he reached the city on 10 April 1841.[19] As he traveled, the visions of little girls in St. Louis came back to him again when he learned that on 27 February his wife, at Arlington, had given birth to another baby girl, this one named Eleanor Agnes Lee (1841–1873). She would subsequently be known simply as "Agnes."

Completed in 1831, Fort Hamilton, New York, his new home, nonetheless required major improvements and finishing treatments to bring it up to speed, and Lee's job was to supervise the improvements. He also oversaw work at Fort Lafayette, both forts sitting at "the Narrows" between the upper and lower parts of New York harbor. At the same time, future Union general Henry J. Hunt was an artillerist at Fort Hamilton. He later wrote that Lee "was the vestryman of the little parish church of Fort Hamilton, of which the post-chaplain was the rector, and as thorough in charge of his church as of other duties."[20] During the period, Mary Custis Lee gave birth to the couple's sixth child, Robert Edward Lee, Jr. (1843–1914), born at Arlington on 27 October 1843, and usually called Rob. Lee's stay at Fort Hamilton lasted until mid-1846, when the Mexican War erupted and disrupted the lives of all officers in the U.S. Army. During this period, on 10 February 1846, his seventh and last child was born at Arlington, Mildred Childe Lee (1846–1905), whom Lee called "Precious Life." Successful and admired for his work, Lee was nonetheless restless and bored with the peacetime maintenance of fortifications. "I am very solitary, and my only company is my dog and cats," he wrote his wife on 18 January 1846. "But 'Spec' [a dog] has become so jealous now that he will hardly let me look at the cats. . . . Lies down in the office from eight to four without moving, and turns himself before the fire as the side from it becomes cold."[21] He longed for more excitement from the army than he had thus far received. He was about to get his wish.

Tensions between the United States and Mexico had been flaring for several years. On 9 May Bvt. Brig. Gen. Zachary Taylor forwarded dispatches to Washington announcing that his troops had clashed with Mexican infantry on 25 April along the Rio Grande, inside territory claimed as held by the United States by President Polk. By 13 May Congress declared war on Mexico. Taylor clashed with more troops at Palo Alto and Resaca de la Palma and the president called for 20,000 volunteers to march southward. A flurry of activity broke out among U.S. Army troops, anticipating their active role in the continuing war in a southern, dusty desert. Lee had never yet seen combat. Throughout all this excitement, he sat idle at Fort Hamilton. Until 19 August, that is, when he received orders to report to San Antonio de Bexar, Texas, and join Brig. Gen. John E. Wool's staff as an engineer.

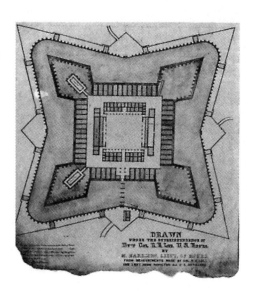

His army career was about to take an abrupt turn. On 31 August he drew up and signed his last will and testament.

Lee reached San Antonio on 21 September, reporting to Wool, the old inspector general who had reviewed his work on the forts near Norfolk (and after whom Fort Wool would be named). The campaign that followed was bloodless. On 28 September 1,954

On 22 April 1847 U.S. troops occupied the castle of Perote, which Lee described as "very strong, with high, thick walls, bastioned fronts, and [a] deep, wide ditch." Lee supervised this engineering drawing of the captured fortification.

National Archives and Records Administration

troops under Wool, accompanied by Lee and other staff officers, moved toward the Rio Grande. The forces met a flag of truce and an armistice, following Taylor's battle at Monterey. This expired, however, and the column pressed on. It penetrated to 365 miles inside enemy territory without seeing a single Mexican soldier in hostile action. Wool turned to attack a force near Saltillo, he believed, but again found no enemy.

About 16 January 1847, Lee's staff assignment changed. He was now ordered to join Maj. Gen. Winfield Scott, commander-in-chief of the army, at Brazos. Now he would see action. "I have been to Tampico," he wrote Custis and Rooney from the USS *Massachusetts*, off Lobos, Mexico, on 27 February. "I saw many things that reminded me of you. The river was so calm and beautiful, and the boys were about in boats, and swimming their ponies.

Heavy action erupted at Churubusco on 20 August 1847, where U.S. forces assaulted a bridgehead protected by a water-filled ditch. Lee served with gallantry.

Library of Congress

. . . We had a grand parade on General Scott's arrival. The troops were all drawn up on the bank of the river, and fired a salute as he passed them."[22] By early March the general staff was chosen. Scott referred to it affectionately as his "little cabinet."[23] It included Totten, the chief of engineers, Ethan Allen Hitchcock, the inspector-general, Henry Lee Scott, the assistant adjutant general, and Lee, the noted engineer.

In February Taylor had defeated the Mexican forces at Buena Vista. But the Mexicans would not surrender, and guerrilla actions broke out, complicating diplomatic solutions. Therefore, Polk ordered Scott to move on Mexico City itself by way of Vera Cruz. Scott's route of landing at Vera Cruz and proceeding to Jalapa, Perote, Puebla, and finally Mexico City would be a long and difficult operation.[24]

Hitchcock recorded in his diary a close call for Lee outside Vera Cruz on 19 March. "Capt. R. E. Lee, one of the engineers, and an admirable officer," he wrote, "had a narrow escape with his life yesterday. Returning from a working party with Lieut. P. T. Beauregard, he turned a point in the path in the bushes, and suddenly came upon one of our soldiers who no doubt mistook him for a Mexican and challenged 'Who comes there?' 'Friends!' said

Captain Lee. 'Officers' said Beauregard at the same time, but the soldier, in trepidation and haste, levelled [sic] a pistol at Lee and fired. The ball passed between his left arm and body,—the flame singeing his coat, he was so near."[25]

The siege of Vera Cruz lasted from 9–29 March. Scott could not afford an immediate attack and so initiated a sustained bombardment of the city and its protective forts. He used several of his own guns along with naval weapons borrowed from the nearby ships. The Mexican commander Santa Anna reinforced defensive positions inland between Vera Cruz and Perote at Cerro Gordo. Scott's army approached this heavily fortified position during the second week of April, Lee taking a lead role in finding a way to turn the enemy's left flank over the rough mountain roads. "Captain Lee has been out all day searching for a path or passes by which the forts on the heights can be turned," wrote Hitchcock on 12 April. "Reports not wholly favorable."[26] Scott himself wrote on 16 April that "The reconnaissances were conducted with vigor under Captain Lee, at the head of a body of pioneers, and at the end of the third day, a passable way for light batteries was accomplished."[27]

The following day Scott divided his force; Brig. Gen. David E. Twiggs followed Lee's guidance in maneuvering through the mountains until he approached a hill called La Atalaya. Against his orders and against Lee's judgment, Twiggs attacked and took the position. But the mismanaged attack and poor coordination allowed the Mexican forces to scatter in retreat. Encamped at

The heavily fortified national military academy at Chapultepec proved a key position in the defense of Mexico City. On 12 September 1847 a massive attack toward the position commenced, Lee having argued against it.

Library of Congress

Finally, on 14 September 1847, Winfield Scott and his staff, Lee included, entered Mexico City. Scott reviewed U.S. troops in the Zócalo, the Aztec's principal square, in the shadow of the Cathedral of Mexico. The Treaty of Guadalupe Hidalgo, signed 2 February 1848, ceded New Mexico and California to the United States.

Library of Congress

Perote on 27 April, Lee recorded, "The advance of the American troops, under Generals Patterson and Twiggs, were encamped at the Plano del Rio, and three miles to their front Santa Anna and his army were intrenched in the pass of Cerro Gordo, which was remarkably strong. . . . On the 17th I led General Twiggs' division in the rear of a hill in front of Cerro Gordo, and in the afternoon, when it became necessary to drive them from the hill where we intended to construct a battery at night, the first intimation of our presence or intentions were known."[28] Later, Scott wrote: "I am compelled to make special mention of the services of Captain R. E. Lee, Engineer. This officer, greatly distinguished at the siege of Vera Cruz, was again indefatigable, during these operations, in reconnaissances as daring as laborious, and of the utmost value. Nor was he less conspicuous in planting batteries, and in conducting columns to their stations under heavy fire of the enemy."[29]

Santa Anna reinforced at Puebla, which Scott approached by early May, scattering the Mexican cavalry and pushing Santa Anna back to Mexico City. He then encamped for three months to await reinforcements. On 7 August Scott began his advance toward the Mexican capital, where he met resistance at El Peñon, a fortified hill ten miles east of the city. "Capt. Robert E. Lee, with an escort of one company of dragoons, made another reconnaissance yesterday afternoon, returning late," wrote Hitchcock on 13 August. "He had been in the direction of Mexicalcingo to see if the city cannot be entered from that way so as to leave the fortifications at the Piñon to the right. He could not push his observations far enough to determine."[30] Four days later he again mentioned Lee: "Captain Lee's reconnaissance today has settled the route of advance in General Scott's mind. He is going southward to Chalco."[31]

Twiggs moved against El Peñon, and the remainder of Scott's army moved to San Augustin by 17 August. On 19 and 20 August attacks erupted at Contreras and Churubusco, the latter concentrating on a strategic bridgehead. "At night Captain Lee—'the' engineer—came to town to report to General Scott the opinion of General Persifor F. Smith that he could make a movement at 3 A.M. and storm the enemy's batteries," wrote Hitchcock. "This plan was approved, and, though it was raining all night, Lee went back and at 3 o'clock this morning the movement commenced."[32] After an armistice, called for by Santa Anna to regroup, Scott attacked on 8 September at El Molino del Rey, wrongly believing it was a cannon foundry.

The crucial attack came at Chapultepec on 13 September, where the huge stone fortress and buildings of the Mexican national military academy proved a formidable position to capture. Wrote Hitchcock on the 12th: "Both Major Smith and Captain Lee, though the latter favored the plan yesterday morning, expressed in the afternoon some doubt whether our guns could do more than demolish the upper part of the building within the main works at Chapultepec and thought an assault with scaling ladders would be necessary to reduce the place."[33] On the 13th Lee, "reeling in his saddle without sleep, rode ahead to reconnoiter the causeway."[34] Scott wrote that Lee "bore important orders for me until he fainted from a wound and the loss of two nights' sleep at the batteries."[35] Lee was slightly wounded on the 13th and had to leave the field due to loss of blood.[36] Victorious, Scott and his staff entered Mexico City the following day and Santa Anna was deposed. On 18 September Scott wrote the secretary of war, William L. Marcy: "At the end of another series of arduous and brilliant operations, of more than forty-eight hours' continuance, this glorious army hoisted, on the morning of the 14th, the colors of the United States on the walls of this palace. . . ."[37] Eventually, the guerrilla warfare died out and the Treaty of Guadalupe Hidalgo ended the war.

In response to the commendations that might come from his service, Lee on 8 April wrote his father-in-law. "I know how these things are awarded at Washington, and how the President will be besieged by clamorous claimants. I do not wish to be numbered among them."[38] Despite his army's victory, Scott was on 18 February 1848 relieved of command and sent home. Lee said he was "turned out like an old horse to die."[39] On 12 June 1848 the last American soldier departed the Mexican capital. For his heroic participation in the Mexican War, Lee received three commissions: brevet major, U.S.A. for Cerro Gordo, Mex., to rank from 18 Apr. 1847; brevet lieutenant colonel, U.S.A. for Contreras and Churubusco, Mex., 20 Aug. 1847; and brevet colonel, U.S.A. for Chapultepec, Mex., 13 Sept. 1847.

The war behind him, Lee returned to Arlington and the pleasures of his family. On 30 June 1848 he wrote his brother Smith Lee. "Here I am, my dear Smith, perfectly surrounded by Mary and her precious children, who seem to devote themselves at staring at the furrows in my face and the white hairs in my head. . . . Some of the older ones gaze with astonishment and wonder at me, and seem at a loss to reconcile what they see and what was pictured in their imaginations."

CHAPTER THREE

∾

The Coming of the War

Fᴏʀ Lᴇᴇ ᴛʜᴇ sᴛᴏʀᴍ ᴄʟᴏᴜᴅs ᴏF ᴏɴᴇ ᴡᴀʀ ʜᴀᴅ ᴘᴀssᴇᴅ,
yet those that would foretell another loomed on the horizon.
On 3 July 1848 he was assigned to duty in the chief engineer
Totten's office in Washington, and he spent much of the summer
redrawing maps made during the Mexican campaigns. He settled into a peaceful routine of enjoying the company of his
family, a relative luxury as evidenced by his earlier duties.
Then, on 13 September, Lee was assigned to duty in
Baltimore to oversee the construction of a new harbor fort
which came to be known as Fort Carroll, after Charles
Carroll, last surviving signer of the Declaration. Several rec-
ommendations had proposed a fort on Sollers's Point Flats
to complement the fabled Fort McHenry, site of the writing
of Francis Scott Key's "Star Spangled Banner." On 15
November he reported to Baltimore, then a bustling city of
200,000, ready for duty.

But no action resulted. Lee was sidetracked on a trip to
Boston with the board of engineers and when he returned the
weather was so cold and materials so scarce that he halted con-
struction plans until the following spring. Returning to
Washington, Lee continued his work on the Mexican War engi-
neering maps and, in January 1849, departed for a surveying trip to
Florida to plan possible coastal forts there, from Pensacola to
Cumberland Island. He returned about 1 April to Baltimore to get

The second portrait of Lee was painted
by Robert W. Weir about 1853. It
depicts him in the uniform of a brevet
colonel of engineers. For a color
reproduction, see the color photograph
section.
The Valentine Museum, Richmond

29

The second photograph of Lee, a cartes-de-visite made by Mathew Brady about 1850–1852, shows the dashing officer in civilian garb prior to his superintendency of West Point. He holds white gloves and a top hat.

Eleanor S. Brockenbrough Library, The Museum of the Confederacy, Richmond

the Fort Carroll project underway, his family following from Arlington shortly thereafter. The Lees moved into a small brick house in Baltimore at 908 Madison Avenue, and the accommodations were a far cry from Arlington. Lee himself wrote that his room was "hardly big enough to swing a cat in."[1]

The work on Fort Carroll commenced. The atmosphere was hot and steamy and swamplike on the shoals between the city and the Patapsco River. Piles had to be driven deep into the mushy bottom to support the fort's masonry walls. Massive granite footings were sunk into the ooze and wharves constructed. Progress sped on rapidly. By late July, however, Lee came down with a feverish illness that was probably malaria.[2] It was his first recorded sickness of significance. He repaired to Ravensworth and then to Arlington until early August, when he returned to Baltimore. He then proceeded to Newport, Rhode Island, for an inspection tour, then to Brooklyn, and finally back to Baltimore by the end of August, having suffered through the whole trip. Thereafter, punctuated by a holiday trip to Arlington and two journeys to Washington, Lee stayed relentlessly on top of the massive construction project.

Relative monotony gave way to a strange episode that developed in the final months of 1849. In New York, Cuban revolutionaries were planning to assault Cuba and looked long and hard for a competent U.S. military officer to lead the unlikely expedition. The plan was hatched chiefly by Narciso López, a Spanish general and later a Cuban patriot. A force of several hundred men assembled at Round Island, near Pascagoula, and President Taylor then issued a proclamation prohibiting the invasion of any friendly country from American soil. Still searching for a leader, López offered the command to Jefferson Davis about February 1850, who declined but recommended Lee. After checking with Davis, he also declined.[3]

By midsummer 1850 Custis emulated his father's career by applying to West Point, where he won a cadetship "at large," in part due to his father's political influence. His younger brother Rooney looked toward the academy as well. On 4 May Lee wrote Custis: "So long as I . . . see [my children] strive to respond to my wishes, and exertions, for their good and happiness I can meet with calmness and unconcern all else the world may have in store for me."[4] Later in the same month, the calmness was broken. An inspection turned up liquor in Custis's room, which humiliated Lee. The situation blew over, however, and the following 28 December, from

Arlington, an again proud father wrote Custis, "[The children] were in upon us before day on Christmas morning, to overhaul their stockings. Mildred thinks she drew the prize in the shape of a beautiful new doll . . . Rooney got among his gifts a nice pair of boots . . . I need not describe to you our amusements, you have witnessed them so often; nor the turkey, cold ham, plum-pudding, mince-pies, etc., at dinner."[5]

The construction at Carroll was moving along well despite some problems such as piles plagued by worms and the perennial problem of halting appropriations from Congress. And then came another of the surprises of Lee's military career, in a telegram from Totten on 27 May 1852. The following September the constructor of Fort Carroll would report to the U.S. Military Academy at West Point to succeed Henry Brewerton as superintendent. For Lee, it was an immense thrill, but he also felt ill-prepared for the job. He wrote Totten, asking the chief engineer to reconsider. Totten did no such thing. As the Academy's ninth superintendent, Lee would oversee the institution where twenty-three years earlier he had graduated with such high esteem, where his eldest son now followed in his footsteps. Accepting the assignment on 1 September, he would preside over the venerated institution until 31 March 1855.

As autumn washed over the land and Lee reported for duty to West Point, his engineering career was over. He now managed a growing institution that had witnessed grand expansion since his own cadetship. Problems existed. Too many cadets were ill-prepared, important subjects were omitted from the curriculum, and the program of studies was disjointed. Few horses could be found on the grounds and the academy needed a riding school of sorts. To these considerations and many others, Lee devoted himself in a daily routine that included an immense amount of correspondence, politicking with Washington, overseeing the institution's finances, and dealing with the myriad concerns relating to the academy's faculty, or academic board.

The Lee family settled in at the superintendent's house at West Point, although Agnes and Annie stayed at Arlington for several months in the winter of 1852. The family cherished being near Custis again, and his performance in classes began to improve. Yet when family members traveled away for periods, Lee wrote them

A reworking of the Brady pose mounted on this cartes-de-visite produced a handsome result.
Leyburn Library, Washington and Lee University

longingly. "You do not know how much I have missed you and the children, my dear Mary," he wrote in February 1853. "In the woods, I feel sympathy with the trees and birds, in whose company I take delight, but experience no pleasure in a strange crowd."[6] On 25 February he wrote Annie: "My limited time does not diminish my affection for you, Annie, nor prevent my thinking of you and wishing for you. I long to see you through the dilatory nights. At dawn when I rise, and all day, my thoughts revert to you in expressions that you cannot hear or repeat."[7]

As the work at West Point continued apace, family sorrow visited the Lees. In April 1853 they found that Mary's mother, Mary Custis, was rapidly declining in health. Her situation had been worsening for some time, actually, and an alarming message received at West Point sent Mary home to Arlington to care for her mother. By the time she arrived, however, the elder Mary was dead. "She was all that a mother could be," Lee wrote his wife, "and I yield to none in admiration for her character, love for her virtues, and veneration of her memory."[8] The experience with their grandmother's death resonated deeply in the children's lives. Four months later, while visiting Ravensworth on 6 August, Agnes described seeing the tombs of her great uncle and aunt. "I confess I felt something like fear or rather awe steal over me as I sat on that mouldy wall surrounded by dark cedars and other trees," she penned, "the poisonous vines waving over and around me and looking down upon that mass of rank and poisonous weeds while my thoughts sank to those who rested beneath the tombs."[9]

Soon after Mary's death came commencement at West Point and the beginning of a long, hot summer. Those graduating included future luminaries James B. McPherson, John Bell Hood, and a man who would thirty-five years later be buried in front of the Lees' house, Philip Sheridan. During the commencement examinations, on 8 June, a number of enterprising businessmen from New York applied to Lee to dig for money allegedly buried on the grounds of the academy. On Lee's recommendation, the freshly appointed secretary of war, Jefferson Davis, authorized the excavations if half of the treasure recovered went to the Academy.[10]

On 5 July Lee returned to Virginia for much needed rest. Twelve days later he and daughters Mary and Annie, the girls having reached confirmation age, were confirmed at Christ Church in Alexandria. Lee had since childhood been religious and believed in a personal relationship with God. Now events conspired to

Long purported to be a post-Mexican War pose predating the Brady image, this cartes-de-visite is actually a retouched variant of the Brady photo itself. It was signed by Lee, probably in the last year or two of his life, as the copy was produced after the Civil War by Boude and Miley in Lexington.

Eleanor S. Brockenbrough Library, The Museum of the Confederacy, Richmond

deepen this religious conviction—the death of his mother-in-law, the experience with battle in the Mexican War, the responsibility of a family and of caring for the careers of the future officers of the U.S. Army.

The summer break over, the Lees returned to West Point and resumed their normal life. It was a fairly uneventful period in which Lee had increasing time to spend with his own family and watch over the development of his youngest son, Rob. During this period, on 16 September, Lee wrote a curious letter. "I can advise no young man to enter the Army," he wrote, reacting to an acquaintance's application to cadetship for a relative. "The same application, the same self-denial, the same endurance, in any other profession will advance him faster and farther."[11] On the 29th he reported on needs for the academy's library, highlighting works important for engineers.[12] His own reading during the period consisted of such diverse works as *Putnam's Monthly*, the *Pickwick Papers*, Jared Sparks's *American Biography*, Cross's *Military Laws*, James Russell Lowell's *Poems*, Brown's *Domestic Architecture*, and O'Meara's *Napoleon at St. Helena*.[13]

The Lees loved throwing parties for cadets and visitors during their stay at West Point, particularly during the holiday season.[14] Agnes described one in her diary entry of 8 November: "Last Sat. papa had a dinner party to some of his classmates, it was at first intended for a gentleman's dinner or 'he dinner' as papa calls them . . . they to be sure need not be very exquisite but must be just right for papa's scrutinizing eye."[15] Aside from the usual work, Lee had to contend with a variety of disciplinary actions relating to cadets who sneaked away to drink at Benny Havens's Tavern near the academy or otherwise violated the rules. Cracking down somewhat on previously lax attitudes, Lee punished rule breakers relatively severely for the good of the institution. Among those who had sneaked out and gone drinking all night on 16 December was Fitzhugh Lee, the superintendent's nephew. Consistent in his treatment, Lee recommended dismissal or a court-martial, and Fitz Lee narrowly escaped having his military career terminated. He then pulled the same stunt again, was caught, and again court-martialed. He escaped dismissal narrowly once again, and proceeded with a stained but workable military career that led him to the Confederacy.

With the New Year came a recommendation on 10 January from Joseph P. Taylor to Jefferson Davis for Rooney Lee's appoint-

An uncredited engraving showing Lee before the war, based on the Brady photograph taken about 1850–1852, was published in *Battles and Leaders of the Civil War*.
Author's Collection

ment to the academy.[16] Sixteen days later came the first recorded connection between Lee and Thomas J. Jackson. The former wrote to the Board of Visitors, University of Virginia: "Understanding that Major Thomas J. Jackson late of the U.S. Army is a candidate for the vacant chair of mathematics in the University of Virginia, I take pleasure in bearing testimony to his character and merit." Lee called his conduct "exemplary" and his services "distinguished."[17] Eight years later the two men would form a team that represented the strategic nucleus of the Confederacy.

For now, however, Lee dealt with the issues at West Point that needed immediate attention. At this time he was a strong proponent of expanding the curriculum from four to five years. The proposal had been recommended by the Academic Board and by Boards of Visitors for several years. The five-year curriculum was approved by Totten on 8 August 1854 and by Secretary of War Davis on 5 September. In response to calls for a more extended course in English, Lee stated that English was taught in the first year to overcome the "present low standard" of students entering the academy.[18]

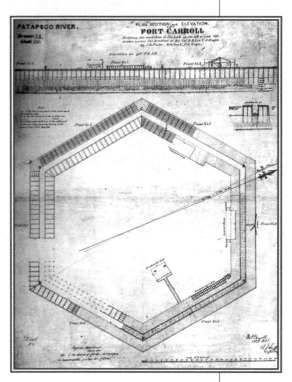

This plan of Fort Carroll, Maryland, on the Patapsco River, shows the construction as it stood on 30 September 1851. Future Union Maj. Gen. John G. Foster drew the plan; Lee supervised the work and signed it at lower right.
National Archives and Records Administration

The Lee family continued a high standard. Custis graduated first in the class of 1854 and entered the engineer corps, making his father warmly proud. During Custis's cadetship and his father's superintendency, Washington had grown concerned over the relatively small size of the regular army, some 14,216 men. The expansive frontier duties, including dealing with hostile Indians, constructing fortifications, and improving defenses along the coasts, required a larger standing army. So argued Jefferson Davis. Congress listened and acted to create four new regiments, two each of infantry and of cavalry.

On 3 March 1855 Lee's long career in the army took yet another abrupt turn. Albert Sidney Johnston would command the Second Cavalry as colonel and Lee would become his immediate subordinate as lieutenant colonel of the regiment. In an instant his long career as a engineering staff officer halted and his superintendency ended. He would now be a line officer somewhere on the frontier. No longer would he be living with his family. The family held several celebratory functions before seeing the father depart. On 11 March Agnes recorded, "We have had so many [dinner parties] . . . that the whole

Arlington's majestic Greek revival architecture and outstanding overlook of the Potomac Valley and Washington City made it one of the great Virginia homes during the 1850s. Ironically, the portion of cemetery that grew up in Arlington's front yard would, twenty-three years after Lee's surrender, receive the grave of the Union Maj. Gen. Phil Sheridan.

David J. Eicher

family are heartily sick of them. We declare they are Pa's delight but he maintains he dislikes them very much." On the same day, after rejoicing over her father's promotion, she wrote in her diary, "But second thoughts—Papa's going way out West, and—and leaving West Point, that I now almost consider as home, was very sad. We all regret it now."[19] Yet Lee did not hesitate for an instant and reported for duty at Louisville on 20 April, commanding the regiment in Johnston's temporary absence.

The new cavalry unit almost immediately repaired to Jefferson Barracks near St. Louis, and shortly after arriving Lee was assigned to a court-martial board at Fort Riley, Kansas. On 27 October the Second Cavalry commenced its journey to Texas without him, whose continued court-martial duty sent him to Carlisle Barracks, Pennsylvania, and back to West Point. He finally joined his regiment at Camp Cooper, Texas, on the Brazos River, on 9 April 1856. Three days later he wrote Mary, at home at Arlington: "We are on the Comanche Reserve, with the Indian camps below us on the river belonging to Catumseh's band, whom the Government is endeavoring to humanize. It will be uphill work, I fear."[20]

The grave of Mary Lee Fitzhugh Custis (1788–1853), mother-in-law of Lee, at Arlington. Her passing initiated a period of sadness at Arlington House that would extend through to the tumultuous years that preceded the war.
David J. Eicher

The duty at Camp Cooper was characterized by heat, desolation, a lack of good food, a complete absence of any buildings (which therefore had to be constructed), and frequent encounters with snakes. One of his subordinates, John Bell Hood, often accompanied Lee on rides throughout the region. Hood later recalled that Lee told him, "Never marry unless you can do so into

George Washington Custis Lee (1832–1913), called simply Custis, followed in his father's footsteps by attending the U.S. Military Academy at West Point. This is the earliest image of him, taken 1850–1854 as a cadet.

Virginia Historical Society, Richmond

a family which will enable your children to feel proud of both sides of the house." The phrase stuck with Hood, who summarized his affection for Lee: "His uniform kindness to me whilst I was a cadet, inclined me the more willingly to receive and remember this fatherly advice; and from these early relations first sprang my affection and veneration which grew in strength to the end of his career."[21]

Lee wrote his wife and children frequently during this period of isolation. On 4 August he described his surroundings to Agnes: "Oh, that I could see you, kiss you, squeeze you! But that cannot be Agnes and I must not indulge in wishes that cannot be gratified.... it is so hot in my tent now that spermaceti candles become so soft as to drop from the candlesticks. Sturine [sic] candles, have melted, and become liquid in the stand ... on the right of the entrance of the tent, stands an iron camp bed. On the left a camp table and chair. At the far end a trunk. On the side near the entrance a water bucket, basin, and broom, clothes hang around within easy reach of all points, and a sword and pistol very convenient."[22] "I hope your father continued well and enjoyed his usual celebration of the Fourth of July," he wrote Mary on the same day. "Mine was spent, after a march of thirty miles on one of the branches of the Brazos, under my blanket, elevated on four sticks driven into the ground, as a sunshade."[23] Ironically, although separated from his family, he advised Almira Hancock, wife of the future Union Maj. Gen. Winfield Scott Hancock, not to desert "your post, which is by your husband's side. I consider it fatal to the future happiness of young married people, upon small provocation, to live apart.... The result is invariably that they cease to be essential to each other."[24]

The dreary service was made even less palatable when news reached Lee that his younger sister, Catherine Mildred Childe, had died in Paris. Of the news, he wrote, "It has cut short my early wishes and daily yearnings, and so vividly does she live in my imagination and affection that I cannot realize she exists only in my memory."[25]

The clouds of unhappiness only seemed to thicken. Following President Pierce's message to Congress, Lee wrote Mary from Fort Brown, Texas, on 27 December. The president had indicated that Northerners were interfering with Southern institutions. "I was much pleased with the President's message," he wrote. "These people must be aware that their object is both unlawful and foreign to them and to their duty, and that this institution, for

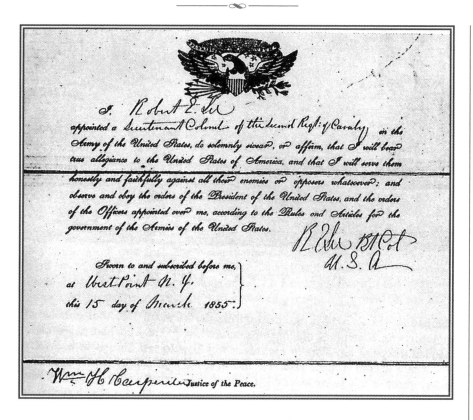

On 15 March 1855 Lee signed his oath of allegiance to the United States on acceptance of his commission as lieutenant colonel, U.S.A., Second Cavalry. Six years later he would lead one of the greatest armies in the world against U.S. forces.

National Archives and Records Administration

which they are irresponsible and non-accountable, can only be changed by them through the agency of a civil and servile war."[26]

As with most non-abolitionists of the day, Lee believed that slavery existed because God had willed it, that blacks were better off enslaved in America than free in Africa, and that if abolition came it would be willed by God and not sparked prematurely by Northern fanatics. The war between pro- and anti-slavery forces had been accelerating wildly in "Bleeding Kansas," and now open political fights were looming on the floor of Congress as officers in the army debated the issues of slavery, state rights versus Federal authority, and the political, economic, and philosophical direction of the country's future. As the decade of the 1850s waned, it seemed that the United States could unravel.

Lee spent time on duty at San Antonio, Custis was now on frontier duty, Rooney had left school and accepted a commission in the army, and Mary was growing increasingly ill. "Systematically pursue the best course to recover your lost health," Lee wrote his wife. "I pray and trust your efforts and the prayers of those who love you may be favorably answered."[27] In October 1857 he learned that George Washington Parke Custis, his father-in-law, had died at Arlington. With his wife ill, Lee took a leave from the army, returned to Arlington, and pulled the family's affairs into order.

The grave of George Washington Parke Custis (1781–1857), father-in-law of Lee and step-grandson of George Washington, at Arlington. In 1817 Custis finished building Arlington. Lee joined the Custis family at Arlington in 1831 after marrying Custis's daughter Mary Anne Randolph Custis.

David J. Eicher

In October 1859 Lee commanded a mixed group of marines and militia troops as they surrounded the Armory Enginehouse at Harpers Ferry, Virginia (since rebuilt and relocated), and forced John Brown's surrender. The slave insurrection envisioned by Brown was an utter failure; shortly after being captured, he was hanged in nearby Charles Town.

David J. Eicher

When he arrived at Arlington on 11 November, he found that not only was Parke Custis dead and his wife ill, but that Mary was becoming virtually crippled by arthritis. Moreover, settling Parke Custis's estate turned into a mess, the papers being out of order and Arlington having fallen into a serious state of disrepair. The family would therefore be squeezed in terms of land and cash to return Arlington to its previous state. Various problems with other family properties and holdings consumed an amazing amount of Lee's time, and he temporarily became a farmer as well as executor during the period.

Late 1858 and early 1859 constituted a gloomy time for the Lees. They revived Arlington only by accepting contributions from family members. During this ebb tide, Lee wrote Rooney, who was on duty in California, "Hold onto your purity and virtue. They will proudly sustain you in all trials and difficulties, and cheer you in every calamity."[28] On 23 March Rooney married his cousin Charlotte Wickham at Shirley on the James River. Rooney and his wife would establish a household at another Lee family structure, the White House on the Pamunkey. Still, Mary continued in bad health, and the daughters ailed with infections. And he wrestled with what to do with the sixty-three slaves at Arlington, who belonged to several families, as he could not employ that many. He sent them to southern Virginia where they could be used and were less likely to escape. Two of them had tried and were captured.

Meanwhile, alarm over widespread slave rebellion, militantly driven by the Northern abolitionists, was infusing the Southern character. Lee reassumed his duties. After attending a court-martial board in New York, he returned home and on 17 October was notified by James E. B. Stuart, a lieutenant who would several years later command the cavalry of the Army of Northern Virginia, of a slave insurrection. The uprising immediately threw the army and the populace into a panic: Lee was to lead an expedition of infantry, marines, and militia to put down the affair. Unknown as yet to Lee, John Brown, a fanatical and delusionary abolitionist from Kansas, led a band of twenty-one followers including five blacks to Harpers Ferry, Virginia, site of a U.S. arsenal and armory, to capture hostages, arms, and initiate an uncontrolled rebellion of slaves, believing they would rise across the land against their masters. Brown and his band were holed up in the arsenal engine house, a small brick structure.

In the words of Jeb Stuart, "Colonel Lee was sent to command the forces at Harpers Ferry. I volunteered as his aid. . . . I was deputed by Colonel Lee to read to the leader, then called *Smith*, a demand to surrender immediately . . . he opened the door about four inches, and placed his body against the crack, with a cocked carbine in his hand: hence his remark after his capture that he could have wiped me out like a mosquito. . . . I left the door and waved my cap and Colonel Lee's plan was carried out."[29]

Brown and his conspirators were captured, tried, and Brown eventually hanged. On 1 December Lee wrote his wife from Harpers Ferry, "I arrived here . . . yesterday about noon, with four companies from Fort Monroe. . . . The feelings of the community seemed to be calmed down, and I have been received with every kindness. . . . This morning I was introduced to Mrs. Brown, who . . . had come to have a last interview with her husband."[30]

The alarm spread by Brown's "raid" vastly outweighed its importance. Paranoia seeped through Southern plantations, where slaves outnumbered the whites in many cases. It was another in the

On 18 October 1859 Lee wrote Brown and his followers, holed up in the Enginehouse, that "it is impossible for them to escape . . . that if compelled to take them by force he cannot answer for their safety."
National Archives and Records Administration

series of events that drove a wedge between North and South and seemed to signal to Southerners the eventuality of separation. In the new year of 1860, Lee traveled to San Antonio, arriving by 19 February. He would now spend a year on the Texas frontier as the country was coming apart. On 13 March he wrote Custis, worried over his prospects: "I fear you do not find much comfort in your position or occupation. . . . You must make friends while you are young, that you may enjoy them when old. You will find when you become old, it will then be too late."[31]

For many of Lee's own friendships in the army, and for many spread over the country at large, it was already too late.

CHAPTER FOUR

An Uneventful Year for Granny Lee

T HE SPRING AND SUMMER OF 1860 PASSED WITHOUT remarkable events in San Antonio. Back in Virginia, Lee's first grandchild arrived, named Robert Edward Lee II (1860–?) by parents Rooney and Charlotte. Several weeks later, from Fort Mason, Texas, he wrote Rooney: "I have received your . . . pleasing account [of the] christening of your boy. So he is called after grandpa, the dear little fellow. I would wish him a better name, and hope he may be a wiser and more useful man than his namesake."[1] The mundane service and isolation from his family gnawed at his disposition, and when in July his friend Joe Johnston was commissioned brigadier general, Lee felt left behind. Now thoughts turned abruptly toward the November election, and Southerners felt nervously threatened by the "black Republican ticket" of Abraham Lincoln and Hannibal Hamlin. Secession emerged as an alternative in more and more conversations centered on the apparent political trauma of the South. The alarm over Lincoln's potential victory was well-founded: in the autumn elections he won the presidential office. In the wake of this event, Lee was split by political loyalties to the South and his official sense of duty to the United States Army. He withdrew as an isolationist, watching and waiting.

The year 1861, one of the most tumultuous in U.S. history, would be relatively uneventful for Lee, at least compared with the three years that followed. In January he turned fifty-four years old, stood five feet eleven inches in height, and weighed 170 pounds.

This reworked engraving based on the Brady photo taken about 1850–1852 was widely circulated during the first year of the war. The uniform has been painted on and the engraver has attempted to portray Lee as a major general in the Virginia militia — note the initials VA on the hat. The print was issued initially in Baltimore.
Library of Congress

41

This reworking of the Brady photograph taken about 1850–1852 also saw wide circulation during 1861. It is a retouched engraving by A. H. Ritchie, with a painted uniform and epaulettes.
National Archives and Records Administration

This engraving by the Charles Magnus Co. in New York is based on the Brady pose.
Leyburn Library, Washington and Lee University

His hair and mustache were black, with a sprinkling of gray, and he had not yet grown a beard. By this time Southern states had left the Union—first South Carolina, forcing Col. Robert Anderson's garrison at Fort Moultrie to move out into Charleston Harbor, to Fort Sumter. Other states joined the embryo of a new Confederacy—Mississippi, Florida, Alabama, Georgia, Louisiana, and Texas. As the country came apart, Lee's allegiance began to transform; he fixed his gaze on native Virginia, hoping desperately that she would remain loyal, but contemplating a bolt from the U.S. Army himself. On 23 January he wrote home from Fort Mason: "I received Everett's *Life of General Washington* . . . and enjoyed its perusal. How his spirit would be grieved could he see the wreck of his mighty labors! . . . As far as I can judge by the papers, we are between a state of anarchy and civil war. May God avert us from both."[2] On the same day he wrote one of his sons: "The South, in my opinion, has been aggrieved by the North. I feel the aggression, and am willing to take every proper step for redress."[3]

In early February Lee received orders to report to Winfield Scott in Washington by 1 April. He was thus relieved from duty in the Department of Texas.[4] On 9 February the provisional government of the Confederate States of America was organized at Montgomery, Alabama. Jefferson Davis was provisional president, Alexander H. Stephens of Georgia provisional vice president. On 13 February Lee left Fort Mason for San Antonio, from which he would journey northward. Asked whether he would join the new Confederacy, Lee responded, "I shall never bear arms against the Union, but it may be necessary for me to carry a musket in defense of my native state, Virginia, in which case I shall not prove recreant to my duty."[5]

Caroline Baldwin Darrow, the wife of a friend, witnessed his arrival in San Antonio. "About 2 o'clock that afternoon Colonel Robert E. Lee arrived in his ambulance from Fort Mason, Texas," she wrote on 18 February, "on his way to Washington . . . he asked, 'Who are those men?' 'They are McCulloch's,' I answered. 'General Twiggs has surrendered everything to the State this morning, and we are all prisoners of war.' I shall never forget his look of astonishment, as with his lips trembling and his eyes full of tears, he exclaimed, 'Has it come so soon as this?' . . . He returned at night and shut himself in his room, which was over mine, and I heard footsteps through the night, and sometimes the murmur of his voice, as if he were praying."[6]

He reached New Orleans by 25 February and the safety and relative serenity of his family at Arlington on 1 March. He now entered a period of contemplation at Arlington that would stretch through the following seven weeks, through which the country would erupt in civil war and Lee would make the most fateful decision of his life.

Lee retained his shoulder straps as colonel, U.S.A., First Cavalry, a grade and assignment he retained for a mere six weeks before resigning to accept command of the Virginia militia. The relics are now displayed at Lee Chapel. *David J. Eicher*

He met with Winfield Scott shortly after arriving, and the two talked for about three hours. Preparations for war were everywhere in Virginia, with militia companies drilling and supplies gathering in key spots, although the state had not yet seceded. The relatively passive inaugural address of Abraham Lincoln's was nonetheless taken as hostile toward Virginia's interests. Back in San Antonio, Bvt. Maj. Gen. David E. Twiggs had surrendered the garrison to local forces and so was cashiered from the army, allowing the promotion of Col. Edwin V. Sumner to brigadier general, and in turn permitting the promotion of Lt. Col. Lee to colonel, vice Sumner, in the First Cavalry, to rank from 16 March. About the same time he received a letter from Confederate War Secretary Leroy P. Walker, offering a commission as brigadier general in the

In 1861 Washington was a rather unimpressive conglomeration of buildings with rural aspects extending into the city's heart. This wartime view shows cattle grazing on what is now the National Mall. The Treasury Building appears conspicuously at right; the dim outline of Lincoln's White House appears above center. *Library of Congress*

On 18 February 1861 Jefferson Finis Davis (1808–1889) of Mississippi, a fourth cousin-in-law of Lee, was inaugurated Provisional President of the Confederate States in Montgomery. He would prove to be both close and supportive of Lee as well as a poor administrator.

National Archives and Records Administration

Alexander Hamilton Stephens (1812–1883) of Georgia became provisional vice president of the Confederacy in February 1861. Uncooperative with Jefferson Davis and absent from Richmond through much of the war, Stephens greatly damaged the Confederate cause.

Library of Congress

On 21 February 1861 Leroy Pope Walker (1817–1884) became provisional secretary of war for the Confederacy. He resigned on 16 September due to poor performance and poor health, although he briefly led troops in the field afterward.

Library of Congress

Confederate States Army.[7] Lee did not reply. He could not accept fighting with the Union against the South, nor fighting the Union with the South, but he could see defending Virginia's interests. And then came Sumter.

Tensions between the Federal government and citizens in South Carolina were about to boil over. On 12 April Confederate forces, led by G. T. Beauregard, opened a bombardment on Sumter, which ended after thirty-four hours without battle casualties. Anderson's Federal troops stationed on the fort surrendered, agreeing to retreat north, and Lincoln called for 75,000 volunteers. The war was now real; solid. On 17 April the Virginia convention, meeting in secret session in Richmond, voted to secede. On 18 April U.S. forces surrendered at Harpers Ferry, after destroying much of the arsenal and armory, preventing the capture of vast stores by pro-Confederates. The next day the U.S. Navy began a blockade of Southern ports. The same day Lee had to pay a bill in Alexandria and told a merchant, "I must say that I am one of those dull creatures that cannot see the good of secession."[8]

Also on 18 April Lee rode into Washington and met his third cousin-in-law, once removed, Francis Preston Blair, Sr., at Blair House a short distance northwest of Lincoln's Executive Mansion. He then went across Pennsylvania Avenue to the War-Navy-State Building and talked again with Scott. Much has been made of the meeting with Blair by a multitude of writers, most of it erroneous. A standard claim is that Blair "offered command of the Union army" or the title of "general-in-chief" to Lee, on Lincoln's behalf. No such thing occurred. Later, he wrote about the meeting. "Nor did I ever have a conversation with any but one gentleman, Mr. Francis Preston Blair, on the subject [of Union command], which was at his invitation, and, as I understood, at the instance of President Lincoln," he wrote. "After listening to his remarks, I declined the offer made to me to take command of the army that was to be brought into the field; stating, as candidly and as courteously as I could, that, though opposed to secession and deprecating war, I could take no part in an invasion of the Southern States. I went directly from the interview with Mr. Blair to the office of General Scott; told him of the proposition that had been made to me, and my decision."[9] He referred only to command of a field army, not all of the armies, or the assignment as general-in-chief. The informal offer, not within the legal power of Blair to make, was probably intended to feel out Lee on the possibility of heading the army that militia general Charles Sandford and later Brig. Gen. Irvin McDowell commanded, the Federal army that turned up at First Bull Run. Whether the Federal government would have entertained passing such a command to Lee, however, whose sympathies were well known, is highly doubtful.

On 20 April the Navy Yard at Norfolk was partially destroyed and then captured by Confederates. On this day Lee wrote an important letter to his old chief Scott. "Since my interview with you on the 18th inst.," he wrote, "I have felt that I ought no longer retain my commission in the Army. I therefore tender my resignation, which I request you will recommend for acceptance. It would have been presented at once but for the struggle it has cost me to separate myself from a service to which I have devoted the best years of my life, and all the ability I possessed.

"During the whole of that time—more than a quarter of a century," he continued, "I have experienced nothing but kindness from my superiors and a most cordial friendship from my comrades. To no one, General, have I been as much indebted as to yourself for uniform kindness and consideration, and it has always been my ardent desire to merit your approbation. I shall carry to the grave the most grateful recollections of your kind consideration, and your name and fame shall always be dear to me.

"Save in defense of my native State, I never desire again to draw my sword.

"Be pleased to accept my most earnest wishes for the continuance of your happiness and prosperity, and believe me, most truly yours, R. E. Lee."[10]

He also wrote his sister, Ann Lee Marshall, on 20 April. "I am grieved at my inability to see you," he wrote. "I have been waiting for a 'more convenient season,' which has brought to many before deep and lasting regret. Now

Stephen Russell Mallory (1813–1873) served as a U.S. senator in antebellum days before becoming Confederate provisional secretary of the Navy on 28 February 1861.
Library of Congress

John Henninger Reagan (1818–1905) brought his background on the Texas frontier to his post as Confederate provisional postmaster general on 6 March 1861.
Library of Congress

A variant of the Ritchie engraving based on the famous 1850–1852 Brady photograph. The popularity and widespread circulation of this image in the North made it a dominant picture of Lee early in the war.
Library of Congress

On 19 April 1861 in his bedroom at Arlington, Lee faced the momentous decision to resign from the U.S. Army and accept command of the Virginia state forces in Richmond.

David J. Eicher

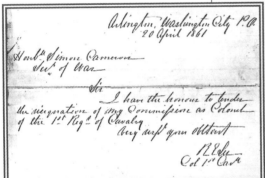

On 20 April 1861 Lee sent this letter to Secretary of War Simon Cameron, resigning as colonel of the First U.S. Cavalry.

National Archives and Records Administration

we are in a state of war which will yield to nothing. The whole South is in a state of revolution, into which Virginia, after a long struggle, has been drawn; and though I recognize no necessity for this state of things, and would have forborne and pleaded to the end for redress of grievances, real or supposed, yet in my own person I had to meet the question whether I should take part against my native State.

"With all my devotion to the Union and the feeling of loyalty and duty of an American citizen, I have not been able to make up my mind to raise my hand against my relatives, my children, my home. I have therefore resigned my commission in the Army, and save in defense of my native State, with the sincere hope that my poor services may never be needed, I hope I may never be called on to draw my sword. I know you will blame me; but you must think as kindly of me as you can, and believe that I have endeavored to do what I thought right.

"To show you the feeling and struggle it has cost me, I send you a copy of my letter of resignation. I have no time for more.

An embroidered Confederate general officer's collar insignia belonging to Lee seems not to have been worn by him; in photographs he always wore a colonel's insignia (three stars) on a lay-down collar. This relic belongs to the Lee Chapel collection.

David J. Eicher

May God guard and protect you and yours, and shower upon you everlasting blessings, is the prayer of your devoted brother, R. E. Lee."[11]

On 22 April Lee traveled to Richmond, staying at the

Spotswood Hotel, and was commissioned major general and commander in chief of the Virginia Provisional Army, a commission that lasted, due to other, unfolding events, until 8 June. After receiving his commission, Lee stood at the Houdon statue of Washington in Richmond's capitol and said gravely, fearing that the seceded states would again secede from *each other*, "I hope we have seen the last of secession."[12] He had faced the same issue of conflicting loyalties thrust upon his father and now abandoned his father's political philosophy. Light-Horse Harry had chosen Union over separatism, but Lee had become a defender of state rights.[13]

On 23 April Lee established an office and issued his General Orders No. 1, as follows: "In obedience to orders from His Excellency, John Letcher, Governor of the state, Maj. Gen. Robert E. Lee assumes command of the military and naval forces of Virginia."[14] On the same day Thomas J. Jackson, in Richmond, wrote his wife Mary Anna: "Colonel Robert E. Lee of the army is here, and has been made major-general. This I regard as of more value to us than to have General Scott as commander . . . I regard him as a better commander than General Scott."[15] On 27 April the

In 1861 Winfield Scott (1786–1866), hero of the Mexican War, was an aged general-in-chief of the U.S. Army. Although writers have alleged that Scott wanted Lee as his successor, Lee's background made such a thing virtually impossible given the situation, and no offer of command of the U.S. Army was made to Lee.

National Archives and Records Administration

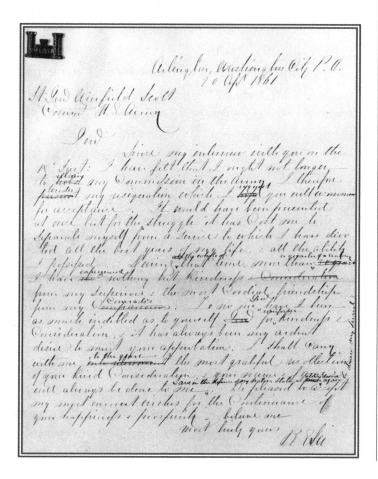

On 20 April 1861 Lee wrote to his old chief Bvt. Lt. Gen. Winfield Scott explaining his difficult decision to resign from the army and sending his heartfelt wishes for their past association.

Eleanor S. Brockenbrough Library, The Museum of the Confederacy, Richmond

This unusual early engraving by the New Yorker John A. O'Neill provides a doctored face and peculiarly embellished hair.

Library of Congress

Custis Lee resigned his commission as lieutenant in the U.S. Army on 2 May 1861 and during the initial months of the war served as an engineer on forts around Richmond and later as a staff officer for the Confederate President, Jefferson Davis.

National Archives and Records Administration

Southern diarist Mary Boykin Chesnut wrote, "General Lee, son of Light Horse Harry Lee, has been made general-in-chief of Virginia. With such men to the fore, we have hope."[16] Nearly a month later, John B. Jones, a clerk in the Richmond war office, wrote of Lee: "The North can boast of no such historic names as we, in its army."[17]

On 25 April Lee's resignation from the U.S. Army was accepted, so for three days he held concurrent commissions in the U.S. Army and the Provisional Army of Virginia. On 30 April he wrote Mary: "On going to my room last night I found my trunk and sword there, and opening them this morning discovered the package of letters and was very glad to learn that you were all well and as yet peaceful. I fear the latter state will not continue long."[18]

And it wouldn't. Lee now had the unenviable task of organizing his state forces for war. The most populous state in the South, Virginia had 1,596,652 people in 1860, 1,047,579 of whom were whites. Defending Virginia's vast territory would be a daunting accomplishment. Following the captures of Harpers Ferry and Norfolk, Lincoln on 15 April had given Southern forces twenty days to "disperse and return peaceably to their homes." No such thing would happen, of course. Through May 1861 Lee prepared for battle, believing "the war may last ten years."[19]

Richmond bristled with activity and many officers and citizens flocked to the city to prepare for war, some describing the commander of state forces. "In Richmond I saw for the first time Gen. R. E. Lee," wrote W. W. Blackford, "and a handsomer man than he was, mounted on a superb bay stallion he then rode, I never saw."[20] "[Lee's] office was on the third or fourth story of, I think, the Mechanics' Institute," wrote John Bell Hood of his visit of 5 May, "and he had around him, it seemed to me, every cobbler in Richmond, giving them instructions as to the manner of making cartridge boxes, haversacks, bayonet scabbards, &c. He was studiously applying his great mind to this apparently trivial but most important work."[21] Also in May, Walter H. Taylor, who would become a devoted staff officer of Lee's, met the general for the first time. "I was at breakfast at the Spotswood Hotel when he entered the room and was at once greatly attracted and greatly impressed by his appearance," wrote Taylor. "[He had] strikingly handsome features, bright and penetrating eyes, his iron-gray hair closely cut, his face cleanly shaved except a mustache, he appeared every inch a soldier and a man born to command."[22]

On 5 May Mary Custis Lee wrote Scott, revealing the painful splintering of the family's relations. "No honors can reconcile us to this fracticidal war which we would have laid down our lives freely to avert," she penned. "Whatever may happen, I feel that I may expect from your kindness all the protection you can in honor afford."[23] About 14 May she left Arlington and traveled to Ravensworth. From Richmond, her husband wrote: "I grieve at the necessity that drives you from your home."[24]

On 14 May Lee was commissioned brigadier general in the Army of the Confederate States of America (A.C.S.A., the "regular army" of the Confederate States). The press was beginning to enthuse over this Virginia soldier, the Charleston *Daily Courier*, on the 14th, describing his "broad, expansive forehead . . . fine profile . . . keen expressive dark brown eye . . . nose, slightly on the Roman style of architecture . . . and a mouth full of spirit and determination."[25] Yet the praise was not universal. "No one admires Genl. Lee more than I do," Albert T. Bledsoe, soon to be assistant secretary of war, wrote Jefferson Davis. "But I fear he is too despondent. His remarks are calculated to dispirit our people. I have heard such remarks myself, and energetically dissented from them. . . . He overrates the power of the North to attack, & underrates the means & power of the South to resist."[26]

Two days later Congress authorized six officers as general, A.C.S.A., including Lee, but he would not be confirmed by the Confederate Senate until 31 August. Meanwhile, he was awash in paperwork. "His correspondence, necessarily heavy, was constantly a source of worry and annoyance to him," wrote Taylor. "He did not enjoy writing . . . after a day's work at his office he would enjoy above all things a ride on horseback."[27]

On 21 May Richmond became the capital of the Confederacy, and Jefferson Davis arrived in town eight days later. "On my arrival in Richmond," he wrote, "General R. E. Lee, as commander of the Army of Virginia, was found there, where he had established his headquarters. He possessed my unqualified confidence, both as a soldier and a patriot, and the command he had exercised over the Army of Virginia, before her

Lee's nephew Fitzhugh Lee (1835–1905) was serving as an instructor at West Point in early 1861. He resigned his commission on 21 May 1861 and joined the staff of Joseph E. Johnston, in which capacity he served at First Bull Run. He was commissioned lieutenant colonel of the First Virginia Cavalry the following month.
National Archives and Records Administration

Walter Herron Taylor (1838–1916) joined Lee's staff in the spring of 1861 and remained with him until Appomattox. The youthful aide and assistant adjutant general rose to the grade of lieutenant colonel and was in closer daily contact with his commanding general than perhaps any other officer.
Eleanor S. Brockenbrough Library, The Museum of the Confederacy, Richmond

Samuel Cooper (1798–1876), Lee's brother-in-law, became in 1861 the senior general officer of the Confederate army and the adjutant and inspector general. Cooper married a sister of Lee's sister-in-law.

Library of Congress

Lee's brother and Fitzhugh's father Sidney Smith Lee (1802–1869) enlisted in the Federal navy as a young man. In 1861 he was commissioned captain in the Confederate navy and subsequently served at Norfolk, Drewry's Bluff, and at the fortifications surrounding Richmond.

Library of Congress

accession to the Confederacy, gave him that special knowledge which at the time was most needful."[28] Two days later Federal soldiers occupied Alexandria and Arlington. The house would never again be used by the Lees. On 25 May 1861 Lee wrote Mary: "I sympathize deeply in your feelings at leaving your dear home . . . I fear we have not been grateful enough for the happiness there within our reach, and our heavenly Father has found it necessary to deprive us of what He has given us."[29] On 30 May Mary received a letter from Irvin McDowell, the Union general at Arlington. "With respect to the occupation of Arlington by the United States troops," wrote McDowell, "I beg to say it has been done by my predecessor with every regard for the preservation of the place. I am here temporarily in camp on the grounds, preferring this to sleeping in the house."[30]

On 31 May Lee held a strategy conference with G. T. Beauregard and President Davis. He had surveyed defenses at the railroad junction of Manassas and from 6–8 June appraised the defensive batteries on the waterways near Richmond. "I have just returned from a visit to the batteries and troops on James and York rivers, etc., where I was some days. I called a few hours at the White House. Saw Charlotte and Annie. Fitzhugh [Rooney] was away, but got out of the cars as I got in. Our little boy seemed very sweet and seemed glad to kiss me a good-bye. . . . I should like to retire to private life, if I could be with you and the children, but if I can be of any service to the State or her cause I must continue."[31]

Continue he would. June brought the first set of clashes between opposing armies in Virginia, at Fairfax Station (1 June), Philippi (3 June), Big Bethel (10 June), and Vienna (16 June). Now Virginia Governor John Letcher transferred the Virginia forces to the national army of the Confederacy.

The immediate threat from Federal forces would be a movement southward from Manassas Junction toward Richmond. Lee had hastily organized a defensive force, helped to initiate a Confederate naval force, protected Norfolk, and helped to reinforce Manassas, Harpers Ferry, and Fredericksburg. About 40,000 Confederate troops were in Virginia's fields. Arms, ammunition, cannon, powder, and other supplies had been furnished for $3.8 million, all in about eight weeks. When it was finished, Lee seemed to embrace a fatalistic view of the risks ahead. He wrote Mary, "God's will be done."[32]

Lee's role now became that of an advisor to Jefferson Davis.

Assisting him were Walter Taylor, Robert H. Chilton, John A. Washington, and George Deas. He did not enjoy this peculiar staff service in Richmond and wished to lead troops in the field. A major Federal approach might come from the valley, from Manassas, or from the Virginia Peninsula. A former staff member of Lee's, Brig. Gen. Robert S. Garnett, had gone to western Virginia to occupy the mountain passes at Laurel Hill and Rich Mountain.

In mid-May 1861 Federal troops occupied Arlington House. This image made in May 1864 shows Union Brig. Gen. Gustavus A. DeRussy (third from left) and his staff on the portico at Arlington.
Library of Congress

By early July Federal Maj. Gen. George B. McClellan moved into position opposite Rich Mountain. McClellan routed Garnett's force at Laurel Hill on the 7th and at Rich Mountain on the 11th, and two days later Garnett was killed at Corrick's Ford on the Cheat River. A significant Union force under Brig. Gen. Irvin McDowell

Rooney Lee's beloved White House on the Pamunkey fell into Federal hands in May 1861. The building would be used as headquarters for Union Maj. Gen. George B. McClellan, the area transforming into a supply depot and river landing. Little more than a year later the house would be burned to the ground. James F. Gibson made this image on 17 May 1862.
Library of Congress

This steel engraving by A. H. Ritchie, also based on the Brady photograph, misidentifies Lee as a major general of the "Confederate" army.

Library of Congress

Mary Custis Lee (1835–1918), the first of four daughters of Lee and Mary Custis Lee, was independent and driven. As with the other Lee girls, she never married. This image was made by Henry Glosser in New York in the 1850s.

Leyburn Library, Washington and Lee University

finally approached Manassas and the first major battle of the war erupted on 21 July along Bull Run. It was a tactical victory for the Confederacy and shattered the Northern morale when McDowell's army retreated back to Washington. The victorious Confederate commanders were Gens. Joseph E. Johnston and G. T. Beauregard.

At First Bull Run, Thomas J. Jackson solidified his standing as a legend when Brig. Gen. Barnard E. Bee uttered the phrase, "There stands Jackson like a stone wall. Rally behind the Virginians!" But Jackson also was wounded in the right hand, which caused him pain and partial paralysis and rendered the circulation imperfect. To alleviate the pain, he sometimes raised his arm straight up, particularly while riding on horseback.[33] Six days later Lee wrote Mary about the battle: "That indeed was a glorious victory and has lightened the pressure on our front amazingly. Do not grieve for the brave dead. Sorrow for those they left behind— friends, relatives, and families."[34]

On 28 July came another turn for Lee, when he departed for western Virginia with Taylor and Washington to regain control of events in that mountainous region. He needed to coordinate operations and ensure that commanders were working well together—a bland assignment. William W. Loring, Henry A. Wise, John B. Floyd, Albert Rust, and subordinate officers were bickering to the point where nothing was getting done. On 4 August he wrote Mary from Huntersville, and after mentioning that he had traveled on the same road in 1840, he commented that "if any one had then told me that the next time I travelled that road I would have been on my present errand, I should have supposed him insane."[35]

Meanwhile, Lee's reputation was growing in a direction far different than the mythic-soldier model of Stonewall Jackson. On 6 August the Memphis *Daily Appeal* described the overseer of western Virginia: "His life, since he assumed the chief command of the Virginia forces, has been a model of soldierly patience and energy and watchfulness. Six o'clock in the morning has seen him regularly enter his office, which, with rare exceptions, he has not left, save at meal times, till eleven at night. A man of few words, of unvarying courtesy, but of a singularly cold and distant manner. . . ."[36]

This same week at Valley Mountain, the young Virginia soldier John H. Worsham recalled seeing the visitor for the first time. "General Robert E. Lee . . . joined us here and pitched his headquarters tent about one or two hundred yards from our company. He soon won the affection of all by his politeness and notice of the soldiers." Articles of food and gifts sent to Lee were "sent to some sick soldier as soon as the messenger got out of sight." He considered the case of a soldier accused of being asleep on guard duty, an offense that could have seen him shot. "When [the officers] approached General Lee's tent, they saw he was alone and writing at a table." On being informed of the offense, Lee said "Captain, you know the arduous duties these men have to do daily. Suppose the man who was found on his post asleep had been you, or me. What do you think should be done to him?"[37]

On 9 August Lee described his temporary home to Mary. "The mountains are beautiful," he wrote, "fertile to the tops, covered with the richest sward of bluegrass and white clover, and inclosed fields waving with the natural growth of timothy. The habitations are few and the people sparse. This is a magnificent grazing country."[38] A few days later Stonewall Jackson wrote Colonel Bennett, auditor of Virginia: "My hopes for our section of

Eleanor Agnes Lee (1841–1873), known simply as Agnes, was the third Lee daughter. The most studious and reflective of the daughters, Agnes died tragically at age thirty-two of acute gastroenteritis. This photo was made about 1861.

Eleanor S. Brockenbrough Library, The Museum of the Confederacy, Richmond

Mildred Childe Lee (1846–1905) was the fourth of the Lee daughters. She was high-spirited and enthusiastic in a wide range of endeavors and, like the other Lee girls, never married. This view was made in Baltimore by Stanton and Butler. Another daughter, incidentally—Annie—was apparently never photographed. Suffering an eye injury at an early age, she died young, in October 1862 at age twenty-three.

Leyburn Library, Washington and Lee University

The John Brockenbrough House in Richmond, built in 1818, served as the White House of the Confederacy. Here Jefferson Davis established both office and living space, and Lee often attended military meetings. This image was made after the city's fall in 1865.

Library of Congress

Joseph Eggleston Johnston (1807–1891), a very distant relative of Lee's, emerged as an early hero in the war. Former U.S. quartermaster general, Johnston became the fourth ranking officer in the Confederate army, won plaudits for First Bull Run, and commanded the Army of Northern Virginia after its formation, before a wound allowed Lee to take command.

National Archives and Records Administration

Robert Selden Garnett (1819–1861) was the first general officer to be killed or mortally wounded in the war. He served briefly on Lee's staff before commanding troops in western Virginia during the summer of 1861. He was mortally wounded on 13 July at Corrick's Ford, dying the same day.

Library of Congress

the state [western Virginia] have greatly brightened since General Lee has gone there. Something brilliant may be expected."[39]

But difficulties lay ahead. Federal Brig. Gen. William S. Rosecrans had a sizable force in the vicinity of Cheat Mountain to attack southeastward toward the upper Shenandoah Valley. Rains were relentless, and mud was everywhere. On 31 August Lee was confirmed as general, C.S.A., to rank from 14 June. He became the third most senior officer in the army, following Samuel Cooper and Albert Sidney Johnston. On 1 September he wrote Mary, who was now at "Audley," in Clarke Co., Va., with Mrs. Lorenzo Lewis: "We have a great deal of sickness among the soldiers, and now those on the sick-list would form an army. The measles is still among them . . . The constant cold rains, with no shelter but tents . . . with impassable roads, have paralyzed our efforts."[40]

Nonetheless, he planned his first battle, fought at Cheat Mountain, 11–13 September. He went forward with his forces and clashed with the enemy first at Conrad's Mill, and the action proceeded up Cheat Mountain. John A. Washington, along with Rooney, conducted a reconnaissance on the 13th, during which Washington was killed and Rooney's horse wounded. On top of this disheartening news, Confederate objectives had failed at Cheat Mountain and nearby at Tygart's Valley. For the moment, at least, the campaign had failed. Newspapers attached a sobriquet to Lee that he most certainly did not appreciate: "Granny Lee," taunting his supposed timidity. Conditions were depressing.

On 26 September he wrote Mary from a camp at Sewell's Mountain: "It is raining heavily. The men are all exposed on the mountain, with the enemy opposite to us. We are without tents, and for two nights I have lain buttoned up in my overcoat. To-day my tent came up and I am in it. Yet I fear I shall not sleep for thinking of the poor men."[41] In early October Thomas J. Goree, a young Confederate soldier who would join James Longstreet's staff, was skeptical of the commander. "Gen. Lee has quite a reputation," he wrote, "but he has not sustained it. He is a great military man in theory, but he has never had any practice. I very much fear that Rozencrantz [sic] will out-general him."[42]

With cold weather approaching, Lee could barely attempt another offensive movement; stalemate was in the air. Disappointment was the order of the day, and he settled in, got to know his men, whom he lived with closely, and grew a gray beard. The second possibility for an attack, this time in early October at Sewell's

The Virginia State Capitol, designed by Thomas Jefferson and constructed beginning in 1785, served as the Confederate Capitol during the war years. Inside met the Confederate Congress, and Lee accepted command of the Virginia state forces. During the war the Virginia legislature and governor also continued to hold their business here. This image was made in 1865.

Library of Congress

Mountain, also failed. "Poor Lee!" editorialized the Charleston *Mercury* on 16 October. "Rosecrans has fooled him again . . . are the roads any worse for Lee than Rosecrans? . . . The people are getting mighty sick of this dilly-dally, dirt digging, scientific warfare; so much so that they will demand that the Great Entrencher be brought back and permitted to pay court to the ladies."[43]

Nonetheless, the campaign over, he returned on 30 October to Richmond. He visited Mary, at Shirley, for the first time since leaving her in April. "He came back, carrying the heavy weight of defeat," wrote Jefferson Davis. "And unappreciated by the people whom he served, for they could not know, as I knew, that, if his plans and orders had been carried out, the result would have been victory rather than defeat."[44]

In truth, a Southern victory in western Virginia may have been irrelevant. Before year's end the region's citizens initiated a movement to break away from Virginia, becoming a separate state loyal to the Union.

On 1 November Jefferson Davis learned that a large Federal naval force was moving southward toward the South Atlantic coast, allegedly to Port Royal Sound, South Carolina. Four days

Robert Mercer Taliaferro Hunter (1809–1887), a former U.S. senator, congressman, and speaker of the house, participated in the provisional Confederate Congress in 1861 before becoming provisional secretary of state on 25 July 1861.

Library of Congress

A rather crude wood engraving by A. H. Ritchie was based on the Brady 1850–1852 photo and appeared in *Harper's Weekly* in August 1861. The work was titled *The Rebel General Lee*.

Author's Collection

THE REBEL GENERAL LEE.—[PHOTOGRAPHED BY BRADY.]

John Augustine Washington (1821–1861), a friend and relative of Lee's from northern Virginia, served on the general's staff during 1861, serving as an assistant adjutant general with the grade of colonel, until he was killed on 13 September at Cheat Mountain, Virginia.

Robert E. Lee Memorial Association, Stratford Hall Plantation

On 31 August 1861 Confederate Secretary of War Leroy P. Walker sent Lee notification of his appointment as general, A.C.S.A., to rank from 14 June. Contrary to popular misconception, this is simply the notification of appointment letter — not the commission itself.

Eleanor S. Brockenbrough Library, The Museum of the Confederacy, Richmond

later Lee was given the assignment of commanding the Department of South Carolina, Georgia, and eastern Florida, a duty that would last until 5 March 1862. He was not happy with the assignment and, due to the public relations damage he had suffered during the western Virginia campaigns, neither were South Carolina authorities. After his arrival, however, opinions changed. South Carolina Governor Francis W. Pickens

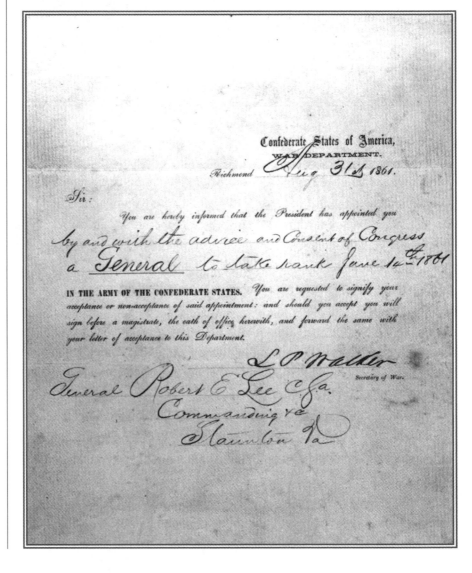

wrote Jefferson Davis on 24 November, saying, "I take this opportunity to say from the interviews I have had with Genl. Lee that I have a very high estimation of his science, patriotism, and enlightened judgment. I am also delighted with his high bred cultivated bearing. If he has a fault it is over caution which results from his scientific mind."[45]

In the words of Jefferson Davis, Lee arrived in Charleston and on 1 December "His vigorous mind at once comprehended the situation. . . . Directing fortifications to be constructed on the Stono and the Edisto and the Combahee, he fixed his headquarters at Coosawhatchie, the point most threatened, and directed defenses to be erected opposite Hilton Head."[46] Ten days later Lee and his staff witnessed the great fire in Charleston, when much of the city burned. "While crossing the Ashley River in an open rowboat," wrote Taylor, "as we approached the city we observed the light of the fire, but did not attach much importance to it." Later, while dining at a hotel, "we became aware of a great excitement prevailing outside, manifested by the rapid rush of people and the noise of passing engines and vehicles."[47]

Christmas 1861 would be spent again away from the family, this time in Coosawhatchie. "I cannot let this day of grateful rejoicing pass without some communion with you," he wrote Mary, "as to our old home, if not destroyed it will be difficult ever to be recognized. Even if the enemy had wished to preserve it, it would almost have been impossible. With the number of troops encamped around it, the change of officers, the want of fuel, shelter, etc., and all the dire necessities of war, it is vain to think of its being in a habitable condition. I fear, too, the books, furniture, and relics of Mount Vernon will be gone."[48] On the same day, he wrote one of his daughters. "Having distributed such poor Christmas gifts as I had around me," he penned, "I have been looking for something for you. . . . I send you some sweet violets that I gathered for you this morning while covered with dense white frost, whose crystals glittered in the bright sun like diamonds."[49]

On 29 December Lee cautioned Charlotte Wickham Lee, Rooney's wife, about traveling with Rooney to Fredericksburg. "I

William Wing Loring (1818–1886), "Blizzards," lost an arm in the Mexican War and in 1861 battled Stonewall Jackson over the Romney expedition in western Virginia. Later in the war he was sent to the west.
Library of Congress

A steel engraving based on a variant of the Brady photograph appeared in *Frank Leslie's Illustrated Newspaper*. *Author's Collection*

This ornate 1851 Navy Colt revolver was carried by Lee during the war.

The Museum of the Confederacy, Richmond; photograph by Katherine Wetzel

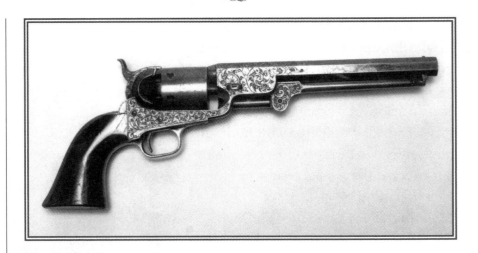

George A. Deas (?–1870) served as an assistant adjutant general on Lee's staff and was briefly chief of staff of the Virginia militia. He rose to the grade of colonel.

Robert E. Lee Memorial Association, Stratford Hall Plantation

am afraid the enemy will catch you," he wrote, "and besides there are too many young men there. I only want you to visit the old men—your grandpapa and papa. . . . You will have to get out the old wheels and looms again, else I do not know where we poor Confederates will get clothes."[50]

Apparent fortunes for the young Confederacy, and for Lee, would take a huge upswing in the coming year, however. In 1862 it appeared that God's will would indeed favor the South.

CHAPTER FIVE

❦

The Emergence of Military Genius

This striking tintype of the General was made probably early in 1862. It has often previously been printed as a mirror image, as it was copied from an image taken in reverse. It is shown here correctly for the first time.
Robert E. Lee Memorial Association, Stratford Hall Plantation

THE YEAR 1862 WAS LEE'S YEAR. ITS EARLY MONTHS progressed rather unremarkably, yet events would conspire to lift him into a position of great opportunity by midyear. And this year would mark the pinnacle of Lee's military career and the greatest period of optimism for the infant Confederacy before events began to work against it. Progress would be slow early in the year.

Still in the Deep South in January, Lee had the opportunity to visit his father's grave. "While at Fernandia I went over to Cumberland Island and walked up to 'Dungeness,' the former residence of General Green [sic]," he wrote Mary on 18 January. "It was my first visit to the house, and I had the gratification at length of visiting my father's grave. He died there, you may recollect, on his way from the West Indies, and was interred in one corner of the family cemetery. The spot is marked with a plain marble slab, with his name, age, and date of his death."[1]

Again writing Mary on 28 January from Coosawhatchie, he remarked on the difficulty of warding off the large Federal fleet endangering coastal forts held by Confederates. "The enemy's gunboats are pushing up the creek to cut off communication between [Savannah] and Fort Pulaski on Cockspur Island," he wrote. "There are so many points of attack, and so little means to meet them on water, that there is but little rest."[2] Scarcely more than a week later, in Savannah, he again worried in a letter to Mary: "Guns are scarce,

Thomas J. "Stonewall" Jackson (1824–1863) eclipsed even Lee's reputation as a Confederate hero during the early months of the war. A distant relative of Lee's, his legendary campaign in the Shenandoah Valley in 1862 and subsequent service with Lee's force at Second Bull Run, Antietam, Fredericksburg, and Chancellorsville, comprise a sterling record of generalship.
National Archives and Records Administration

as well as ammunition, and I shall have to break up batteries on the coast to provide, I fear, for this city. . . . I hope, however, we shall be able to stop [the enemy], and I daily pray to the Giver of all victories to enable us to do so."[3]

Meanwhile, events were unfolding badly for the Confederacy out west. Defeats at Fort Henry and Fort Donelson in Tennessee forced the evacuation of large tracts of Kentucky and western Tennessee. The victorious Federal commander was a little known Illinois officer, Brig. Gen. Ulysses S. Grant. "The news from Tennessee and North Carolina is not all cheering, and disasters seem to be thickening around us," Lee wrote Mary from Savannah on 23 February. "I fear our soldiers have not realised the necessity for the endurance and labour they are called upon to undergo, and that it is better to sacrifice themselves than our cause."[4]

Confederate soldiers indeed were becoming depressed, and impatience through the long winter marked the Manassas line held by Gen. Joseph E. Johnston in northern Virginia. Disagreements between Jefferson Davis, who was micromanaging military events, Secretary of War Judah P. Benjamin, and Johnston, seemed to be calling for a reorganization of the important Virginia command structure. "I trust that General Lee will be secretary of war," wrote Stonewall Jackson to Alexander R. Boteler on 3 March.[5] Lee was indeed called back to Richmond, not to be war secretary but to act

At Yorktown, Confederate forces delayed the Union army in a siege that lasted nearly a month. This view, taken on 1 July 1862 by George N. Barnard, shows a Confederate naval gun in the foreground and Nelson Church, used as a hospital, in the background.
Library of Congress

Grapevine Bridge, built from logs and swamp vines 27–28 May 1862 by the 5th New Hampshire Infantry, suggests the improvised nature of the Peninsular campaign. David B. Woodbury made this image in 1862.
Library of Congress

as a military advisor to Jefferson Davis, an arrangement that would last until 31 May. Instead, George Wythe Randolph was appointed secretary of war. "I have been placed on duty here to conduct operations under the direction of the President," Lee wrote Mary on 14 March, from Richmond. "It will give me great pleasure to do anything I can to relieve him and serve the country, but I do not see either advantage or pleasure in my duties. But I will not complain, but do my best."[6]

With Custis, Rooney, nephew Fitzhugh, and brother Smith all in Confederate service, it was now time for Lee's youngest son, Rob, to enter the army. "I went with [Rob] to get his overcoat, blankets, etc. . . . and he has gone to the adjutant general's office of Virginia to engage in the service," Lee wrote Mary on 16 March. "God grant it may be for his good. . . . I hope our son will make a good soldier."[7]

Two major operations in Virginia unfolded in the spring of 1862. Stonewall Jackson conducted his legendary campaign in the Shenandoah Valley against Federal Maj. Gens. Nathaniel P. Banks, John C. Frémont, James Shields, and others. Jackson baffled much larger Union forces in a succession of actions throughout the Valley in April and May. Meanwhile, Maj. Gen. George B. McClellan, commanding the Federal Army of the Potomac, moved forces and supplies to Fort Monroe on the peninsula and anticipated a heavy campaign northwestward along the peninsula to capture

John Bankhead Magruder (1807–1871) completely fooled the force under Maj. Gen. George B. McClellan at Yorktown. Following the latter part of the Peninsular campaign, where he failed tactically, Magruder was assigned to commands in the west.
National Archives and Records Administration

The railroad at Fair Oaks Station, which marks the position of one of the most peculiar battles marked by a succession of errors. The plan to destroy the Federal Fourth Corps fell apart when James Longstreet employed the wrong roads for approaches. What was planned for dawn began only after noon.

David J. Eicher

At the end of May 1862 the armies faced off in two actions at Fair Oaks and Seven Pines, where Joseph E. Johnston hoped to crush the isolated Federal Fourth Corps. In the action during the afternoon of 31 May Johnston was wounded; the command passed to Maj. Gen. G. W. Smith and then to Lee. This view, taken in June 1862 by George N. Barnard, shows the distinctive twin houses on the Seven Pines battlefield along with a Federal 32-pounder field howitzer.

Library of Congress

Richmond. This movement began on 17 March. On 4 April McClellan initiated an advance up the peninsula, elements of his 50,000 combat-ready troops meeting Maj. Gen. John B. Magruder's 13,000 troops, about to be joined by Johnston's main force of 43,000. As the president's advisor, Lee "thought that the Peninsula had excellent fields of battle for a small army contending for a great one, and that we should for that reason make the contest with McClellan's army there."[8] The Confederate defenses around Yorktown were poor but Magruder shifted troops nearly constantly and bluffed McClellan as to the size of his force. A siege resulted, which lasted until 3 May. Meanwhile, news from the west continued to be bad, as Confederate forces at Shiloh, Tennessee, retreated southward from the field and the commander, Gen. Albert Sidney Johnston, was mortally wounded.

As McClellan readied for a massive bombardment of the Confederate lines with heavy siege guns, Johnston frustrated the plan by swiftly withdrawing. Union forces pursued and attacked the Confederate rear near Williamsburg on 5 May. This was successfully repulsed, but now McClellan had open routes to approach Richmond. His advance was glacial due to heavy rains and muddy roads. With a force of 105,000 facing Johnston's 60,000, McClellan

In June 1862 George McClellan's Peninsular campaign brought what Lee feared most: a mini-siege of Richmond. The Federal army approached within eight miles of the city. In the end it withdrew to Harrison's Landing, however, and would not return so close to the Confederate capital for nearly another three years. This view was made in 1865.

National Archives and Records Administration

moved to a position along the Chickahominy River and occupied the White House, Rooney's home, as his headquarters. Jackson's continued success in the valley prevented McClellan from even heavier reinforcement.

McClellan halted before attempting a movement to the south of Richmond and then attacking to the north. At this time, on 31 May, Johnston attacked the isolated Third and Fourth Army Corps under Maj. Gen. Erasmus D. Keyes at Fair Oaks and Seven Pines. Keyes was struck from three directions and badly damaged, but poor weather, mud, and finally darkness prevented a rout. Jefferson Davis and Lee rode out from the city and watched the battle unfold, seeing the Army of Northern Virginia in action. For Lee, the key event occurred near the end of the battle: Johnston was wounded, two pieces of shell striking him and placing him in great pain. For a portion of one day, Maj. Gen. Gustavus W. Smith assumed command of the army. His subsequent attack was bungled, and on 1 June Lee was ordered into the field to take command. His legendary pairing with the Army of Northern Virginia now began. "Now with our inferior forces & resources," wrote Edward Porter Alexander, a young Confederate officer who would serve on Lee's staff, "our only hope is to

Gustavus Woodson Smith (1821–1896) commanded the Army of Northern Virginia for several hours following Joseph E. Johnston's wounding at Seven Pines. Thereafter, command passed to Lee. Later in 1862 Smith served temporarily as Confederate secretary of war.
Library of Congress

This striking Lee photograph was made probably sometime in late 1862 or early 1863 by either Minnis and Cowell of Richmond or Bendann of Baltimore. It may have been taken in the field. Lapels tucked under the second button suggest the uniform was new, as they would not stay in place unless restrained.

National Archives and Records Administration

This image from a cartes-de-visite made in 1862 or early 1863 by Tanner and Van Ness, Lynchburg, is a retouched engraving made from the Minnis and Cowell or Bendann image.

The Valentine Museum, Richmond

James Longstreet (1821–1904) served Lee as ably as any other officer. He demonstrated great fighting ability during the Peninsular campaign, at Second Bull Run, Antietam, and at Fredericksburg. Critically wounded in the Wilderness, he sat out for several months before returning to command the army's First Corps.

National Archives and Records Administration

Robert Hall Chilton (1815–1879) served in 1862 as chief of staff to Lee as well as inspector general of the Army of Northern Virginia. A commission as brigadier general eluded Chilton during most of the war; after receiving it he performed mostly desk duty.

Library of Congress

bounce [the enemy] and whip him somewhere before he is ready for us, and that needs audacity in our commander. Has Gen. Lee that audacity?"[9] Meanwhile, Mary and two of the Lee girls went to "Marlbourne," home of the fiery secessionist Edmund Ruffin, where they stayed for some weeks, inside territory held by the Federal army, until moving on to Richmond, with permission of Union officers.[10]

On 1 June Lee assumed command of the Department and Army of Northern Virginia, a command that would last until his surrender at Appomattox Court House.[11] "The unfortunate casualty which has deprived the army in front of Richmond of its immediate commander Genl. Johnston," Davis wrote Lee, "renders it necessary to interfere temporarily with the duties to which you were assigned.... You will assume command of the armies in Eastern Va. and in North Carolina and give such orders as may be needful and proper."[12]

Lee established his headquarters at Dabb's House about two miles from Richmond on the Nine Mile Road. On 3 June a conference was held at "The Chimneys" at Seven Pines, and several officers suggested retreating closer to Richmond because they were exposed to Federal artillery. "General Lee said to me," wrote Charles Marshall, a staff officer, "'if we leave this line because they can shell us, we shall have to leave the next line for the same reason, and I don't see how we can stop this side of Richmond.'"[13] "When General Lee took command it was my first sight of him," wrote Moxley Sorrel, a staff officer of Longstreet's. "Up to a short time before Seven Pines he had worn for beard only a well-kept mustache, soon turned from black to grizzled. When he took us in hand his full gray beard was growing, cropped close, and always well tended.... Withal graceful and easy, he was approachable by all; gave attention to all in the simplest manner. His eyes— sad eyes! The saddest it seems to me of all men.

The General was always dressed well in gray sack coat of Confederate cloth, matching trousers tucked into well-fitting riding boots—the simplest emblems of his rank appearing, and a good, large black felt army hat. . . . He rarely wore his sword, but his binoculars were always at hand. Fond of the company of ladies, he had a good memory for pretty girls. His white teeth and winning smile were irresistible."[14]

Lee was now well-known but had yet to win the confidence of the masses. He seemed solid, lacking brilliance, and not particularly lucky. He did not yet emerge as a hero.[15] The people had Stonewall Jackson, but Southerners needed more heroes. Not only were Richmonders physically endangered but daily life for average citizens and even for the wealthy was becoming difficult. "Lee has assumed command," wrote Alexander Cheves Haskell on 3 June. "We must whip the Yankees now and get into their country. Food and forage are getting very scarce."[16] In the War Office on the same day, the clerk John B. Jones wrote, "Gen. Lee henceforth assumes command of the army in person. This may be hailed as the harbinger of bright fortune."[17] "When General Lee took command there was really very little known of him generally," wrote Porter Alexander. "He had made great reputation in Mexico as a staff officer & an engineer, but in our war he had had, as yet, but one command, & that had been unfortunate. . . . And now that he was put in command of the army, some of the newspapers—particularly the Richmond *Examiner*—pitched into him with extraordinary virulence, evidently trying to break him down with the troops & to force the president to remove him." Porter Alexander continued with his description of the transition. "There now began a gradual breakup of Gen. Johnston's staff & organisation of Gen. Lee's," he wrote, "Lee brought some men, perhaps Walter Taylor, [Charles] Marshall, [Armistead L.] Long & [Charles] Venable, his aids, &c., with him, but I can't recall exactly; & Johnston's heads of departments, of course, stayed on. For at first it was supposed that Johnston would return to command as soon as his wounds healed."[18]

To initiate Lee's command, Jefferson Davis offered a new horse. The commander already had a favorite in the soon-to-be-famous Traveller. On 3 June he answered the

Edward Porter Alexander (1835–1910) joined Lee's staff in 1862 as chief of artillery and later performed the same assignment for James Longstreet's corps. Alexander's lucid, balanced accounts of many eastern battles shed great light on the Lee story.
Library of Congress

The Episcopal Reverend William Nelson Pendleton (1809–1883), who vaguely resembled Lee, acted as a nominal chief of Lee's artillery operations from 1862 to his capture at war's end. Pendleton's daughter married Edwin G. Lee, Lee's first cousin, once removed; his son served on Stonewall Jackson's staff.
Library of Congress

Armistead Lindsay Long (1825–1891) fought in western Virginia before joining Lee in Charleston. After Lee assumed command of the Army of Northern Virginia, Long served as a military secretary. Losing his eyesight after the war, Long painstakingly wrote *Memoirs of Robert E. Lee* using a slate.
Library of Congress

Lafayette Guild (1825?–1870), medical director on Lee's staff for the final three years of the war, appears in a prewar daguerreotype. The image is necessarily a mirror image, as evidenced by the hat insignia.
Eleanor S. Brockenbrough Library, The Museum of the Confederacy, Richmond

president: "I am extremely grateful for your kind offer of your fine horse & feel most sensibly the kind consideration & thoughtfulness that prompted it. But I really do not require one at this time & would infinitely prefer your retaining him & allow me to enjoy the sense of your kindness & to call for him when I am in want. My gray [Traveller] has calmed down amazingly, gave me a very pleasant ride all day yesterday. . . ."[19] Two days later he again wrote Davis, this time thinking strategy. "After much reflection I think that if it was possible to reinforce Jackson strongly," he wrote, "it would change the character of the War. This can only be done by the troops in Georgia, S.C. & N.C. Jackson could in that event cross Maryland into Penn—it would call all the enemy from our Southern Coast & liberate those states."[20]

He now found himself backed up against Richmond with McClellan's huge army just eight miles from the city, and what he feared most was a siege and entrapment of the capital. So he planned to force McClellan to retreat by a tactical turning movement. By endangering McClellan's communications with his base on the York River, this movement would force him either to withdraw or attack. Jackson, drawn in from the valley, would act as the turning force. On 14 June Col. Alexander Boteler of Jackson's staff rode south to meet Lee, who suggested that Jackson abandon the valley and join him on the peninsula. Boteler hesitated, and said "if you bring our Valley boys down here at this season among the pestilential swamps of the Chickahominy the change from their pure mountain air to this miasmic atmosphere will kill them off faster than the Federals have been doing." Lee laughed and said, "I can see that you appreciate General Jackson as much as I myself do, and it is because of my appreciation of him that I wish to have him here."[21]

Soldiers and civilians alike grew impatient. "If we do not [strike] a blow—a blow that will be felt—it will soon be all up with us," wrote Charles Venable on 16 June. "The Southwest will be lost to us. We cannot afford to shilly-shally much longer. . . . They call Mars Robert 'Ole Spade Lee,' he keeps digging them so. General Lee is a noble Virginian. . . . You let Mars Robert alone. He knows what he is about."[22] The entrenching operations undertaken by the Army of Northern Virginia indeed earned Lee the derisive sobriquet "king of spades" in the press. Some of the army, however, began calling him "Marse Robert," a distinctly Southern term that referred to a plantation master. It fit the life of a soldier as well as a slave, in that both meant absolute obedience to absolute authority. Robert Stiles, a young soldier, wrote, "The proviso with which a ragged rebel accepted the doctrine of evolution, that 'the rest of us may have descended or ascended from monkeys, but it took a God to make Marse Robert.'"[23] On 22 June, from Dabbs, Lee wrote Charlotte Wickham Lee, describing his own appearance. "My coat is of gray, of the regulation style and pattern, and my pants of dark blue, as is also prescribed, partly hid by my long boots," he wrote. "I have the

A variant engraving made from the 1862–3 Minnis and Cowell/Bendann photo adds somewhat softer facial features than the previous effort.
Library of Congress

same handsome hat which surmounts my gray head (the latter is not prescribed in the regulations) and shields my ugly face, which is masked by a white beard as stiff and wiry as the teeth of a card."[24] Curiously, although the General commented on his "regulation style" coat, he never wore the correct collar insignia of a Confederate general officer, three stars within a wreath. Instead, he habitually wore the three plain stars of a colonel, a grade he never held in the Confederacy and only briefly, in 1861, in the U.S. Army. Perhaps the coat he normally wore with its "lay-down" collar (rather than the typical "stand-up" collar) and incorrect grade insignia was a gift, perhaps made for him by admirers, and he simply wore it as a gracious gesture. In no known case did he go unrecognized on the battlefield due to this curiosity.

In any case, the next evening Jackson arrived from the valley and held a conference with Lee, Longstreet, D. H. Hill, and A. P. Hill. The generals decided that a siege would make holding Richmond impossible and therefore they must take the offensive, attempting the turning movement using Jackson as the key. The attack began in late June 1862 and went poorly, transforming into weakly coordinated frontal attacks against McClellan's army.[25]

The resulting battles, a mostly separate action occurring each day for a week, came to be known as the Seven Days. The first action, on 25 June, acquired the name Oak Grove. Rain fell sporad-

The Sarah Watt House near Gaines's Mill, built about 1835, served as Union Maj. Gen. Fitz John Porter's headquarters during part of the action on 27 June 1862. A portion of the Army of Northern Virginia, troops from Georgia and Texas, penetrated the Federal line near this spot.
David J. Eicher

On 27 June 1862 the third battle of the Seven Days erupted at Gaines's Mill. Uncoordinated attacks were the rule but finally, shortly before darkness, the Army of Northern Virginia threw back the Union line. John Reekie photographed the ruins of Gaines's Mill in April 1865.

Library of Congress

When it abandoned its base of supplies at the White House on the Pamunkey, the Union army burned Rooney Lee's house, leaving only brick chimneys standing. The destruction occurred on 28 June 1862.

National Archives and Records Administration

ically and Federal artillery opened fire along the Chickahominy River, Jackson still approaching with his force. Attacks and counterattacks across the Williamsburg Road decided nothing, and the artillery eventually ceased in the evening as a rainbow appeared. Lee planned his great attack for the following morning.

The second of the Seven Days, 26 June, brought bad news. The battle fought on this day at Mechanicsville and along Beaver Dam Creek was poorly coordinated, and Jackson was delayed at Ashland. He failed to reach the field until late afternoon, rather than early morning. This collapsed the Confederate plan, despite Magruder's and Benjamin Huger's competent performance on the right of the Confederate line. During the morning, the artillerist William T. Poague witnessed an unusual encounter between Lee and his son and namesake. "We occupied the field of Cold Harbor overlooking Grapevine Bridge. Here General Lee, followed by well mounted and well dressed staff, rode up to the battery and asked for Private Robert Lee. He could not be found for some time. At last someone found him asleep under a caisson. As he came up to the general, blinking and rubbing his eyes and as dirty as he well could be, the general broke into a broad smile, saying, 'Why Robert, I scarcely knew you, you've changed so much in appearance.' The staff all grinned tittered and all of us

enjoyed the interview between the splendid looking, handsomely mounted general and his son."[26] Late in the afternoon, before Jackson's arrival, John Bell Hood encountered Lee in the field. "I moved on with all possible speed," he wrote, "through field and forest, in the direction of the firing, and arrived, about 4:30 P.M., at a point, on the telegraph road, I should think not far distant from the centre of our attacking force. Here I found General Lee, seated upon his horse. He rode forward to meet me, and, extending his usual greeting, announced to me that our troops had been fighting gallantly, but had not succeeded in dislodging the enemy; he added, 'This must be done. Can you break his line?'"[27]

But success evaded the Southern army. The following day, 27 June, brought the battle of Gaines's Mill, the third of the Seven Days. Maj. Gen. Fitz John Porter's Federals, despite their successful repulse of Confederate attacks the previous day, withdrew along the Union left. Early in the morning, Robert Stiles witnessed a council between Lee and Jackson. "The two generals greeted each other warmly, but wasted no time upon the greeting," he wrote. "They stood facing each other, some thirty feet from where I lay, Lee's left side and back toward me, Jackson's right and front. Jackson began talking in a jerky, impetuous way, meanwhile drawing a diagram on the ground with the toe of his right boot. He traced two

The cost of the Peninsular campaign had been terrific for both armies. In the battle of Gaines's Mill alone, 8,751 Confederate soldiers were killed or wounded and 6,837 Federals. This grisly image made near Gaines's Mill sometime between 1862–1865 shows the remains of several soldiers.

Library of Congress

The noted special artist Alfred R. Waud sketched Lee watching the action at Thoroughfare Gap during the Second Bull Run campaign. The resulting engraving was produced for *Harper's Weekly*.

Author's Collection

sides of a triangle with promptness and decision; then starting at the end of the second line began to draw a third projected toward the first. This third line he traced slowly and with hesitation, alternately looking up at Lee's face and down at his diagram, meanwhile talking earnestly; and when at last the third line crossed the first and the triangle was complete, he raised his foot and stamped it down with emphasis, saying 'We've got him.'"[28] Jackson pursued but was again slow and used the wrong road, becoming lost. He finally attacked, aided by Longstreet, late in the afternoon, and pushed back the Federals. But the battle was not yet decisive and much of the Federal army remained in reserve. The commander himself wrote Jefferson Davis following this action: "Profoundly grateful to Almighty God for the signal victory granted to us, it is my pleasing task to announce to you the success achieved by the army today. The enemy was this morning driven from his strong position behind Beaver Dam Creek and pursued to that behind Powhite Creek and finally, after a severe contest of five hours, entirely repulsed from the field. Night put an end to the contest. I grieve to state that our loss in officers and men was great. We sleep on the field, and shall renew the contest in the morning."[29]

On the 4th day, 28 June, the armies clashed at Garnett's Farm. McClellan assembled his army and moved southward to change his base to the James River. Confederates chased only after their commander was sure of McClellan's intention. On this day McClellan abandoned the White House, and Rooney's charming homestead was burned to the ground, leaving only chimneys.

A more significant action returned on the 5th day, 29 June, at Savage's Station. Magruder struck three Federal corps at this position and expected help from Jackson, who again was lethargic in showing up and offering support. Instead he rested and reconstructed Grapevine Bridge, although he didn't really need it to cross the Chickahominy. As a result, Magruder's attacks melted away. The Federal army continued to move south and fought another action on the 6th day, 30 June, at the White Oak Swamp, or Frayser's Farm. Huger, Magruder, and Jackson all made critical mistakes in carrying out their missions, however, and again the possibility for a decisive attack evaporated. During this action both Lee and President Davis were close to the fighting. "While awaiting the nearer approach of Jackson or the swelling volume of Huger's fire," wrote James Longstreet, "the President, General Lee, and General A. P. Hill, with their staffs and followers, rode forward near my line and joined me in a little clearing of about three acres, curtained by dense pine forests. All parties engaged in pleasant talk . . . very soon we were disturbed by a few shells tearing and screaming through the forests over our heads, and presently one or two burst in our midst, wounding a courier and killing and wounding several horses."[30]

This rather crude, retouched lithographic cartes-de-visite of Lee was probably produced in 1862 or early 1863. It was derived from the 1862–3 Minnis and Cowell/Bendann photo and this lithographic copy may have been taken by J. W. Davies in Richmond and rephotographed for sale by E. and H. T. Anthony in New York.
National Archives and Records Administration

What turned into the final chance for destruction of the Federal force came on the 7th day, 1 July, at Malvern Hill. McClellan's force had backed up into an excellent position and ringed a ridge with artillery. The Army of Northern Virginia anticipated knocking out the Union guns and following up with an infantry assault, but the superior action of the Federal artillery made short work of this idea. First canceling an attack, Lee later ordered another when he thought the Federals were withdrawing. Poorly coordinated, the attacks failed miserably and contributed to alarmingly high casualties. "At Willis's Church I met Gen. Lee," wrote Porter Alexander. "He bore grandly his terrible disappointment of the day before & made no allusion to it."[31]

The Judith Henry House on the Bull Run battlefield, "Spring Hill," burned during the first battle. In 1862 Lee's forces won a decisive victory on the old battlefield; a Federal stand on this hill allowed the Yankees an organized retreat. The rebuilt house stands next to the Bull Run Monument, erected in 1865.
David J. Eicher

Confederate troops at Second Bull Run held fast in the "Deep Cut," part of an unfinished railroad bed that ran through the battlefield in August 1862. Federal Maj. Gen. Fitz John Porter's attack on Stonewall Jackson here utterly failed. When troops ran low on ammunition, they hurled rocks.

David J. Eicher

The campaign ended as McClellan retreated to Harrison's Landing and both armies began to recover from the dizzying blows. Although the Federal army had not been whipped, and the campaign had been poorly managed, Lee had faced a much larger force directly endangering the Confederate capital and had turned it away. The shadows of "Granny Lee" and the "King of Spades" were gone overnight—now Lee was a savior of the Confederate cause. "No captain that ever lived could have planned or executed a better plan," read an editorial in the Richmond *Daily Dispatch* on 9 July.[32] Nine days later, the Richmond *Daily Whig* proclaimed: "[Lee] amazed and confounded his detractors by the brilliancy of his genius, the fertility of his resource, his energy and daring. He has established his reputation forever."[33] "Lee was an aggressive general, a fighter," wrote Moxley Sorrel. "To succeed, he knew battles were to be won, and battles cost blood, and blood he did not mind in his general's work. Although always considerate and sparing of his soldiers, he would pour out blood when necessary or when strategically advisable."[34] The cost was high, however: Confederate casualties amounted to more than 26,000, nearly thirty percent of the available men, as opposed to McClellan's loss of twenty percent casualties.

As McClellan sat at Harrison's Landing, Maj. Gen. John Pope took command of the Union Army of Virginia. He was assigned the protection of Washington and the Shenandoah Valley, and the task of drawing Confederate forces away from Richmond. This he did. Jackson moved north to Gordonsville by mid-July and then was followed by month's end by A. P. Hill, spurred on by McClellan's inactivity. During this period Lee was feeling ill and tired.[35] Jackson arrived at Cedar Mountain on 9 August and

The Henry P. Matthew House, known as the "Stone House," was a prominent landmark during Second Bull Run. The vicinity of this structure served as Union Maj. Gen. John Pope's headquarters; after the battle, it functioned as a major hospital site.

David J. Eicher

clashed with his old nemesis from the valley, Nathaniel P. Banks. Aided by A. P. Hill, Jackson pushed back the Federals but stopped short of his aim of crushing Federal army corps one by one. Lee now sent the bulk of the remainder of his army north to strike Pope before McClellan could react.

On 18 August at Clark's Mountain, Lee and Longstreet together watched the Yankees, using field glasses. "Watching without comment till the clouds grew thinner and thinner," wrote Longstreet, "as they approached the river and melted into the bright haze of the afternoon sun, General Lee finally put away his glasses, and with a deeply-drawn breath, expressive at once of disappointment and resignation, said: 'General, we little thought that the enemy would turn his back upon us this early in the campaign.'"[36]

Several days later, the two armies faced off on opposite sides of the Rappahannock. The bold plan hatched by Lee sent Jackson on a turning movement to threaten the enemy's communications, thus forcing a withdrawal. He wanted to force Pope back to Washington rather than fight a large battle. When Jackson felt too much pressure, he launched another turning movement, this time using Longstreet. A massive assault took place when Lee realized that Pope was simply continuing to attack Jackson.[37]

The battle erupted on 29 August along the old battleground at Bull Run, when Jackson was assaulted on the Confederate left, while Longstreet held back

This striking retouched variant of the 1862–3 Minnis and Cowell/Bendann image was produced by E. and H. T. Anthony in New York.
Eleanor S. Brockenbrough Library, The Museum of the Confederacy, Richmond

John Bell Hood (1831–1879), a courageous and reckless fighter, rose to divisional command in the Army of Northern Virginia. He lost the use of his left arm at Gettysburg and lost his right leg at Chickamauga. Hood subsequently led the Confederacy's great western army to disaster at Franklin and Nashville.
Library of Congress

Perhaps the only photograph of a major Civil War engagement, this view at Antietam was made by Alexander Gardner probably in the late afternoon of 17 September 1862, or possibly the following day. Taken from a ridge near McClellan's headquarters, the Pry House, the view looks south-southwest. The parked artillery in the field below belongs to the Union Fifth Corps, held in reserve. Smoke and dust from troops is visible at right. The soldier with field glasses is looking toward the center of the battlefield.
Library of Congress

The most vicious area of battle at Antietam was a sunken farm road near the Henry Piper House that came to be called Bloody Lane. Confederate infantry used the road as a natural breastwork; waves of Union attacks from the north failed before finally capturing the position. The bodies piled into the road afterward gave the location its infamous name.

David J. Eicher

Lee established headquarters at Antietam in a group of tents in a little clearing in the western part of Sharpsburg. A stone monument now marks the spot.

David J. Eicher

The Lutheran Church in eastern Sharpsburg hosted a brief meeting of Lee and several subordinate officers. Built in 1768, the building served as a signal station and, following the battle, a hospital. During the battle the church was struck by artillery repeatedly. Alexander Gardner photographed the church on 21 or 22 September 1862.

Library of Congress

from attacking as he should have. The first day of Second Bull Run may have become an important victory for Lee. Still, he was encouraged. At 9 P.M. he telegraphed Jefferson Davis: "So far this army has steadily advanced and repulsed the frequent attacks of the enemy. . . . Many prisoners are captured and I regret quantities of stores to be destroyed for want of transportation. . . . We have Ewell, Trimble, and Taliaferro wounded. The latter slightly, the others not mortal."[38] Early the next afternoon Jackson was again hit in force, but artillery from Longstreet perplexed the Union attack and Longstreet thrust a major counterattack that pushed the Federals back onto Henry House Hill, where more than a year earlier Jackson had earned his name.

At 10 P.M. Lee telegraphed Davis: "This Army achieved today on the plains of Manassas a signal victory over combined forces of Genls McClellan and Pope. . . . We mourn the loss of our gallant

dead in every conflict yet our gratitude to Almighty God for his mercies rises higher and higher each day, to Him and to the valour of our troops a nations [sic] gratitude is due."[39] Hood, commanding a division under Longstreet, encountered Lee at the end of the battle. "I found [Gen. Lee] in an open field, near a camp-fire of boards kindled for the purpose of reading dispatches," he wrote. "He was in high spirits, doubtless on account of the brilliant and complete victory just achieved by his Army. He met me in his usual manner, and asked what had become of the enemy. I replied that our forces had driven him almost at a double-quick, to and across Bull Run, and that it was a beautiful sight to see our little battle-flags dancing after the Federals, as they ran in full retreat. He instantly exclaimed, 'God forbid I should ever live to see our colors moving in the opposite direction.'"[40]

Second Bull Run was a major victory for the Army of Northern Virginia. Before he could relish it, Lee suffered a painful accident the very next day. At Stewart's Farm, he suffered a fall, spraining one hand and breaking several bones in the other. Both hands went into splints, one into a sling, and he could not ride a horse for nearly two weeks.[41] He was wearing a poncho standing in the rain with Traveller, holding the horse's reins, when someone shouted "Yankee cavalry!" and a number of prisoners rushed across a nearby embankment, startling the horse. Lee stumbled and fell,

Centerpiece of the Antietam battlefield, the Dunkard Church was so named for a German Baptist Brethren sect that immersed, or dunked, its converts. The structure was savagely fought around during the whole of 17 September, and in 1921 was blown down by a storm. The building was reconstructed in 1962.
David J. Eicher

Another variant image from the 1862–3 Minnis and Cowell/Bendann image was widely distributed throughout the Confederacy and served as the central portrait for the "Military Medallion" (see image on page 133).
Eleanor S. Brockenbrough Library, The Museum of the Confederacy, Richmond

Confederate dead lie scattered along the rail fence on the Hagerstown Pike, north of the Dunkard Church, following the battle of Antietam. Alexander Gardner made the photo on 19 September 1862.
Library of Congress

This lithograph by A. Robin was also derived from the 1862–3 Minnis and Cowell/Bendann image, and was widely distributed in the postwar years. It captures Lee's facial details only crudely.

Author's Collection

A general officer and secretary of war, George Wythe Randolph (1818–1867) left behind only a brief career in the Confederacy. A grandson of Thomas Jefferson and fourth cousin-in-law of Lee's, Randolph served in the field in the late winter of 1862 before accepting the cabinet position. He resigned in November of the same year due to ill health.

Library of Congress

partly catching the reins, and when he arose his hands had been injured.

In the wake of Second Bull Run, the Lincoln government sent John Pope packing. McClellan and the Army of the Potomac absorbed the remnants of Pope's army and reorganized. Lee took his army north of the Potomac and grouped about Frederick, Maryland, by 7 September. He laid the groundwork for his first gigantic raid into the North. To bring the war away from Virginia, gain support from pro-Confederate civilians in Maryland, perhaps win foreign recognition, and maintain the psychological momentum, Lee boldly moved 55,000 men into Maryland. If he could capture Harpers Ferry and move to Hagerstown, his army could sever the main east-west railroad line. He could then "turn my attention to Philadelphia, Baltimore, or Washington, as may seem best for our interests."[42] The army could also "live at the enemy's expense," foraging off the countryside and thereby providing a movable base of supplies—but one that also had to keep moving.[43]

"The present position of affairs, in my opinion," Lee wrote Jefferson Davis on the 8th, "places it in the power of the Government of the Confederate States to propose with propriety to that of the United States the recognition of our independence. For more than a year both sections of the country have been devastated by hostilities which have brought sorrow and suffering upon thousands of homes, without advancing the objects which our enemies proposed to themselves in beginning the contest. . . . The rejection of this offer would prove to the country that the responsibility of the continuance of the war does not rest with us, but that the party in power in the United States elect to prosecute it for purposes of their own."[44] On the 12th, Davis advised Lee to issue a form of proclamation to the citizens of Maryland, telling them that the Confederacy "is waging a war for self-defense," that it has "sought peace," that the "Mississippi River should be free for all navigation," that the Confederacy, "after recent victories, asks only that the United States cease the war and allow the Confederacy to exist in peace," that "the Confederacy has been forced to invade to defend citizens and property," and that "people of the invaded states must take responsibility for the continuing war."[45]

The citizens of Maryland did not react as Davis and Lee had wished. McClellan moved slowly in pursuit and on 13 September, at Frederick, received an incredible gift—a Federal soldier had found D. H. Hill's copy of Lee's Special Orders No. 191, outlining

Under the command of the incompetent Maj. Gen. Ambrose E. Burnside, the Army of the Potomac encamped opposite Fredericksburg in mid-November 1862. On 11 December they crossed the Rappahannock River and faced Lee's army in one of the largest battles of the war.

National Archives and Records Administration

his plan for the Maryland campaign. Astonishingly, McClellan pursued only cautiously after waiting sixteen hours before doing anything. The Confederate high command learned that the order had been found and consequently, finding the Federal army in force at the foot of South Mountain, made a stand at Turner's Gap.[46] The battle of South Mountain took place there and at Fox's Gap and Crampton's Gap on 14 September. Meanwhile, Jackson, sent by Lee to capture Harpers Ferry, accomplished this on the 15th. By again boldly dividing his army, Lee had succeeded in reading the overcaution of his adversary and making use of it. Time now benefited the Army of Northern Virginia as it held fast near Sharpsburg, receiving elements slowly coming in from Harpers Ferry.[47]

On 16 September Jackson and Maj. Gen. John G. Walker arrived at Lee's headquarters at Sharpsburg. "The thought of General Lee's perilous situation," wrote Walker, "with the Potomac River in his rear, confronting, with his small force, McClellan's vast army, had haunted me through the long hours of the night's march . . . he was calm, dignified, and even cheerful. If he had had a

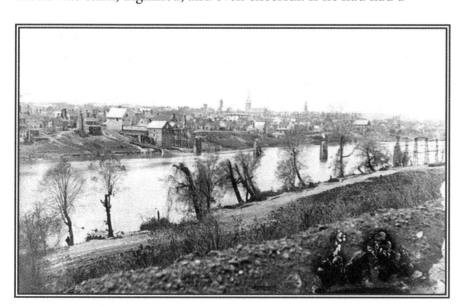

The ensuing battle at Fredericksburg, fought under harshly cold conditions, really consisted of two distinct actions: a large attack on Stonewall Jackson's forces at Prospect Hill, and a frontal assault toward Longstreet's troops on Marye's Heights. The former succeeded for a time before Jackson's forces pushed back Meade; the latter was a fruitless slaughter for the Yankees. Timothy O'Sullivan photographed the town in March 1863.

Library of Congress

A single field piece marks the position of Lee's Hill between Marye's Heights and Howison's Hill. Here on 13 December Lee watched Federal troops being hurled back by a wave of gray-clad infantry, after which he said: "It is well war is so terrible, or we should grow too fond of it."

David J. Eicher

well-equipped army of a hundred thousand veterans at his back, he could not have appeared more composed and confident."[48]

The battle of Antietam, the bloodiest single day of the war, erupted on 17 September as McClellan found the Army of Northern Virginia outside of Sharpsburg along Antietam Creek. It began with a powerful attack from Maj. Gen. Joseph Hooker's First Corps from the north at dawn, striking Jackson in force. Hood counterattacked and soon a series of vicious waves in the northern part of the field pressed back and forth, amassing heavy casualties. "General Lee and I stood on the top of the crest with our glasses, looking at the movements of the Federals on the rear left," wrote Longstreet. "I noticed a puff of white smoke from the mouth of a cannon . . . the cannon-shot came whisking through the air for three or four seconds and took off the front legs of the horse that [D. H.] Hill sat on and let the animal down upon his stumps."[49]

D. H. Hill's men lay down in a sunken farm lane to the south where they fought savagely with a division of the Second Corps. Aided by powerful deployment of Union artillery, by noon the Confederate center had been captured and numerous wounded and demoralized troops thrown back into Sharpsburg. About this time Lee, in the streets of Sharpsburg, encountered his son Rob. "General Lee was dismounted," Rob later wrote, "with some of his staff around him, a courier holding his horse. Captain Poague, commanding our battery, the Rockbridge Artillery, saluted, reported our condition and asked for instructions. The General, listening patiently, looked at us—his eyes passing over me without any sign of recognition—and then ordered Captain Poague to take the most serviceable horses and men. . . . As Poague turned to go, I went up to speak to my father. When he found out who I was he congratulated me on being well and unhurt. I then said: 'General, you are going to send us in again?' 'Yes, my son,' he replied with a smile. 'You must all do what you can to help drive these people back.'"[50] "General Lee rode away as quietly and composedly as if nothing special was going on," wrote Poague. "His equanimity and self possession under the awful stress of that fearful day were marvelous."[51]

To the south, Maj. Gen. Ambrose E. Burnside was delayed in attempting to cross the creek at the lower bridge and push his Ninth Corps westward. He finally succeeded by midafternoon only to be met by a crushing counterattack from A. P. Hill, who had just arrived on a long forced march. Thus ended the momentum of the potential Federal envelopment of the Confederates into Sharpsburg and the day was over, both sides terribly bruised and in need of recovery. Some 4,808 men lay dead on the fields; of Lee's 51,844 engaged, he lost 2,700 killed, 9,024 wounded, and 2,000 missing, amounting to a frighteningly high twenty-six percent casualties. McClellan, who had mismanaged his attacks badly and not even engaged the Fifth Corps, suffered sixteen percent casualties. As night fell, Moxley Sorrel described the meeting of Lee and Longstreet. "Longstreet, big, heavy, and red, grimly stern after this long day's work, that called for all we could stomach, rolled in on his clumsy carpet slippers. Lee immediately welcomed him with unconcealed joy. 'Here comes my war horse just from the field he has done so much to save!' his arm affectionately around 'Peter's' shoulder."[52]

"Lee was not satisfied with the result of the Maryland campaign," wrote Longstreet, "and seemed inclined to attribute the failure to the Lost Dispatch."[53] "My hands are improving slowly," he wrote Mary after the battle, "and with my left hand I am able to dress and undress myself, which is a great comfort. My right is becoming of some assistance, too, though it is still swollen, and sometimes painful. . . . I am now able to sign my name."[54]

Following the campaign the Army of Northern Virginia moved back to Opequon Creek and gathered food and stragglers. McClellan stayed north of the Potomac and tested his value with the War Department, arguing daily about this and that. By November the Army of Northern Virginia had, by regrouping, grown to 85,000, still much smaller than the Federal army but a powerful force, especially if used defensively. His hands still slowly recovering, Lee enjoyed a visit with Custis in October and then received terrible news—his daughter Annie had become ill in Warren White Sulphur Springs, North Carolina, and died on 20 October. "The death

Powerful Union guns overlooked the city of Fredericksburg in December 1862 from the front yard of Chatham at Falmouth. Despite the Federal artillery, foolish tactics helped to enable a great Confederate victory that devastated Northern morale.
David J. Eicher

The J. Horace Lacy Estate, "Chatham," where Lee had years earlier courted Mary, was used in 1862 as headquarters for a number of Union generals. The house sits atop a ridge at Falmouth, overlooking the Rappahannock opposite Fredericksburg. Timothy O'Sullivan captured the house on a glass plate in March 1863.
Library of Congress

of my dear Annie was, indeed, to me a bitter pang," he wrote a daughter on 24 November, "but 'the Lord gave and the Lord has taken away: blessed be the name of the Lord.' . . . I have always counted, if God should spare me a few days after this Civil War was ended, that I should have her with me."[55]

On 7 November, Burnside received a telegram directing him to command the Army of the Potomac. McClellan had argued too much and too long. For the Army of Northern Virginia, Burnside was a better choice—not timid like McClellan but simply incompetent as an army commander. On 17 November the first elements of the Federal army arrived opposite Fredericksburg at Falmouth. Longstreet maneuvered south to oppose them and Jackson was still in the valley.

The resulting battle at Fredericksburg on 13 December was a Federal disaster, the outcome of an ill-conceived plan that was poorly executed. The scheme was taken advantage of fully by Lee, Longstreet, and Jackson, who performed admirably in an action that consisted of two main elements—the "slaughter" of Fredericksburg as Federals fruitlessly charged Longstreet at Marye's Heights, and the battle against Jackson to the south at Prospect Hill and Hamilton's Crossing.

Burnside began crossing troops, exposed to sniper fire, on pontoon bridges on 10 December and completed the operation under a fog two days later. They would need to fight uphill through a city and into a heavily fortified position posted with ample Confederate artillery. "The enemy," Lee wrote Mary on the 11th, "after bombarding the town of Fredericksburg, setting fire to many houses and knocking down nearly all those along the river, crossed over a large force about dark, and now occupies the town."[56] Had Burnside scouted more efficiently, even he may not have executed the plan. Maj. Gen. George G. Meade spearheaded the attack on Jackson's line, driving forward successfully before a counterattack pushed him back after noon. Jackson attempted a major

Placed centrally on Marye's Heights, John L. Marye's house, "Brompton," hosted Confederate artillery during the Fredericksburg battle. Below the heights stood the stone wall attacked in vain by Federal troops. Following the battle Marye's house served as a hospital. The house was photographed by James Gardner in May 1864.

Library of Congress

counterattack that was thwarted by Federal artillery. Maj. Gen. William B. Franklin, commanding the Union left flank, then stayed in position but was inactive.

Meanwhile, on the Union right flank, elements under Hooker advanced through the streets of Fredericksburg after fog lifted, in the late morning. "It is rarely vouchsafed to any one to witness so grand a tableau as was presented to our gaze on that December morning," wrote Walter Taylor, "when the curtain of fog was lifted and the sun lit up the scene with the bright effulgence of its rays. As if by magic, the hosts of the grand Federal army were disclosed in martial array extending from the city down the river as far as the eye could reach."[57] The Yankees moved toward the Confederate defenses on an open plain and over a deep ditch with only two available footbridges, allowing Longstreet's artillery to focus squarely on them. The Federal objective, the base of Marye's Heights, afforded Confederate defenders with a sunken road protected by a stone wall that was a natural defensive stronghold. Lee watched the battle from "Lee Hill" about 1,000 yards southwest of Marye's Heights. Before the attacks on Marye's Heights began, "We noted the thin, pale smoke of infantry fire fading in the far away of their left," wrote Longstreet, "the heavy clouds rising from the batteries on both sides of the river, the bright armored ranks and banners . . . only a few [artillery] shots were sent when the troops that had been lying concealed in the streets of the city came flying out by both roads in swarms at double time and rushed towards us. Every gun that we had in range opened upon the advancing columns and ploughed through their ranks . . . one shell buried itself close under the parapet at General Lee's side, as he sat among the officers of his staff, but it failed to explode."[58] And then came the fruitless attacks. "Presently, however, as was anticipated, the spirited charge was reversed," wrote William N. Pendleton, "and blue figures by thousands were seen recrossing, 'double quick,' with faces to the rear, the space they had traversed, and hundreds of gray pursuers hastening their speed. While younger spectators near us gave impressions to their feelings by shouts, clapping of hands, &c., the gratified yet considerate and amiable commander turned to myself, and with beaming countenance said 'It is well war is so terrible, or we should grow too fond of it.'"[59]

Because of Franklin's inactivity, Lee shifted troops northward to further support the heights, and Hooker's attacks were knocked to pieces. Beaten severely, taking twice the casualties of the

Lee made the cover of the *Southern Illustrated News* on 13 December 1862, although the paper identified him as "Robert Edmund Lee, Commander-in-Chief of the Confederate Forces," mistaking both name and assignment.
Author's Collection

A portion of the stone wall used by Confederates as a defensive barrier below Marye's Heights at Fredericksburg. One portion of the battle witnessed poorly coordinated, hopeless Union assaults on this position, each of which withered in the murderous fire from Lee's army.
David J. Eicher

This striking and unique image probably resulted from the same late 1862 or early 1863 sitting with Minnis and Cowell or Bendann. The copyright stamp on this cartes-de-visite copy bears a claim by Minnis and Cowell in 1863, registering the image in the eastern district of Virginia. The image stands out for the fully-buttoned coat and the extremely rare aspect of showing the General's right side.

Eleanor S. Brockenbrough Library, The Museum of the Confederacy, Richmond

Confederates (half of which occurred at the base of Marye's Heights), Burnside wished to attack again the next day but was talked out of it by his subordinates. The last major operation of the year was a signal victory for the Army of Northern Virginia. At 9 P.M. Lee telegraphed James A. Seddon, the secretary of war. "About 9 A.M. the enemy attacked our right, and as the fog lifted, the battle ran from right to left; raged until 6 P.M.; but, thanks to Almighty God, the day closed (with the attacks) repulsed along the whole front. Our troops behaved admirably, but, as usual, we have to mourn the loss of many brave men. I expect the battle to be renewed at daylight. Please send this to the President."[60] "[The enemy] went as they came," he wrote Mary on 16 December, "in the night. They suffered heavily as far as the battle went, but it did not go far enough to satisfy me."[61]

The year had been a magnificent one for Lee, for the Army of Northern Virginia, and for the Confederacy. In its struggle for survival, the Confederate States had found its leading field commander. Lee had pushed the invading Federal army back from the front door of the Confederate capital. Major victories at Second Bull Run and Fredericksburg had stunned the Federal morale. At Antietam the raiding Confederates had held their own against a much larger army even if they had not achieved their potential goals. New situations and challenges were poised on the horizon for the coming year—one that would test Lee's abilities as a militarist like never before. On Christmas day, writing from the field at Fredericksburg, he shared some of his innermost feelings with Mary. "What a cruel thing is war," he penned, "to separate and destroy families and friends, to mar the purest joys and happiness God has granted us in this world; to fill our hearts with hatred instead of love for our neighbors, and to devastate the fair face of this beautiful world!"[62] In these terms, the coming months would only bring a graver, more desperate war.

CHAPTER SIX

The Glorious Summer of Battle

THE SUN SHONE BRIGHTLY ON CONFEDERATE FORTUNES at the outset of 1863. In the West, Gen. Braxton Bragg fought a large pitched battle against Maj. Gen. William S. Rosecrans at Stones River, Tennessee, on 31 December 1862 and 2 January 1863. Although a strategic disappointment for the South—after which Bragg retreated southward to Tullahoma—it was perceived by many as a victory due to heavy Federal losses. Farther west, Yankees under Maj. Gen. U. S. Grant had pushed southward along the Mississippi River opposite the stronghold of Vicksburg, but the garrison under Lt. Gen. John C. Pemberton, assisted by Nathan Bedford Forrest and Earl Van Dorn, held the Northerners at bay. The situation was slightly worrisome in North Carolina, where a raid by Union Maj. Gen. John G. Foster spread alarm.

Back near Fredericksburg, on 18 January, the Federal army under Burnside began to move. Lee was apprehensive and began two days of intense scouting, after which the Yankees reformed and deactivated. Burnside had found the roads hopelessly mired, and the expedition came to be called the "Mud march." Lee then began to fortify the whole Rappahannock line, a process that continued for several weeks. Although Confederate fortunes were strong, Lee warned Richmond that the coming months would perhaps decide the war. "The enemy will make every effort to crush us between now and June," he wrote, "and it will require all our strength to resist him."[1]

Early in 1863 Lee posed for his first formal portrait as a Confederate general officer. Minnis and Cowell took the photograph in Richmond. Lee wore his field sword and field glasses, and held a black felt hat.
National Archives and Records Administration

An engraving based on the Minnis and Cowell photograph appeared in *Harper's Weekly* on 2 July 1864. The engraving presents only crude facial aspects by comparison with the photo. *Author's Collection*

The Yankees were not exactly doing their best. Lincoln replaced the incompetent Burnside with the hotheaded and intemperate Maj. Gen. Joseph Hooker. "General Hooker is obliged to do something," Lee wrote Agnes on 6 February. "I do not know what it will be. He is playing the Chinese game, trying what frightening will do. He runs out his guns, starts his wagons and troops up and down the river, and creates an excitement generally. Our men look on in wonder, give a cheer, and all again subsides *in statu quo ante bellum*."[2]

It was clear that Hooker planned no action until springtime weather arrived. Meanwhile, shortages began to significantly affect the Army of Northern Virginia. Food shortages posed the biggest problem, for horses as well as the soldiers, and shortages of horses and artillery supplies were becoming serious. Moreover, the condition of the railroads in Virginia had deteriorated rapidly. "General Lee writes anxious letters to which he endorses that he has long foretold the scarcity [of food], that transportation is the present difficulty," wrote Robert G. H. Kean, chief of the Bureau of War, on 1 April. "The railroads are worn out. . . . General Lee has fought all winter *against* this, and now the evil, which much might have been done to remedy during the winter months, is nearly irremediable, and the campaign about to begin."[3]

During the first week of April Lee caught a bad cold, which was worsened by the environment inside his tent. Doctors moved him to the nearby Yerby House, thinking he had developed pericarditis. He experienced occasional sharp chest pains, sustained a fever, and felt sore in his back and arms. By 11 April he was able to ride Traveller again, although his legs were weak and his pulse rate was about ninety beats per minute. The next day a worrisome cough seemed to improve.[4] The doctors "were tapping me all over like an old steam boiler before condemning it," he wrote.[5]

Throughout this month the armies had been maneuvering on opposite sides of the Rappahannock. But the army could discern no clear Federal movement. During these last calm days before the storm, on 27 April, Stonewall Jackson's wife Mary Anna attended a prayer meeting at her husband's headquarters. There she met Lee for the first time. "I remember how reverent and impressive was General Lee's bearing, and how splendid he looked, with his splendid figure and faultless military attire," she wrote. "General Lee was always charming in the society of ladies, and often indulged in a playful way of teasing them that was quite amusing. He claimed the privilege of kissing all the pretty young girls, which was regarded by them as a special honor."[6] And then came the storm. On the morning of 29 April, a distant rumble marked the initiation of Hooker's crossing of the Rappahannock. The campaign of Chancellorsville had begun.

At this time, Lee sought to protect the Virginia Central Railroad, maintain his communications with the Shenandoah Valley, and gather supplies from the area north of Richmond. To prevent a siege of the capital, he determined to hold his line of defense along the Rappahannock and not to allow Hooker to turn his left flank. Instead of falling back, he made a risky attempt to turn Hooker's turning movement.[7]

Hooker's plan to turn Lee's left flank developed into a sound one: Maj. Gen. John Sedgwick placed the First and Sixth Corps opposite Fredericksburg and crossed below the city. Maj. Gen. Darius N. Couch and the bulk of the Second Corps crossed at U.S. Ford opposite Chancellorsville, and Maj. Gens. George G. Meade (Fifth Corps), Henry W. Slocum (Twelfth Corps), and Oliver O. Howard (Eleventh Corps), crossed at Germanna Ford and Ely's Ford and marched on Chancellorsville from the north and west.

On 1 May the battle of Chancellorsville, named for a brick tavern house at a crossroads, began in earnest. The area was a difficult one for tactical maneuvers: dubbed the Wilderness, the surrounding dense woods contained thick second-growth oak and pine with brushy undergrowth. At first the fighting was indecisive, with attacks and counterattacks washing back and forth before Union Maj. Gens. Slocum and Winfield Scott Hancock stubbornly held their ground. Hooker then utterly lost his nerve and ordered a withdrawal, which he later countermanded, but it was too late to reassemble the advanced positions. Lee cautiously followed and worried about Sedgwick's possible drive from the east.

Now Lee's characteristic boldness and desire to grasp the offensive took over and he hatched a controversial—and spectacularly successful—plan. Jackson would take half of the army at hand, some 26,000, and march around the Union right flank, attacking it in force from the west. Early in the morning of 2 May, Lee and Stonewall Jackson had a fateful conference to discuss tactics. "Some time after midnight I was awakened by the chill of the early morning hours, and, turning over, caught a glimpse of a little flame on the slope above me," wrote James Power Smith, a staff officer of Jackson's. "Sitting up to see what it meant, I saw, bending

Another wood engraving based on the Minnis and Cowell photo is more successful in terms of realism. This one appeared in the *Illustrated London News* for 4 June 1864, and the engraver was Frank Vizetelly. The piece was titled *General Robert Edmund Lee, Commander-in-Chief of the Army of the Confederate States of America*, mistaking both Lee's name and assignment. *Author's Collection*

Frank Vizetelly, correspondent for the *Illustrated London News* and a guest of J. E. B. Stuart's, sketched Lee in the field sometime early in 1863. This engraving, published in *Harper's Weekly* on 14 March 1863, was the result.

Author's Collection

over a scant fire of twigs, two men seated on old cracker boxes and warming their hands over the little fire. I had but to rub my eyes and collect my wits to recognize the figures of Robert E. Lee and Stonewall Jackson."[8]

Hooker strengthened his line at Hazel Grove and by early afternoon Jackson had reformed for attack after the early morning march. "The enemy has made a stand at Chancellor's, which is about two miles from Chancellorsville," Jackson wrote Lee at 3 P.M. "I hope, as soon as practicable, to attack. I trust that an ever-kind providence will bless us with success."[9]

Jackson completed his amazing flank march to the west of the Union army and struck at 6 P.M., pushing back the Yankees initially before they regrouped and uncoordinated movements by Jackson's subordinates decelerated the action. About dark Jackson set off to reconnoiter a route to entrap Hooker, but returning, he was accidentally shot by his own troops, hit in his left humerus and right hand. His left arm was amputated at an aid station on the Orange Turnpike and Stonewall was put into an ambulance that would take him toward Richmond. "At 12 midnight I started for General Lee's . . . to inform him of the state of our affairs, making a wide detour, as the enemy had penetrated our lines," wrote Jedediah Hotchkiss, Jackson's topographer. "He was much distressed [about Jackson] and said he would rather a thousand times it had been himself. He did not wish to converse about it."[10] Finally, Lee told Hotchkiss, "I know all about it and do not wish to hear any more—it is too painful a subject."[11]

The next day Lee wrote his fabled lieutenant. "I have just received your note informing me that you were wounded," he wrote. "I cannot express my regret at the occurrence. Could I have directed events, I should have chosen for the good of the country to have been disabled in your stead."[12]

On this morning of 3 May the battle of Chancellorsville raged on without Jackson. The Federal battle line now had a bulge extending to the south around Chancellorsville Tavern and Fairview, another house site, after Hooker withdrew from Hazel Grove. This bulge consisted of the forces of Maj. Gens. Couch, Slocum, and Daniel E. Sickles. Meanwhile, Maj. Gen. James E. B. Stuart assumed temporary command of Jackson's corps to the west, and the divisions of Maj. Gens. Dick Anderson and Lafayette McLaws to the east, with Maj. Gen. Jubal A. Early opposing Sedgwick at Fredericksburg. As the Confederate assaults achieved some initial success, the Federal commander Hooker leaned on a column of the tavern. Just then a shell hit the column, knocking Hooker senseless. "About this time General Lee rode up with some of his staff from the direction of Salem Church followed by Confederate infantry," wrote the artillerist William T. Poague. "Cheering broke out and was taken up by the various bodies of Confederate troops as they converged at this central point."[13] By midmorning Hooker ordered a withdrawal, just as Sedgwick was having success pushing westward from Fredericksburg.

By late afternoon Sedgwick battled his way across the Fredericksburg battlefield of the previous December to Salem Church, Early retreating southward; Sedgwick faced McLaws instead. About this time a courier rode up to Lee and staff with the news about Sedgwick. "When his eye fell upon General Lee he made directly for him, and I followed as fast as I could," wrote Robert Stiles. "He dashed to the very feet of the commanding general, indeed almost upon him, and gasping for breath, his eyes starting from their sockets, began to tell of dire disaster at Fredericksburg—Sedgwick had smashed Early and was rapidly coming in on our rear. I have never seen anything more majestically calm than General Lee was . . . something like a grave, sweet smile began to express itself on the General's face, but he checked it, and raising his left hand gently, as if to protect himself, he interrupted the excited speaker, checking and controlling him instantly, at the same time saying very quietly: 'I thank you very much, but both you and your horse are fatigued and overheated. Take him to that shady tree yonder and you and he blow and rest a little. I'm talking to General McLaws just now. I'll call you as soon as we are through.'"[14]

Darkness brought the struggle to a close. On 4 May the Army of Northern Virginia concentrated against Sedgwick but the attack that came in early evening was a piecemeal affair. Following more maneuvering, Lee planned a decisive attack against Hooker for 6 May, but Hooker initiated an early morning retreat. The battle, hailed by many as Lee's masterpiece, was over. The general commanding had the honor to communicate news of the battle to President Davis, which he did as follows: "Yesterday General Jackson, with three of his divisions, penetrated to the rear of the enemy, and drove him from all of his positions from the Wilderness to within 1 mile of Chancellorsville. He was engaged at the same time in front by two of Longstreet's divisions. This

Allegedly the only soldier Lee addressed by his first name, Henry Heth (1825–1899), nicknamed Harry, spent the early months of the war in western Virginia and in Kentucky. He served well at Chancellorsville, his troops sparked the first action at Gettysburg, and he fought on throughout the actions of 1864 and 1865, surrendering at Appomattox.
Library of Congress

Chancellorsville was Lee's master stroke. A key position, Hazel Grove, changed hands three times during the battle. The house that stood at this spot was demolished. When Union forces abandoned the area on 3 May, Lee could unite the divided army and complete his tactical masterpiece.

David J. Eicher

Catherine Furnace was a key battlefield landmark at Chancellorsville. At the time of the battle the iron works had been defunct for sixteen years. The stone stack that remains was a familiar sight to troops under Stonewall Jackson who passed it on their flank march around the Federal right.

David J. Eicher

morning the battle was renewed. He was dislodged from all his positions around Chancellorsville and driven back toward the Rappahannock, over which he is retreating. Many prisoners were taken, and the enemy's loss in killed and wounded large. We have again to thank Almighty God for a great victory. I regret to state that General Paxton was killed, General Jackson [wounded] severely, and Generals Heth and A. P. Hill slightly wounded."[15]

The victory at Chancellorsville dramatically accelerated the confidence of the Army of Northern Virginia and of the Confederate cause, despite the shortages. "The past week has been a most eventful one," Walter Taylor wrote on 8 May. "The operations of this army under Genl. Lee during that time will compare favorably with the most brilliant engagements ever recorded."[16] Yet there was a heavy price to pay for Chancellorsville. Among the army's 13,000 casualties during the campaign would be its greatest hero of the moment, Jackson. Taken by ambulance to Guinea's Station, he contracted pneumonia and declined rapidly on 10 May. On Jackson's deathbed, surgeon Hunter Holmes McGuire recorded the last, wandering, delirious spoken passages of Jackson. Shortly before he died, Jackson called out for A. P. Hill, ordering him to

"prepare for action," and continued, "Pass the infantry to the front rapidly! Tell Major Hawks . . . let us cross over the river, and rest under the shade of the trees."[17] On the same day Lee wrote James A. Seddon, the secretary of war. "It becomes my melancholy duty to announce to you the death of General Jackson," he wrote. "He expired at 3:15 P.M. to-day. His body will be conveyed to Richmond in the train tomorrow, under the care of Major Pendleton, assistant adjutant general. Please direct an escort of honor to meet at the depot, and that suitable arrangements be made for its disposition."[18] To Mary, he wrote on 11 May, "In addition to the deaths of officers and friends consequent upon the late battles, you will see that we have to mourn the loss of the great and good Jackson. Any victory would be dear at such a price. . . . I know not how to replace him. God's will be done!"[19]

W. L. Sheppard's engraving *R. E. Lee and Stonewall Jackson in Council of War on Night of May 1, 1863* appeared in the expansive series *Battles and Leaders of the Civil War*. The graphic drew from James Power Smith's eyewitness account of seeing the two commanders seated on discarded Federal cracker boxes.
Author's Collection

Following Chancellorsville, the eastern armies flowed back into their old defensive positions along the Rappahannock. By now troubling signs began to emerge. The Army of the Potomac was as formidable as ever. Out west, Grant was threatening Vicksburg, capture of which would cut the Confederacy in half and return control of the Mississippi to the Union navy. In May Grant fought a series of battles from Jackson to Champion's Hill to Big Black River before laying siege to the entrapped Pemberton. In Richmond, something needed to be done. Longstreet proposed shifting troops to strike the centrally placed Rosecrans in Tennessee, drawing Grant away from Vicksburg. But Lee refused to look at the war in that broad a context and stuck to his self-appointed priority of focusing on Virginia. "The secretary of war dispatched Gen. Lee a day or two ago, desiring that a portion of his army, Pickett's division, might be sent to Mississippi," wrote the war clerk John B. Jones on 15 May. "Gen. Lee responds that it is a dangerous and doubtful expedient; *it is a question between Virginia and Mississippi; he will send the division off without delay, if still deemed necessary*. The President . . . says it is just such an answer as he expected from Lee, and he approves it. Virginia will not be abandoned."[20]

A stone monument marks the spot where Lee last met with Stonewall Jackson before the latter's untimely mortal wounding. Afterward, Lee wrote Stonewall, "Could I have directed events, I should have chosen for the good of the country to have been disabled in your stead."
David J. Eicher

The situation was thus set for the Gettysburg campaign. Defending Virginia alone would not accomplish anything and would cast time as a Union advantage. So Lee concocted a plan to

William Henry Fitzhugh Lee (1837–1891), called "Rooney," was Lee's second son. Colonel of the Ninth Virginia Cavalry, Rooney rode with J. E. B. Stuart throughout the first two years of the war. Wounded at Brandy Station and subsequently captured, he returned to service in March 1864.

National Archives and Records Administration

launch another raid into the North, as he had in the Maryland campaign the previous autumn, to draw the war away from Virginia, shift Union forces away from the West, perhaps win foreign recognition, and stay on the offensive. This would put time on his side. He reorganized the army and placed Richard S. Ewell in command of Jackson's old corps. On 9 June Stuart, now commanding the army's cavalry, held a grand review at Brandy Station. "A mimic battle had taken place, preceding the real one," wrote John Esten Cooke of Stuart's staff. "The horse artillery, posted on a hill, fired blank cartridges as the cavalry charged the guns; the columns swept by a great pole, from which the white Confederate flag waved proudly in the wind. General Lee, with his grizzled beard and old gray riding cape, looked on, the centre of all eyes; bands played, the artillery roared, the charging squadrons shook the ground, and from the great crowd assembled to witness the imposing spectacle shone the variegated dresses and bright eyes of beautiful women, rejoicing in the heyday of the grand review."[21]

The next day a massive cavalry battle was fought at Brandy Station pitting Stuart's cavalry against the Federal horse soldiers of Maj. Gen. Alfred Pleasonton. About 10,000 men fought on each side, and the result was highly confused. Rooney was badly wounded in the leg and his father saw him borne off the field on a stretcher. Two days later he wrote Charlotte Wickham Lee, Rooney's wife. "I am so grieved, my dear daughter," he wrote, "to send Fitzhugh to you wounded. But I am so grateful that his wound is of a character to give us fully hope of a speedy recovery. . . . As some good is always mixed with the evil in this world, you will now have him with you for a time, and I shall look to you to cure him soon and send him back to me."[22] The army was now in a full northward movement, heading for Pennsylvania, using the Blue Ridge mountains as a screen. Stuart, harassed by Pleasonton, protected the army's advance up to the Potomac River. Hooker cautiously pursued, with relatively good intelligence about the enemy's whereabouts, whereas Lee lacked such knowledge. "Yankeedom is in a great fright at the advance of Lee's army to the Potomac," wrote Robert G. H. Kean on 21 June, "and considers this part of Pennsylvania south of the Susquehanna as good as gone. . . . General Lee's plans are still wrapped in profound mystery, at least to us in Richmond except doubtless the President and Secretary."[23]

On the 23d the Army of Northern Virginia was mostly safe across the Potomac. "I did not know until we commenced marching that Genl. Lee intended to send us back in the Union, but here we are all in the Union again," wrote Clement A. Evans.[24] Four days later the army had dispersed into positions as follows: Longstreet at Chambersburg, A. P. Hill at Greenwood, Early at York, and Ewell below Carlisle. Lee sent a dispatch to Ewell, "If Harrisburg comes within your means, capture it."[25] Stuart, back in Virginia, received a dispatch from Lee providing orders, and the night was dripping rain, and Stuart was asleep. So Henry B. McClellan of Stuart's staff opened it, and "the letter discussed at considerable length the plan of passing around the enemy's rear. It informed General Stuart that General Early would move upon York, Pa., and that he was desired to place his cavalry as speedily as possible with that, the advance division of Lee's right wing."[26] Upset at being caught off guard at Brandy Station, Stuart hatched a plan to ride northeast of the Federal army, now concentrated at Frederick, to capture supplies and restore his reputation. He captured a train of 125 wagons and headed north to link up with the army.

Late on 28 June a spy of Longstreet's, Edward Harrison, reached Chambersburg with alarming news. The Yankees were concentrated about Frederick and Hooker was out—Maj. Gen. George G. Meade was the new commander of the Army of the Potomac. "I was roused by a detail of the provost guard bring up a suspicious prisoner," wrote G. Moxley Sorrel of Longstreet's staff. "I knew him instantly; it was Harrison, the scout, filthy and ragged, showing some rough work and exposure. He had come to 'report to the General, who was sure to be with the army,' and truly his report was long and valuable. . . . [Harrison] described how they were even then marching in great numbers in the direction of Gettysburg, with intention apparently of concentrating there. . . . [Longstreet] was immediately on fire with such news and sent the scout by a staff officer to General Lee's camp near by. The General heard him with great composure and minuteness."[27]

Lee ordered a concentration at Cashtown, which offered a good defensive position and the ability to strike at a flank of the advancing Federal army. On 30 June the visiting British military observer Arthur J. L. Fremantle described the Confederate commander: "This morning, before marching from Chambersburg, General Longstreet introduced me to the Commander-in-chief [sic]. General Lee is, almost without exception, the handsomest man of his age I ever saw. He is fifty-six years old, tall, broad shouldered, very well made, well set up—a thorough soldier in appear-

"My war horse," said Lee of James Longstreet. The senior corps commander of the Army of Northern Virginia was the officer closest to Lee during the war. Only in postwar years when "Pete" Longstreet joined the Republican party and dared criticize Lee in print did he become the target for Lost Cause hatred and revisionist history.

Library of Congress

One of Lee's favorite soldiers, Ambrose Powell Hill (1825–1865) served gallantly through the Peninsular campaign, at Antietam—where his "light division" fairly saved the day—at Gettysburg and through the Wilderness campaign and Petersburg. On 2 April 1865, the war virtually over, Hill was killed by a Federal soldier.

National Archives and Records Administration

ance. . . . He generally wears a well-worn long gray jacket, a high black felt hat, and blue trousers tucked into his Wellington boots. I never saw him carry arms, and the only mark of his military rank are the three stars on his collar."[28] These stars are the ones erroneously identifying Lee as a colonel, the peculiarity of his uniform mentioned previously.

Brig. Gen. John Buford's Federal cavalry had moved into Gettysburg, a town where ten roads converged, and on the early morning of 1 July Confederates under Henry Heth, on a foraging mission, encountered Buford. Sporadic fighting broke out along the Chambersburg Pike and the Cashtown Road northwest and west of town, and slowly escalated as Buford deployed his dismounted cavalry along McPherson's Ridge. "General Lee and myself left his headquarters together," recalled Longstreet, "and had ridden three or four miles, when we heard heavy firing along Hill's front. The firing became so heavy that General Lee left me and hurried forward to see what it meant."[29] Badly outnumbered, the Union troops nonetheless held ground stubbornly until 9:30 A.M., when the First Corps under Maj. Gen. John F. Reynolds arrived. Bringing on a general engagement went against Lee's orders, and he was by now baffled by the continued absence of Stuart. "[Dick Anderson] found General Lee intently listening to the fire of the guns, and very much disturbed and depressed," wrote Longstreet, referring to activities at 10 A.M. "At length he said, more to himself than to General Anderson, 'I cannot think what has become of Stuart; I ought to have heard from him long before now. He may have met with disaster, but I hope not. In the absence of reports from him, I am in ignorance as to what we have in front of us here. It may be the whole Federal army, or it may be only a detachment.'"[30]

It was not yet the whole Federal army. As the Union First and 11th Corps struggled west and north of town, A. P. Hill pushed west toward the town while Ewell approached from the north. Union Brig. Gen. James S. Wadsworth counterattacked and Reynolds, the Union commander of the field in lieu of Meade, was killed. The Federals recognized the importance of Cemetery Hill, a rise south of town, as they were pushed back and retreated through the town. "General Lee witnessed the flight of the Federals through Gettysburg and up the hills beyond," wrote Walter Taylor. "He then directed me to go to General Ewell, and to say to him that, from the position which he occupied, he could see the enemy retreating over those hills, without organization, and in great confusion; that it was only necessary to press 'those people' in order to secure possession of the heights; and that, if possible, he wished him to do this."[31]

Lee established headquarters on the Chambersburg Pike in a series of tents across the road from the Mary Thompson House. The battle, now becoming a monstrous engagement as reinforcements poured in from both directions, continued to go well for the Army of Northern Virginia. A. P. Hill stopped his advance on Seminary Ridge, west of the town, but Ewell pressed southward through to the northern edge of Cemetery Hill. Although his army was not yet concentrated, Lee felt that once the major battle was underway—even if he had not wanted it—it must be pressed to shatter Meade's army. He therefore ordered Ewell to take Cemetery Hill "if practicable," the latter phrase—a favorite of Lee's—unfortunately vaguely leaving the order open to interpretation. Meanwhile, Edward Johnson approached Culp's Hill, a potentially commanding artillery position, but found it occupied.

Lee's plan now evolved further. He would sweep southward and attack the Union left, enveloping it and pushing northward. "When I overtook General Lee, at five o'clock that afternoon," wrote Longstreet, "he said, to my surprise, that he thought of attacking General Meade upon the heights the next day. I suggested that this course seemed to be at variance with the plan of the campaign that had been agreed upon before leaving Fredericksburg. He said, 'If the enemy is there to-morrow, we must attack him.'"[32]

Both armies massed around Gettysburg during the night, the Army of Northern Virginia assuming a north-south line along Seminary Ridge with Longstreet to the south and Hill to the north. The Federals formed a fishhook-shaped line around high ground on Cemetery Hill, Culp's Hill, and extending south to near the two highest elevation features in the region, Little Round Top and Round Top. Longstreet disagreed with his chief, preferring to fight a defensive battle. But Lee had made up his mind. "We were both

Often faulted for failing at Gettysburg, Richard Stoddert Ewell (1817–1872) fought with distinction and boldness throughout the war to Spotsylvania, when failing health forced a leave. For a year he commanded Stonewall Jackson's old corps. Captured at Sayler's Creek in the closing days of the war, Ewell spent his final years as a Tennessee farmer.
Library of Congress

After the war George Edward Pickett (1825–1875) called Lee "that old man [who] had my division massacred at Gettysburg." Despite being graduated last in his West Point class, Pickett served well in the Peninsular campaign and at Fredericksburg. He longed for the glory that would come with an attack such as Pickett's Charge at Gettysburg. When it failed, he was stunned. He ended the war with an incompetent performance at Five Forks.
National Archives and Records Administration

engaged in company with Generals Lee and A. P. Hill, in observing the position of the Federals," John Bell Hood later wrote Longstreet. "General Lee—with coat buttoned to the throat, sabre-belt buckled round the waist, and field glasses pending at his side—walked up and down in the shade of the large trees near us, halting now and then to observe the enemy. He seemed full of hope, yet, at times, buried in deep thought."[33]

By 11 A.M., a relatively late hour, the orders to attack were issued. By 3 P.M. the Confederate artillery opened fire. "So soon as the firing began," wrote Arthur J. L. Fremantle, "General Lee joined [A. P.] Hill just below our tree, and he remained there nearly all the time, looking through his field-glass, sometimes talking to Hill and sometimes to Colonel Long of his staff. But generally he sat quite alone on the stump of a tree. What I remarked especially was, that during the whole time the firing continued, he only sent one message and only received one report. It is evidently his system to arrange the plan thoroughly with the three corps commanders, and then leave to them the duty of modifying and carrying it out to the best of their abilities."[34]

Opportunities were present. The Round Tops were up for grabs. Moreover, Union Maj. Gen. Daniel E. Sickles moved his Third Corps, against orders, out into an exposed salient through the Wheatfield and Peach Orchard. Longstreet's attack came at

The Mary Thompson House photographed by Mathew Brady on 15 July 1863. Lee's headquarters at Gettysburg was established near this structure in a group of tents; a number of Confederate officers used the house intermittently.

Library of Congress

4 P.M. Hood punched through the salient and captured a rocky feature known as the Devil's Den near the base of Little Round Top. About this time Union Maj. Gen. Gouverneur K. Warren discovered the open nature of Little Round Top and ordered it occupied. Uncoordinated attacks and counterattacks moved back and forth across various parts of the field. Ewell failed to attack until nearly dark, Johnson had no success at Culp's Hill, and Confederate casualties were heavy. Lee was clearly not at his best at Gettysburg, and in fact he was bothered intermittently by diarrhea and possibly a recurrence of malaria.[35]

An upturned cannon marks the position at Gettysburg of the General Headquarters, Army of Northern Virginia. The series of tents stood across the Chambersburg Pike from the Thompson House.
David J. Eicher

That night the Federal high command decided to stay and fight another day. At daybreak on 3 July Longstreet pressed to move around the Yankee left and force Meade to attack. Lee was adamant about hitting the Yankees on Cemetery Ridge. Longstreet later recalled their early morning conference. "'General,' said Longstreet, "I have had my scouts out all night, and I find that you still have an excellent opportunity to move around to the right [south] of Meade's army, and maneuvre him to attack us.' He replied, pointing with his fist at Cemetery Hill, 'The enemy is there, and I am going to strike him.' I then felt that it was my duty to express my convictions; I said: 'General, I have been a soldier all my life. I have been with soldiers engaged in fights by couples, by squads, companies, regiments, divisions, and armies, and should know, as well as any one, what soldiers can do. It is my opinion that no fifteen thousand men ever arrayed for battle can take that position.'" General Lee then ordered Longstreet to prepare Pickett's division for attack.[36]

The Confederate attack would strike at the Union center, toward a copse of trees and an angle in a defensive stone wall. About 13,000 troops commanded by Maj. Gen. George E. Pickett, Brig. Gen. Johnston Pettigrew, and Brig. Gen. Isaac R. Trimble would make the charge across more than a mile of open ground, following a stiff artillery barrage designed to soften the Yankee defenses. The 159 Confederate guns opened at 1 P.M. and were answered promptly by Federal artillery from Cemetery Hill to Little Round Top. After an hour, the guns silenced, the Confederates assuming Yankee batteries were running low on ammunition. Then the charge began. It utterly failed. "All accounts of the charge agree that its failure began when the advance had covered about half the distance to the Federal line," wrote Porter

The strategic key at Gettysburg was Little Round Top, a craggy hill littered with boulders that offered a spectacular artillery position. Intense fighting on 2 July resulted in Federal occupation of the heights, an unfortunate occurrence for Lee's army. The image was made by Timothy O'Sullivan on 6 July 1863.

Library of Congress

Alexander, who directed the artillery. "At that point the left flank of Pettigrew began to crumble away and the crumbling extended along the line to the right. . . ."[37]

After ragged and bleeding troops stumbled back, Fremantle approached Lee. "His face, which is always placid and cheerful," wrote Fremantle, "did not show signs of the slightest disappointment, care, or annoyance; and he was addressing to every soldier he met a few words of encouragement, such as 'all this will come right in the end.'"[38] A short time later, he described the commander again. "I saw General Wilcox . . . come up to him and explain, almost crying, the state of his brigade. General Lee almost immediately shook hands with him and said cheerfully, 'Never mind, all this has been my fault, it is I that have lost this fight, and you must help me out of it the best way you can.'"[39] Meanwhile, Stuart had finally arrived and been repulsed east of the town by Federal Brig. Gen. David M. Gregg. Gettysburg was over, the Federal commander not pursuing with even his relatively fresh Sixth Corps and the bulk of both armies in need of recovery. The Army of Northern Virginia had lost a devastating 28,000 men, about one-third of their force, while Meade lost 23,000, about one-fourth of his effective force.

For Lee, it was a defeat from which he would never fully recover. That night, he met with a number of officers to plan the retreat. "I ventured to remark, in a sympathetic tone, and in allusion to his great fatigue: 'General, this has been a hard day on you,'" wrote John D. Imboden. "He looked up, and replied mournfully, 'Yes, it has been a sad, sad day to us,' and immediately relapsed into his thoughtful mood and attitude."[40]

The following day, Lee wrote several missives, one of which constituted a short report to Jefferson Davis. "Upon reaching the vicinity of Gettysburg, found the enemy and attacked him, driving him from the town, which was occupied by our troops," he wrote. "The enemy's loss was heavy, including more than 4,000 prisoners. He took up a strong position in rear of the town, which he immediately began to fortify, and where his re-inforcements joined him. On the 2d July, Longstreet's Corps, with the exception of one division, having arrived, we attempted to dislodge the enemy, and, though we gained some ground, we were unable to get possession of his position. The next day, the third division of General Longstreet having come up, a more extensive attack was made. The works of the enemy's extreme right and left were taken, but his numbers were so great and his position so commanding, that our troops were compelled to relinquish their advantage and retire. It is believed that the enemy suffered severely in these operations, but our own loss has not been light.

"General Barksdale was killed," he continued. "Generals Garnett and Armistead are missing, and it is feared that the former is killed and the latter wounded and a prisoner. Generals Pender and Trimble are wounded in the leg, General Hood in the arm and General Heth slightly in the head. General Kemper, it is feared, is mortally wounded. Our losses embrace many other valuable officers and men. General Wade Hampton was severely wounded in a different action in which the cavalry was engaged yesterday."[41] He then wrote another long letter asking to be relieved of command. Davis did not take him up on this. On the same day, another setback befell the Confederacy when Vicksburg capitulated to Grant. It marked the beginning of a bleak period for Confederate morale, especially as life on the home front had become nearly intolerable with shortages, substitutions, and a downwardly spiraling economy. It was a burst for Yankee morale and cast a gloom over the Confederacy, yet the Confederate mili-

A Confederate sharpshooter lies dead in the Devil's Den at Gettysburg. The photograph was made by Timothy O'Sullivan on 6 July 1863. It is a contrivance, the body having been moved from a different location for effect.
Library of Congress

At Gettysburg, the Angle served as a focus for the attack by Pickett, Pettigrew, and Trimble on the third day of the battle. Federal artillery at this position and stretching far to the north and south raked those troops in Pickett's Charge, forcing Lee's army to retreat southward.

David J. Eicher

tary machine remained viable and most of the Confederate States had not yet fallen into Northern occupation.[42]

On 13–14 July Lee finally retreated southward across the rain-swollen Potomac. "The General's anxiety was intense," wrote Moxley Sorrel of the crossing. "He expected to be attacked at the passage of the river. . . . General Lee, like every one, had been up the whole night, and his staff officers were stretched in sleep on the ground. . . . Just then a heavy gun was fired lower down, filling the gorge of the river with most threatening echoes. 'There,' said the General. 'I was expecting it, the beginning of the attack.'"[43] But no attack came—only a period of prolonged inactivity for the Army of Northern Virginia. In the wake of Brandy Station, where he had been wounded, Rooney was captured at "Hickory Hill," near Hanover Court House. He was placed into Federal captivity near the site of the White House, his old home. "I can appreciate your distress at Fitzhugh's situation," Lee wrote Charlotte Wickham Lee from Culpeper Court House at month's end. "I deeply sympathise with it, and in the lone hours of the night I groan in sorrow at his captivity and separation from you. But we must bear it, exercise all our patience, and do nothing to aggravate the evil."[44]

On 8 August Lee again attempted to tender his resignation. "Everything, therefore, points to the advantages to be derived from a new commander," he wrote Davis, "and I the more anxiously urge the matter upon Your Excellency from my belief that a younger and abler man than myself can be readily obtained."[45] Davis replied, "I am truly sorry to know that you still feel the effects of the illness you suffered last Spring, and can readily understand the embarrassments you experience in using the eyes of others, having been so accustomed to make your own reconnaisances. . . . To ask me to substitute you by some one in my judgment more fit to command, or who would possess more of the confidence of the army or of the reflecting men in the country is to demand for me an impossibility."[46] By 2 September some were questioning Lee's continued popularity. The war clerk John B. Jones wrote, "[Lee] rode out with the President yesterday, but neither were greeted with cheers. I suppose Gen. Lee has lost some popularity among idle street walkers by his retreat from Pennsylvania."[47]

While the situation was quiet in Virginia, matters were heating up in Tennessee and Georgia. Union forces under Rosecrans moved to occupy Chattanooga and threatened Gen. Braxton Bragg, south of the city in northern Georgia. Longstreet was ordered south to help support Bragg. The resulting battle along Chickamauga Creek was a tremendous Confederate victory, spurred by Longstreet's frontal attack that coincided with confused Union orders. "My whole heart and soul have been with you and your brave corps in the late battle," Lee wrote Longstreet, from near Orange Court House on 25 September. "It was natural to hear of Longstreet and [D. H.] Hill charging side by side, and pleasing to find the armies of the East and West vying with each other in valor and devotion to their country."[48] The Union army retreated in chaos to Chattanooga but regrouped to stun Bragg at Missionary Ridge and push him southward again in November.

During September and October Lee's health worsened. A severe cold exacerbated the rheumatism in his back. He experienced intense pain when riding his horse. By October his rheumatism was so severe that he was confined to his tent. For some time he could not mount a horse.[49] "I moved yesterday into a nice pine thicket, and Perry [a servant] is to-day engaged in constructing a chimney in front of my tent, which will make it warm and comfortable," he wrote Mary from Camp Rappahannock on 25 October. "I am glad you have some socks for the army. . . . I wish they could make some shoes, too. We have thousands of barefooted men."[50]

The Southern army was concentrated between Gordonsville and the Rapidan River. After minor operations and false starts on a new campaign, Meade moved south on 7 November. The stage for the Mine Run campaign was set. During mid-November Lee rode a

General Robert Edmund Lee by John W. Torsch used as its basis the Minnis and Cowell photographs of 1863. The wood engraving was published in the *Southern Illustrated News* on 17 October 1863. Although the paper erred with Lee's name and his uniform coat, it offered relatively satisfying facial features and beard.
Author's Collection

Confederate prisoners at Gettysburg stand against log breastworks at the Lutheran Theological Seminary on Seminary Ridge. The photo was made by Mathew Brady, possibly on 15 July 1863. The defiance in these soldiers' faces symbolizes the fight left in mid-war for the Confederate cause.
Library of Congress

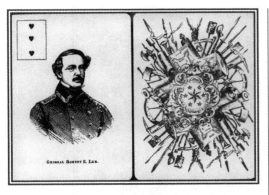

How the soldiers played with General Lee. In 1863 the firm M. Nelson in New York created a set of playing cards featuring Confederate generals, and Lee became the three of hearts.

Author's Collection

James Alexander Seddon (1815–1880) served as a Virginia delegate to the Washington Peace Conference in 1861 and subsequently served in the first Confederate Congress. In November 1862 Seddon became Confederate secretary of war, a position he held until February 1865, when ill health forced him to resign.

National Archives and Records Administration

fair amount but experienced sharp pains and remained stiff.[51] He now took to staying inside a house rather than his customary tent. "The house General Lee occupied was a small frame structure on the side of the road and I found him already up and partially dressed, though it was still long before daylight," wrote William W. Blackford on 26 November. "The room contained little else in the way of furniture than the General's camp bed, a small camp writing table and some camp stools. He was walking backwards and forwards in his shirtsleeves before a bright wood fire, brushing his hair and beard. . . . 'Well, Captain,' said he, 'what do you think they are going to do?' . . . I told him . . . attack. . . . He then resumed his walk and the brushing of his hair for a while and then faced me again and said, 'Captain, if they don't attack us today we must attack them.'"[52]

By late in the month Confederates were constructing winter quarters. Meade marched quickly ahead, crossed the Rapidan, and turned west against A. P. Hill and Ewell. But the plan unfolded more slowly and Confederates reacted, digging in defensive positions. At month's end Meade prepared to attack and then on 2 December Lee launched a turning movement of his own, but Meade had by then retreated. It was an unspectacular ending to a glorious summer of battle. In this last month of 1863 Lee seemed to age considerably and his hair and beard turned white. He still experienced a sharp pain intermittently, particularly on his left side.[53] On 2 December he told Charles Venable, "I am too old to command this army; we should never have permitted these people to get away."[54] Moreover, Mary's illnesses were deepening as well. "I was grieved at the condition in which I found your poor cousin Mary [Custis Lee]," Lee wrote Margaret Stuart from Orange on Christmas Day. "She is now a great sufferer. Cannot walk at all, can scarcely move."[55]

And then came a greater tragedy. Rooney was now imprisoned at Fort Monroe. And on 26 December Lee received a horrifying telegram, announcing the death of Rooney's wife Charlotte. "Custis' dispatch which I received last night demolished all the hopes in which I had been indulging during the day of dear Charlotte's recovery," Lee wrote Mary on 27 December. "It has pleased God to take from us one exceedingly dear to us, and we must be resigned to his [sic] holy will. . . . What a glorious thought it is that she has joined her little cherubs and our angel Annie in heaven! Thus is link by link of the strong chain broken that binds us to earth, and smoothes our passage to another world."[56]

CHAPTER SEVEN

❧

A Modern Kind of War

I N 1864 THE AMERICAN CIVIL WAR TRANSFORMED IN character and the Confederacy began a more desperate fight for its continued existence. The period January–March witnessed relative inaction, with Lee encamped at Clark's Mountain south of the Rapidan and Meade stretched north of the river from Culpeper to Manassas. Supplies, food, and morale for the army were low. On 22 January Lee wrote James A. Seddon, the secretary of war. "Short rations are having a bad effect upon the men, both morally and physically," he wrote. "Desertions to the enemy are becoming more frequent, and the men cannot continue healthy and vigorous if confined to this spare diet for any length of time. Unless there is a change, I fear the army cannot be kept together."[1]

On the same day, in his General Orders No. 7, he communicated to the army a heartfelt message describing the situation as out of his control. He appealed to their patriotic, religious, and manly qualities: "Soldiers! You tread, with no unequal steps, the road by which your fathers marched through suffering, privation and blood to independence! Continue to emulate in the future, as you have in the past, their valor in arms, their patient endurance of hardships, their high resolve to be free, which no trial could shake, no bribe seduce, no danger appall and be assured that the just God who crowned their efforts with success, will in His own good time, send down His blessings to you."[2]

Events for the Lee family took a downturn when on

An exceptionally crisp copy of the full-length Vannerson pose (see the image on page 102) measures an impressive 8 1/4" by 11" and was signed by Lee. On the verso of this copy Edward V. Valentine wrote, "sent through blockade to Berlin in modelling a statuette for a bazaar in Liverpool, E. V. Valentine."

The Valentine Museum, Richmond

In early 1864 Lee sat at Julian Vannerson's studio in Richmond for studies to be used in the execution of a statue to raise war funds. Of the three resulting images, this is perhaps the strongest, clearly showing the General's facial features, graying beard, and uniform coat.

Library of Congress

A striking left profile from the Vannerson session records Lee's folded hands and clearly shows the form of his torso. The images were sent through the blockade to the sculptor Edward V. Valentine in Berlin, where they were received on 5 May 1864, the first day of the battle of the Wilderness.

The Valentine Museum, Richmond

A full-length pose from the Vannerson session shows Lee in long pants over his boots (as opposed to the somewhat similar pose with high boots made by Minnis and Cowell in 1863). This pose served as the primary model for the Valentine statuette. Lee signed this cartes-de-visite copy of the image.

Leyburn Library, Washington and Lee University

Valentine's statuette from the Vannerson poses, 20" tall, was completed 9 November 1864, too late for the Liverpool bazaar. Instead, it was sent to London, exhibited in a well-known shop, and eventually sent to Scotland.

The Valentine Museum, Richmond

11 January the Lincoln administration purchased the title to Arlington house for $26,800. The primary Lee house was now gone. The family moved into a brick house owned by John Stewart at 707 East Franklin Street in Richmond, where they would stay until June 1865. Called "The Mess," Custis and his army friends had used the house before this. By this time Rooney had been exchanged and was back with the Confederate army.

On 22 February Lee traveled to Richmond to confer with President Davis. The Southern diarist Mary Boykin Chesnut, at the White House, recorded the next morning's scene: "At the president's. General Lee breakfasted there. A man named Phelan [James, an Alabama senator] told him all he ought to do, planned a campaign for him. General Lee smiling blandly all the while, though he did permit himself a mild sneer at the wise civilians in Congress who refrained from trying the battlefield in person but from afar dictated the movements of armies."[3]

Five days later Union Brig. Gen. Judson Kilpatrick and Col. Ulric Dahlgren launched a cavalry raid to the outskirts of Richmond in an attempt to liberate Federal prisoners. Papers allegedly found on Dahlgren suggested a plan to assassinate Davis and other Confederate leaders and to burn the city. This of course created high excitement, but on 13 March Robert G. H. Kean wrote, "General Lee's answer put a quietus on the plan if such there was. It was a very calm, sober expression of the opinion that the criminal *intentions* of Dahlgren were not brought home either to his men or their Government. . . ."[4]

In early March the Lincoln government made a fundamental change that would alter the remainder of the war by placing Lt. Gen. Ulysses S. Grant in command of all Federal armies—about 553,000 men in the field. Grant understood the nature of how the war would have to be won far more clearly than his predecessors, and would now focus not on capturing Richmond but on relentlessly pursuing the Confederate armies and crushing their fighting capability. Grant would stay away from Washington and accompany Meade in the field, so that a duel would develop between Lee and the team of Grant and Meade. In April Grant began to concentrate on the Army of Northern Virginia in person. He coordinated movements with Meade west of Fredericksburg and Maj. Gen. Benjamin F. Butler's Army of the James in the rear of Richmond on the James River. Butler's army would focus on eliminating communications to the south, forcing Lee to reinforce the city. This would permit Meade to work against the Confederate forces north of the city.[5] "The General called me into his tent this afternoon to talk over some matters," wrote Walter Taylor on 3 April, "and after discussing some things all relating to Grant's movements & probable intentions he said 'but Colo we have got to whip them, we must whip them and it has already made me better to think of it.'"[6]

Grant's combined strategy called for destroying the Army of Northern Virginia as his chief lieutenant, Maj. Gen. William T. Sherman, pursued and defeated Gen. Joe Johnston's army in Georgia. "Wherever Lee goes, there you will go also," Grant wrote Meade. The Confederate defenses were far too strong for frontal attacks, however, and so Grant adopted a strategy of a series of turning movements against Lee's right flank. The campaign began on 4 May as the first elements of the Army of the Potomac crossed the Rapidan southward into the Wilderness, toward the same battleground where Jackson had been mortally wounded the previous year, and Lee shifted his forces to meet the onslaught. "Genl. Lee is said to express the utmost confidence in our success," wrote Harvey Black, "and Major Bridgford remarked this evening that if any man felt despondent he ought to visit the Old Chief, and he would be

This lithograph, published in 1895 in *The Confederate Soldier in the Civil War*, is based on the Vannerson left profile view.
Author's Collection

Superficially similar to the Vannerson poses and labeled "retouched Vannerson portrait," this image is from an unknown date.
Virginia Historical Society, Richmond

On 5 May 1864 the battle of the Wilderness erupted in Saunders Field, sparked by 12,000 Union troops moving out from the trees. Behind the initial attack, Lee's army faced a massive army spreading east and southeast.

David J. Eicher

As the Wilderness battle began, Federal officers seized the J. Horace Lacy House, "Ellwood," and used it as a headquarters. The thick brush and second-growth woods that gave the region its name made fighting even more chaotic than usual.

David J. Eicher

revived by his very manner and expression of countenance as he promenades in front of his tent."[7] The General wrote Davis on the 4th: "You will already have learned that the army of Gen Meade is in motion, and is crossing the Rapidan on our right, whether with the intention of attacking, or moving towards Fredericksburg, I am not able to say. But it is apparent that the long threatened effort to take Richmond has begun, and that the enemy has collected all his available force to accomplish it."[8]

The bloody battle of the Wilderness that resulted on 5–7 May was sparked when Ewell accidentally encountered Warren along the Orange Turnpike. Lee's army of approximately 64,000 men faced one of the largest field armies assembled in history, about 119,000 with Grant and Meade. To make matters worse, during the campaign, Lee was sick eleven of forty-four days, while Grant was healthy every day.[9] "[Lee] was ill and confined to his tent at the time," wrote Evander M. Law on 5 May, "but, as showing his purpose he had been able to keep the saddle, he was heard to say, as he lay prostrated by sickness, 'We must strike them a blow; we must never let them pass us again.'"[10]

The advantage offered to the Southern army would come from striking the larger force in the confused tangle of the Wilderness where visibility was poor and tactics fell apart in the chaos of action. As yet without Longstreet, Lee did not wish to begin a general engagement, but after the first clashes, Ewell and A. P. Hill struck eastward at the Federals under Warren and Sedgwick along the Orange Turnpike and the Orange Plank Road. The noisy, clumsy approach of an attacking force through the thick underbrush made it an appealing target for defenders. By late afternoon Hancock's Union Second Corps arrived and deployed on the left flank. Capt. John D. Young described A. P. Hill and Lee observing the situation late in the afternoon. "[Lee appeared] intensely disgusted at the turn which affairs had taken," he wrote. "The ridiculous procedure of the ambulance corps, the teamsters, and the camp-followers generally, was singularly well calculated to aggravate this irritated feeling; for those people, supposing the day to have been lost, sought the rear with keen ardor, leaving the road so blockaded with sporadic plunder, and wagons turned upside-down, as to render difficult the movement of the supports. The 'old man' was in no good humor, and had a business look about the eyes as he ordered the guns to be loaded with canister, and trained down the road."[11]

By the morning of the 6th, Burnside's Union Ninth Corps arrived at the Wilderness Tavern, behind the Union center, and Longstreet was finally approaching behind Hill. Vicious activity gave way to a temporary lull about 11 A.M., after which Longstreet coordinated a powerful flank attack that was successful, but during which Longstreet was wounded accidentally by his own men. By late afternoon a reorganized continuance of the attack under Lee's own direction was running out of time, and on the extreme left John B. Gordon launched a successful attack before darkness fell. "To reach our position we had to pass within a few feet of General Lee," William C. Oates wrote of the day. "He sat his fine gray horse 'Traveler' [sic], with the cape of his black cloak around his shoulders, his face flushed and full of animation. The balls were flying around him from two directions. His eyes were on the fight then going on south of the Plank Road between Kershaw's division and the flanking column of the enemy. . . . He turned in his saddle and called to his chief of staff in a most vigorous tone, while pointing with his finger across the road, and said: 'Send an active young officer down there.' I thought him at that moment the grandest specimen of manhood I ever beheld."[12] At another point on 6 May, William T. Poague recalled his commander: "Gregg's Texans came in line of battle at a swinging gait from the rear of our position. They passed through our guns, their right

The Widow Tapp House on the Wilderness battlefield, no longer extant, served as Lee's headquarters. The open field surrounding the house allowed Confederate batteries to fire efficiently into the Union lines.
David J. Eicher

A mini-siege occurred at Spotsylvania from 8–21 May, with the Confederate lines arranged in a "mule shoe" pattern. The action at the Bloody Angle, now marked by monuments, was among the severest of the war.
David J. Eicher

One of the supreme heroes of the Confederacy, James Ewell Brown "Jeb" Stuart (1833–1864) was adored by Lee. Stuart was Lee's third cousin-in-law, once removed. The dashing cavalryman displayed boldness that often confused Federal cavalry until mid-1863. Stuart's death the following spring at Yellow Tavern shocked Lee badly.

Library of Congress

After falling at Yellow Tavern on 11 May 1864, J. E. B. Stuart died the following day in Richmond. He was buried in Hollywood Cemetery, the city's largest and most distinguished burying ground. This image was taken in 1865.

Library of Congress

near the road. General Lee was riding close behind them. Of course our firing to the front had to cease now and only two pieces continued across the road. Soon the Texans began to call to General Lee to go back, and as he seemed not to heed they became clamorous, insisting that if he did not go back they would not go forward. . . . Then, turning Traveller about, he rode quietly to the rear of our line of guns, amid the cheers of the artillerymen."[13]

On 7 May the armies were mainly dormant, separated by a mere three-quarters of a mile. A fire burned across parts of the Wilderness, killing wounded who were too weak to crawl away. The losses from the battle may have been as great as 11,000 Confederates and 18,000 Yankees. In the evening Federal troops began a pullout and raced southward toward Spotsylvania Court House, a key junction of roads, and the site where Light-Horse Harry Lee was imprisoned for a time many years before. A race ensued, and the Confederate First Corps, commanded now by Dick Anderson in Longstreet's absence, hit the Federals along the Brock Road north of the town.

The Confederates won the race to Spotsylvania and immediately began constructing a defensive line. They blocked Meade. Butler vacillated at Bermuda Hundred, wasting valuable time; this allowed Beauregard to counterattack and "bottle him up."[14] On the afternoon of the 8th both armies concentrated toward Spotsylvania. Grant ordered Maj. Gen. Phil Sheridan to take the Union cavalry and move south to the James, which led to a raid from 9–24 May that skirted the outer defenses of Richmond. The raid failed to damage seriously the Confederate cavalry but it did produce a stunning casualty when Maj. Gen. James E. B. Stuart was mortally wounded at Yellow Tavern, north of the city, on 11 May. He died in Richmond the following day. Lee could only say, "I can scarcely think of him without weeping!"[15]

Meanwhile, the situation at Spotsylvania was becoming a micro-siege that would last until 21 May. The Confederate line was formed in a semicircle facing north with Anderson on the left, Ewell at center, and Jubal Early, now commanding Hill's corps, on the right. On 9 May Hancock's Second Corps closed up on the

Union right, assisted by Warren's Fifth Corps and Maj. Gen. Horatio G. Wright's Sixth Corps, while Burnside's Ninth Corps approached from the left. The admired Federal corps commander John Sedgwick had been killed by sniper fire during the day. "We have succeeded so far in keeping on the front flank of that army," Lee wrote Davis on that day, "and impeding its progress, without a general engagement, which I will not bring on unless a favorable opportunity offers, or as a last resort. Every attack made upon us has been repelled and considerable damage done to the enemy. With the blessing of God, I trust we shall be able to prevent Gen. Grant from reaching Richmond. . . ."[16]

On 10 May the Confederates solidified their formidable defenses while Hancock scouted an opportunity for attack. He turned the Confederate army's left flank, imperiling its communications, but did not follow up with a reinforced attack. Instead, frontal assaults were ordered across the line between 4 P.M. and 7 P.M., the most carefully planned attack from Col. Emory Upton against Ewell at 6:10 P.M. This succeeded until a withdrawal became necessary at dark.

After a day of rest, a vigorous Federal attack directed by Hancock and using the Second and Ninth Corps erupted at 4:35 A.M. on 12 May. After the early morning fog dissipated slightly, an enormous rush took place toward the Confederate line, particular-

As Lee's army suffered heavy casualties during the spring of 1864, it became clear that there would be fewer and fewer replacements. Officers suffered a high rate of injury and death, as with Col. Thomas J. Hardin of the 19th Mississippi Infantry, who "fell in battle of Spotsylvania, May 12th, 1864."
David J. Eicher

A dead Confederate soldier at the Widow Alsop's Farm near Spotsylvania Court House, Virginia. Timothy O'Sullivan made the photograph on 20 May 1864. For the Army of Northern Virginia, the price of the May campaign was daily becoming ever higher.
Library of Congress

While Lee's options diminished, U. S. Grant continued his southward movement following Spotsylvania. An image made by Timothy O'Sullivan on 21 May 1864 shows Grant, George Meade, and their staffs at Massaponax Church. Grant is near left, leaning over the pew that was removed to act as a bench.

Library of Congress

Richard Heron Anderson (1821–1879) served gallantly in Longstreet's corps throughout most of the war. When in the Wilderness Longstreet was seriously wounded, Anderson took command of the corps. Later the lieutenant general commanded a new Fourth Corps, a short-lived unit. He died virtually penniless.

National Archives and Records Administration

ly the northernmost salient in the C-shaped line, called the Mule Shoe. The Union soldiers overran the Mule Shoe and vicious hand-to-hand fighting ensued, accompanied by the monstrous clatter of nearly continuous small arms fire. Gordon counterattacked and drove the Federals back, and the Yankee general Wright again struck the Mule Shoe while Confederates worked on a new line of defenses south of the Harrison House. "Lee's position during the day was near Early's lines," reported Charles Venable, "where he observed, from time to time, the movements of the Federal troops in aid of Hancock's attack, and counter-movements of Early's troops. He was with the artillery when it broke Burnside's assault. Lee was present dictating notes and orders in the midst of his guns."[17] Lee and Gordon sat on their horses as a line of enemy advanced toward the Spotsylvania works on this day. As reported by Col. J. Catlett Gibson, a number of men called out, "Come back, General Lee, we won't fight as long as you are before us, come back." Gordon led Traveller's bridle to the rear among shouts of "Three cheers for General Lee and Old Virginia!"

As both armies again rested, the Federal soldiers reset their priorities for an attack early on the morning of 14 May. Warren and Wright had to maneuver through thick woods without roads and heavy rains obscured the operation. Because of these movements the Confederate line shifted reinforcements to the right. Over the next few days this action continued until the line extended from Ewell to the north on the Brock Road to Anderson, down on the Po

Above: Trenches built by Lee's army at Cold Harbor are eroded but easily visible yet today. The last major victory for the Army of Northern Virginia, Cold Harbor signaled the beginning of the trench warfare that would unfold at Petersburg.
David J. Eicher

Left: A wartime view of the Cold Harbor battlefield. Despite Grant's reckless and costly attack on 2 June, Lee was forced to continue moving south to protect Richmond and Petersburg.
Library of Congress

River to the south. Federals under Wright and Hancock shifted northward and attacked again at 4 A.M. on 18 May. This failed utterly due to vigorous Confederate artillery fire. "If the changed circumstances as around Richmond will permit," Lee telegraphed Davis, "I recommend that such troops as can be spared be sent to me at once. Reports from our scouts unite in stating that reinforcements to Genl Grant are arriving."[18]

On 19 May Grant hatched a plan to spring the Confederates from their entrenchments. He would send Hancock speeding to the south and order the rest of the army to follow after a delay that gave Lee the opportunity to chase and destroy Hancock. Concerned with Grant moving directly on Richmond, Lee sent

The awesome spectacle of death on the battlefield is reflected in this April 1865 photograph made at Cold Harbor by John Reekie. Teams of black soldiers are disinterring the remains of fallen soldiers for reburial in cemeteries.
Library of Congress

Federal troops occupy the steps of Arlington in 1864. On 15 June of that year the Federal government established 210 acres on the property as a national cemetery, ensuring that the Lees could never return.

National Archives and Records Administration

Soldiers lounge on the lawn in front of Arlington House in 1864.

National Archives and Records Administration

Ewell to feel the Federal right. This delayed Hancock's departure until 20 May. Both armies moved south on the night of 20–21 May. Total casualties for the Spotsylvania campaign were 10,000 for Lee's army and about 18,000 for the attacking Yankees. "General Lee's indisposition at this time was really serious," wrote Robert Stiles on the night the army moved south, ". . . [having been sent on an errand], I reached . . . Army Headquarters, where I found Colonel Taylor in his tent on his knees, with his prayer-book open

The Northern paper *Harper's Weekly* featured a cartoon showing Grant whipping Lee in its issue for 11 June 1864.

Author's Collection

George Washington (1732–1799)
loomed large over the Lee and Custis
families for decades after his death. Lee
greatly admired the military victor
served by his father. Charles Willson
Peale's portrait, painted from life in
1772, shows Washington in the dress
uniform of a colonel in the Virginia
militia.

Washington/Custis/Lee Collection,
Washington and Lee University,
Lexington, Va.

Thomas Lee (1690–1750) purchased a
block of land in 1717 and in the 1730s
began building "Stratford," later to be
known as Stratford Hall Plantation, the
birthplace of Lee. Light-Horse Harry
Lee, Lee's father, inherited an interest in
the house in 1790. Seventeen years later
Lee was born at the house, but left with
the family for Alexandria at the age of
three, never to return to Stratford.

David J. Eicher

Henry "Light-Horse Harry" Lee (1756–1818), hero of the American Revolution, major general, U.S.A., governor of Virginia, and congressman, painted by Charles Willson Peale. Light-Horse Harry's meteoric downfall affected the remainder of his son Robert's life.

Independence National Historical Park Collection, Philadelphia

Anne Hill Carter Lee (1773–1829) painted by an unknown artist, *ca.* 1800. Significantly, Lee's mother wore a miniature portrait of George Washington, presumably as a mourning tribute relatively soon after his death.

Washington/Custis/Lee Collection, Washington and Lee University, Lexington, Va.

Mary Randolph Custis Lee (1807–1873), Lee's wife and great-granddaughter of Martha Washington, painted in 1838 by William Edward West. Later in life Mary became an invalid due to a string of diseases and chronic rheumatism.

Washington/Custis/Lee Collection, Washington and Lee University, Lexington, Va.

The first portrait of Robert E. Lee (1807–1870), painted in 1838 by William Edward West. The famous image depicts Lee in the dress uniform of a 1st lieutenant of engineers, United States Army.

Washington/Custis/Lee Collection, Washington and Lee University, Lexington, Va.

Mary Custis Lee as a young woman, painted *ca.* 1825 by Auguste Hervieu.

Robert E. Lee Memorial Association, Stratford Hall Plantation

About 1853 Lee sat for this portrait by
Robert W. Weir, a professor of drawing at
West Point. It is the second of only two
portraits of the general painted before
the Civil War, and shows him in the uniform of a brevet colonel of engineers.

Robert E. Lee Memorial Association,
Stratford Hall Plantation

In September 1853 the historian, author,
and artist Benson J. Lossing produced
this watercolor showing Arlington.

Robert E. Lee Memorial Association,
Stratford Hall Plantation

This unusual portrait of Lee was produced
in 1862 by Benjamin Franklin Reinhardt.
Lee's face was allegedly painted from life in
1861 and the portrait finished in England
the following year.

R. W. Norton Art Gallery, Shreveport, La.

Chancellorsville was arguably Lee's master battle. Working in Richmond, the French-born artist Louis Mathieu Didier Guillaume produced this stunning portrait about 1863–1865. *Gen. Robert E. Lee at the Battle of Chancellorsville, Va.,* was produced on commission from M. Knoedler Co. in New York.
R. W. Norton Art Gallery, Shreveport, La.

This scene depicts the imagined last moments spent together by Lee and Stonewall Jackson at Chancellorsville, before Jackson's untimely mortal wounding and death. Everett B. D. Julio created the painting in St. Louis in 1864 and ultimately titled it *The Last Meeting of Lee and Jackson*.

The Museum of the Confederacy, Richmond. Photograph by Katherine Wetzel

This study of Lee was produced about 1864 by the artist Edward Caledon Bruce, in preparation for a now-lost full-length portrait. Its brushy nature suggests a surrealism unlike other wartime portrait studies of Lee.
Virginia Historical Society, Richmond

This striking full-length portrait of Lee is presumed to have been accomplished by W. B. Cox about 1865, based on the strong similarity to another known work by the Missouri artist. The work is based on two photographs taken in Richmond by Julian Vannerson in 1864.
Virginia Historical Society, Richmond

On 9 April 1865 Lee capitulated to Ulysses S. Grant in the front parlor of the Wilmer McLean House at Appomattox Court House, Virginia. Executed about 1866, Louis Mathieu Didier Guillaume's painting *Surrender of General Lee to General Grant, April 9, 1865*, depicts a highly inaccurate version of the surrender room, with far too many officers present and Lee and Grant at a single table. Lee's aide Charles Marshall and Grant's military secretary Ely S. Parker stand at left.

Appomattox Court House National Historical Park, Appomattox, Va.

A recreated camp tent at the Museum of the Confederacy in Richmond displays a collection of items used by Lee during the war, placed on his camp bed and table. They include (left to right): his sash, gauntlets, haversack, holster, saddle cover, tableware, field glasses, Colt Navy revolver, sword belt, hat, saddle, and boots. The table was carved for Lee by his mess boy and has a reversible top that features a checkerboard.

The Museum of the Confederacy, Richmond. Photograph by Katherine Wetzel

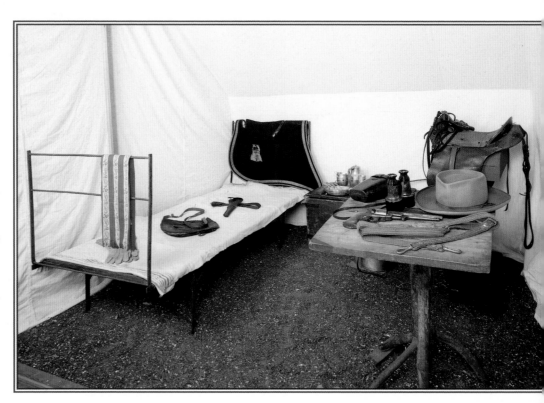

About 1870 John Adams Elder painted this portrait, one that shows a Lee apparently much worn from the war years. The pose shows a clear influence from the last photograph by Michael Miley.
Robert E. Lee IV, McLean, Va.

This portrait by Michael S. Nachtrieb, completed about 1870, was derived from photographs taken by J. W. Davies (the facial features) and Mathew B. Brady (the clothing, following the surrender).
Robert E. Lee Memorial Association, Stratford Hall Plantation

Sometime in the early postwar period George Peter Alexander Healy executed this noble portrait of Lee as president of Washington College.
Robert E. Lee Memorial Association, Stratford Hall Plantation

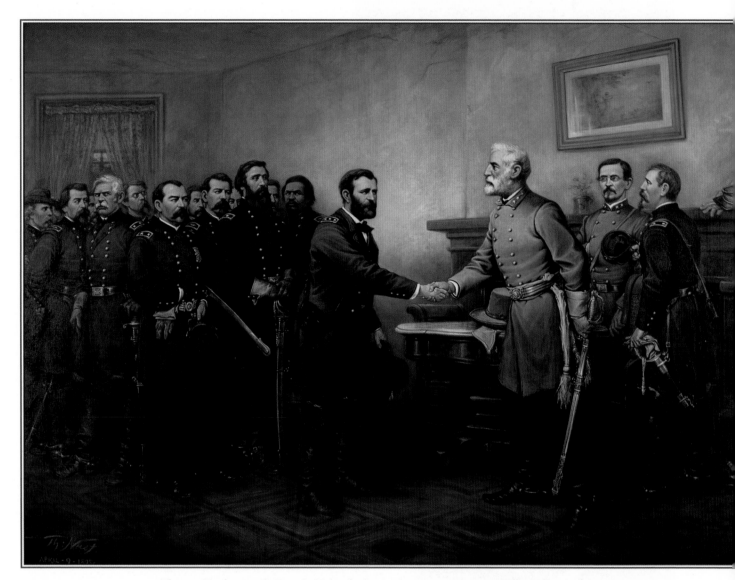

Thomas Nast's portrait *Peace in Union* depicts an Appomattox scene equally as distorted as that of Guillaume. Completed in 1895, the work presents Charles Marshall and Orville E. Babcock to the right of Lee and a group of officers left of Grant that includes George A. Custer, Edward O. C. Ord, Adam Badeau, Phil Sheridan, John A. Rawlins, and Ely S. Parker. *The Galena/Joe Daviess County Historical Society and Museum, Galena, Ill.*

This gentle caricature of Lee by John P. Walker is an idealized view of the commander in the last year of the war. Completed in 1896, the work stands out for its Napoleonic pose.
Virginia Historical Society, Richmond

This striking profile portrait of Lee was executed by Louis Mathieu Didier Guillaume about 1865. It is based on the Julian Vannerson "blockade" profile photograph made in 1864 and was painted for Joseph E. Brown, Confederate governor of Georgia.

R. W. Norton Art Gallery, Shreveport, La.

Robert E. Lee painted by Theodore Pine in 1904. Pine used an array of Lee photographs as a basis for what is generally considered to be the finest twentieth-century rendering of the fabled commander.

Washington and Lee University, Lexington, Va.

This marvelous engraving titled *Lee and His Generals* shows virtually all important Confederate commanders at the same height with the exception of Lee, who stands several inches taller. It was produced in 1907 by the A. B. Graham Co., after G. B. Matthews, and was published by W. B. Matthews in Washington. Pictured (left to right) are Hood, Ewell, Bragg, A. S. Johnston, Hampton, Kirby Smith, Early, A. P. Hill, S. D. Lee, Anderson, Gordon, Holmes, Hardee, Joseph E. Johnston, Buckner, Longstreet, Polk, Lee, Forrest, Beauregard, Jackson, Cooper, Stuart, Taylor, Pemberton, and D. H. Hill.

Hargrett Rare Book and Manuscript Library, University of Georgia, Athens

French-born artist Charles Hoffbauer unveiled *Summer* in 1921, one of four "seasons of the Confederacy" and four accompanying panels that grace the Cheek Mural Gallery at the Virginia Historical Society in Richmond. Lee on Traveller dominates the scene; also appearing (left to right) are Hampton, Ewell, Gordon, Jackson, Fitzhugh Lee, A. P. Hill, Longstreet, Joseph E. Johnston, Pickett, Beauregard, and Stuart.

Virginia Historical Society, Richmond

Executed in 1907 by Eliphalet Frazer Andrews and Marietta Minnigerode Andrews, this handsome portrait of Lee is based largely on the Brady series of photographs taken after Appomattox and on Lee's death mask. *Virginia Historical Society, Richmond*

Arlington, the exquisite mansion overlooking the city of Washington, was initially constructed in 1802–1804 by George Washington Parke Custis. Lee lived at the house after he married Mary Custis in 1831. The Lees abandoned Arlington House at the outbreak of war and three years later the Federal government established Arlington National Cemetery on the grounds. *David J. Eicher*

The mammoth equestrian figures of Jefferson Davis, Lee, and Stonewall Jackson adorn Stone Mountain, east of Atlanta, the largest exposed dome of granite in North America. The dome rises 700 feet above the surrounding plain. In 1916 Gutzon Borglum began work on the sculpture, which measures 90 by 100 feet and which, due to various difficulties, was not finished until 1972.

David J. Eicher

before him, and General Lee in his tent, wide awake, poring over a map stretched upon a temporary table of rough plank with a tallow candle stuck in a bottle for a light. I remember saying to myself, as I delivered my message and withdrew, 'Does he never, never sleep?'"[19]

On 22 May the bulk of the Confederate army reached Hanover Junction along the south bank of the North Anna River. The armies clashed on the following day. Lee became sick on the night of 23–24 May, bothered by intestinal complaints that may have been bilious dysentery. During this illness he testily greeted A. P. Hill, on the 24th, who had reported his losses to the commander. "Why did you not do as Jackson would have done," said Lee, "thrown your whole force upon those people and driven them back?"[20] He was worse on the 25th and was confined to his tent. On the 29th, he was almost too sick to leave headquarters. He had improved slightly after about two days so that he could enter a carriage.[21] The Union soldiers withdrew along the north bank of the Pamunkey on the 26th, and a race again ensued toward Richmond, with the Confederates blocking the way north of Mechanicsville, near the old battlefields of the Peninsular campaign of two years hence, on 28 May. The Yankees arrived two days later. The alarming nature of Grant's repeated turning movements was starting to shake the Confederate commander. "If this army is unable to resist Grant," he wrote Davis on 30 May, "the troops under Gen. Beauregard and in the city will be unable to defend it."[22]

Grant next shifted toward Old Cold Harbor, where Anderson hit Sheridan on 1 June. The Confederate army now had about 59,000 effectives facing Grant's 108,000. The next day both armies shifted toward Cold Harbor, where Lee established a line that was formidable and difficult to flank. The armies were now extended over long northwest-southeast lines and had erected breastworks separated by a tiny gap, only 100 yards at the closest spot. A new, modern kind of war now emerged, one that would characterize the remainder of the conflict: trench fighting. This mode of operations continued until 12 June, punctuated by a thunderous frontal assault by the Federal Second, Sixth, and Eighteenth Corps on 3 June. This attack was a disaster and produced 7,000 dead Yankees in less than an hour. "The dead and dying lay in front of the Confederate lines in triangles," wrote Charles Venable, "of which the apexes were the bravest men who came nearest to the breastworks under the withering, deadly fire."[23]

A straight cartes-de-visite of another J. W. Davies pose, the "floppy tie picture," was retouched as a vignette. The ink is an identification, not Lee's signature.

National Archives and Records Administration

This copy of a cartes-de-visite of the Davies "floppy tie" portrait was signed by Lee.

Leyburn Library, Washington and Lee University

On 18 June Confederate troops at Colquitt's Salient repulsed a major Union attack on the position. The following spring infantry under Maj. Gen. John B. Gordon led the bold assault on Fort Stedman from this position.

David J. Eicher

Pierre Gustave Toutant Beauregard (1818–1893), who went by G. T. Beauregard, was the war's initial hero. Victor at Fort Sumter and at First Bull Run, Beauregard's shifting assignments resulted from a bitter feud with Jefferson Davis. In 1864 he supported Lee by helping to defend Petersburg.

National Archives and Records Administration

"Violet Bank," a small house north of the Appomattox River at Petersburg, served as Lee's headquarters from June–October 1864. During this period Lee was ill frequently and the hopes for Confederate victory faded day by day.

David J. Eicher

Now, on 12 June, Grant's strategy suddenly changed. He shifted his base of operations south of the James River, intending to capture Petersburg and then threaten the final rail line supplying Richmond. The next morning Confederates found the Union trenches empty, and Lee believed it was simply another flanking maneuver. He would soon learn the disturbing truth. Hancock and Maj. Gen. William F. Smith swept south for Petersburg, where Beauregard maintained strong defenses but had few men. On the 15th Smith attacked only after a lengthy reconnaissance and poor artillery support. Nonetheless, he opened a mile-wide gap in the Confederate defenses and had an open shot at Petersburg. But he believed the bulk of the Army of Northern Virginia was about to arrive and so waited for Hancock. Attacks were finally made the next day, but Beauregard had strengthened and they failed. On the 15th, the day of the failed Yankee opportunity, another disappointment befell the Lee family. The U.S. government established 210 acres at Arlington for use as a military cemetery. Any hope for recovering the property for Lee family use was now gone.

On the 18th a major Federal attack erupted only to find that Confederates had withdrawn a mile and established a new line of defenses. Four days later Grant decided to concentrate on the Confederate communications, so the operations against Petersburg were transformed into a siege. It would remain so until days before the end of the war in the eastern theater. The situation for Lee's army was worsening in terms of supplies and morale. "For some few days back we have been only able to get sufficient corn for our animals from day to day," Lee wrote Davis on 16 June. "Any acci-

This simple engraving of Lee and accompanying staff viewing artillery at Petersburg appeared in *The Illustrated London News* on 3 September 1864. The well-known artist Frank Vizetelly produced the engraving.

Author's Collection

dent to the railroads would cut short our supplies. . . . Genl Lawton is doing everything he can, but cannot provide more than about 2000 bushels per day. We require 3200 bushels daily for all our animals—I think it is clear that the railroads are not working energetically & unless some improvement is made, I do not know what will become of us."[24] "Occasionally, when Generals Rodes or Early passed the line, the cry was 'Bread, bread, bread,'" wrote Bryan Grimes on 22 June.[25] Later in the summer, on 9 August, Lee wrote Davis, "The soap ration for this Army has become a serious question—Since leaving Orange C.H. the commissary Lt Col Cole has only been able to make three issues of three days rations each. The great want of cleanliness which is a necessary consequence of these very limited issues is now producing sickness among the men in the trenches, and must affect their self respect & morale."[26] Still, the General reflected optimism. On 30 June, the Lees' anniversary, he wrote Mary from Petersburg. "I trust that you will continue to improve and soon be as well as usual," he wrote. "God grant that you may be entirely restored in His own good time. Do you recollect what a happy day thirty-three

"My bad old man." So said Lee of Jubal Anderson Early (1816–1894), allegedly the only officer who swore in front of the General. Prominent in the Army of Northern Virginia from 1862–1864, Early thereafter fought through the Shenandoah Valley and approached Washington. He was the prototypical "unreconstructed rebel" in postwar years.

Library of Congress

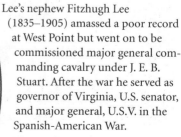

Lee's nephew Fitzhugh Lee (1835–1905) amassed a poor record at West Point but went on to be commissioned major general commanding cavalry under J. E. B. Stuart. After the war he served as governor of Virginia, U.S. senator, and major general, U.S.V. in the Spanish-American War.

Library of Congress

This first portrait of Lee on Traveller was made in Petersburg sometime during the late summer or early autumn of 1864. At the time Traveller was seven years old. Careful examination shows debris from shelling mixed with windblown leaves on the street, and damaged windows behind the General's form.

Douglas Southall Freeman and the Dementi Studio

A larger format version of the "floppy tie" picture records exceptional facial detail and significantly more of the uniform coat.

The Valentine Museum, Richmond

years ago this was? How many hopes and pleasures it gave birth to!"[27]

Lee exploited his base in the Shenandoah Valley by sending Jubal Early north on a raid. Grant diverted two corps, but Early then crossed the Potomac again into Pennsylvania.[28] This raid resulted in actions at Monocacy, Maryland, and Fort Stevens, D.C., where Lincoln was briefly under fire. At the end of July Brig. Gen. John McCausland's troops raided and burned Chambersburg, Pennsylvania. Early's raid for a time shook Northern confidence, but events to the south in Georgia were going badly for the Confederacy. Sherman was closing in on Atlanta, bringing harsh war upon the heart of the Confederacy.

At Petersburg, an unlikely scheme hatched by Federal commanders resulted in tunneling underneath the Confederate lines (a job done by Pennsylvania coal miners) and exploding a massive gunpowder charge, allowing a follow-up attack that would break the strong Confederate defenses. The resulting battle of the Crater on 30 July was a disaster for the Yankees, and Confederates in the counterattack led by Brig. Gen. William Mahone shot many black troops caught in the destruction that followed. On 18 August Grant sent Warren on an expedition to destroy as much of the Weldon Railroad as possible south of the city, where Mahone struck back on the 19th. "I have only one earthly want," the General wrote Custis on 27 August, "that God in His infinite mercy will send our enemies back to their homes."[29]

The final four months of 1864 saw the siege continue. It would be a startlingly bleak period for the Confederacy, with the eventuality of defeat growing daily as the Army of Northern Virginia weakened, great successes were scored by Union soldiers in other theaters (particularly after the fall of Atlanta on 2 September), and the solidarity of the North as demonstrated by the reelection of Lincoln in November. Sherman cut across Georgia on his March to the Sea and John Bell Hood, a year hence one of Lee's finest division commanders, led a disastrous campaign in Tennessee whereby he jeopardized and eventually ruined the great western Confederate army, the Army of Tennessee, at Franklin and Nashville. Now the situation was growing more des-

A key post in Richmond's defense stood at Fort Harrison, where on 29 September 1864 a massed force of Federal troops assaulted and captured the position. The Confederate capital would hold on for only another six months.

David J. Eicher

perate every day. Amidst all the despair, however, one thing had become clear—by his leadership of the great eastern army, Lee had become virtually synonymous with the Confederacy itself. In stark contrast with the first year or two of the war, Robert Edward Lee now symbolized more than anyone or anything else the whole of the Confederate cause. His health during this period was relatively good, and he remained remarkably active at his various headquarters around Petersburg, although he looked much older than even

Union Quartermaster General Montgomery C. Meigs (1816–1892) accelerated his plans to expand Arlington as a cemetery on 3 October 1864, when his son John, a lieutenant in Virginia, was murdered by Confederate troops after he had surrendered. His grave at Arlington holds an elaborate bas-relief statue.

David J. Eicher

Wooden boards marked the graves of most soldiers interred in Hollwood Cemetery in Richmond. This image taken in 1865 shows dozens from Virginia fields in the Confederate section, which expanded rapidly in the 1870s to accommodate Confederate dead brought home from Gettysburg.

Library of Congress

Edwin Gray Lee (1836–1870), Lee's first cousin, once removed, served admirably until resigning in 1862 due to poor health. In 1864 he commanded the post at Staunton until November, when he was given leave for sickness. Lee escaped to Canada after the war and died soon thereafter.

National Archives and Records Administration

In 1864 the Richmond photographer J. W. Davies captured Lee in excellent detail. This copy of a cartes-de-visite was cut and inserted into a badge with ribbons.

Library of Congress

a year before. "The Genl proposed that we should go [to church] to Mr. Gibson's," wrote Walter Taylor on 11 September, ". . . It is quite trying to accompany the General to Church or any public place. Everybody crowds the way and stops on the pavements to have a look."[30]

The attacks on Lee's line continued, and supplies were scarcer than ever. The Confederate lines grew thinner each day. Federal Maj. Gen. Edward O. C. Ord captured Fort Harrison, an important stronghold, on 29 September. In late October Grant attacked positions along the Southside Railroad, the last important Confederate supply route, but failed. The armies settled in for what would become the last winter of the war. The desperation extended to subjects at the core of the Confederate philosophy. "Even Gen. Lee . . . has permitted to be published as his opinion, that there is an imperative necessity for employing slaves to fill our ranks in the army," wrote the fiery secessionist Edmund Ruffin on 27 December. "When he declares the measure to be necessary, it goes farther with me . . . than would any arguments, or any other authority."[31] Given the Confederate attitude toward slavery, that reaction strongly demonstrates how by this time, in the words of one historian, Lee's position in the Confederacy approximated that held by Washington during the American Revolution.[32] Still, time was running out at Petersburg.

CHAPTER EIGHT

∞

The Confederacy Unravels

B Y THE NEW YEAR OF 1865 HEARTS IN THE CONFEDERATE States were heavy, and hopes for a military victory seemed to be fading daily. The cold winter in camps about Petersburg seemed especially cruel as food supplies and forage ran lower day by day and the only thing that grew was desertion. Growing desperation attracted Early back from the Valley, although Lee was forced to dispatch much-needed troops to help bolster Wilmington, North Carolina, the last major seaport supplying Confederate troops, now in danger of Federal capture. On the Petersburg front, significant actions were absent during the cold, but pickets cracked shots and artillerists sent shells here and there, testing and checking the opposite lines. In the Deep South, Sherman had arrived at Savannah and at Nashville the remnants of the Confederate Army of Tennessee under John Bell Hood had been shattered. And Sheridan was still devastating the military value of the Shenandoah Valley.

Two actions took place during this winter of desperation. In December Maj. Gen. Gouverneur K. Warren destroyed a stretch of the Weldon Railroad south of Petersburg. On 5 February 1865 Brig. Gen. David M. Gregg and others led an assault to capture wagon trains that resulted in extending the Union line to the creek called Hatcher's Run. And down South, on 15 January, the stronghold at Fort Fisher collapsed under a furious, coordinated army-navy

The Military Medallion, a popular cartes-de-visite showing Lee and his staff, was produced in droves by Vannerson and Jones in Richmond in 1865. Lee appears at center. Clockwise from top are his staff officers Walter H. Stevens, Charles Marshall, James L. Corley, Briscoe G. Baldwin, Lafayette Guild, Henry E. Young, William N. Pendleton, Henry E. Peyton, D. B. Bridgeford, Walter H. Taylor, Robert G. Cole, and Charles S. Venable.

Library of Congress

A magnificent, studied exposure by Mathew Brady is perhaps the finest portrait of Lee as a general officer. It was made on the porch of the Lee House in Richmond following the surrender at Appomattox.
National Archives and Records Administration

attack and Wilmington was closed as a Confederate port.

The desperation among Confederates in the army and on the home front resulted in a push in Congress to create a new position of general-in-chief of all Confederate armies. The days of Jefferson Davis's micromanagement of military operations would come to an end and Lee was the obvious choice for the position. "The passage in both houses of the measure for making General Lee general-in-chief by large majorities is very distasteful to the President," wrote Robert G. H. Kean on 23 January. "I am told he has approved it *totis vivibus.* Now it is a question whether he will have the hardihood to veto it."[1] Two days later Josiah Gorgas, chief of the Bureau of Ordnance, wrote, "The Virginia legislature has requested the President to appoint Gen. Lee to the command of all our armies. He replies that he would be only too happy if Gen. Lee would undertake it, but he declines. There is a great outcry against the President...."[2] Davis relented, however, and Lee was appointed general-in-chief, C.S.A. to rank from 31 January 1865. "I am indebted alone to the kindness of His Excellency the President for my nomination to this high and arduous office," Lee wrote Samuel Cooper on 4 February, "and wish I had the ability to fill it to advantage."[3] On 9 February he assumed command of all Confederate armies.

The measure would prove to be too little, too late. "[Grant's] present force is so superior to ours," Lee wrote Davis on 29 January, "that if he is reinforced to any extent, I do not see how in our present position he can be prevented from enveloping Richmond. Such a combination is his true policy & therefore I fear it is true."[4] Mary Boykin Chesnut reacted so: "General Lee [is] generalissimo of all our forces. Rather late—when we have no forces."[5]

The situation was indeed grave. So grave that Lee, a relative progressive on the subject, and others, pushed for what at the outset of the war was unthinkable—emancipation for slaves who would fight for the Confederate cause in the field. Edmund Ruffin recorded thoughts on the possibility on 9 January: "Gen. Lee had long been in favor of [the policy], & that too with the understanding of the logical sequence, emancipation."[6] Some Confederates felt that Lee's support for emancipation amounted to a betrayal of the Confederacy. Robert Barnwell Rhett, Jr. was furious; William A. Graham, a North Carolina senator, stated, "with such wild schemes . . . it is time to attempt peace." After the war Lee told the Joint Committee on Reconstruction that he "was always in favor of emancipation—gradual emancipation."[7] Perhaps the greatest liability for such a plan was that Jefferson Davis opposed it. On 13 March the Confederate Congress passed a law, "largely on the endorsement of Lee," to call on the owners of slaves for as many blacks between the ages of eighteen and forty-five as President Davis deemed expedient "to perform military service in whatever capacity he may direct." This could not amount to more than one-fourth the population of slaves in any state.[8]

The enactment of the law developed slowly enough that no black troops ever took the field to fight for the Confederacy. And many people, even some in influential stations, continued to delude themselves about the seriousness of the situation. In January Confederate Senator William S. Oldham served on a

A former U.S. vice president, John Cabell Breckinridge (1821–1875) served many months in the west, briefly assisted Jubal Early in the Shenandoah Valley, and in the spring of 1865 became secretary of war. He was Lee's distant relative. At war's end Breckinridge fled south with Jefferson Davis's party.
National Archives and Records Administration

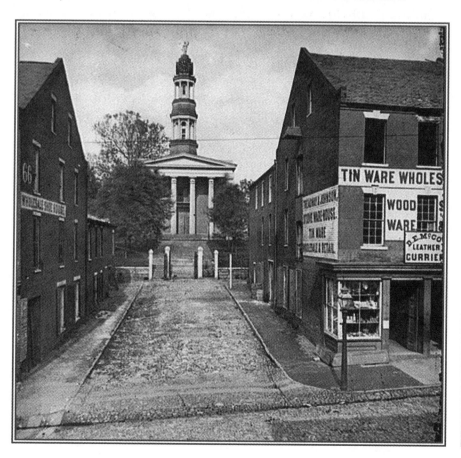

During the siege of Petersburg the Court House, photographed in 1865, served Confederate officers who occupied the structure.
Library of Congress

The Lee Home at 707 East Franklin Street in Richmond housed Mary Custis Lee and various family members from early 1864 to the end of the war. Lee arrived at the house after Appomattox and stayed until September 1865, when the family moved to Lexington. This image is from 1865.

Library of Congress

Gilbert Moxley Sorrel (1838–1901) spent the first actions of the war as a volunteer aide to James Longstreet, and followed his chief through virtually the whole of the contest. Late in 1864 he commanded a brigade in the Army of Northern Virginia; the following February he was shot through the lungs at Hatcher's Run.

Library of Congress

committee to "inquire into our present and future means of self-defense." Congress considered the secret report and "came to the unanimous conclusion and so reported, 'that we were in possession of resources, sufficient to enable us to carry on the war for an indefinite period of time.'"[9] On 12 February the war clerk John B. Jones recorded, "Doubtless Lee could protract the war, and, by concentrating farther South, embarrass the enemy by compelling him to maintain a longer line of communication by land and by sea.... Lee could have an army of 100,000 effective men for years."[10]

On 23 February Lee wrote his old comrade Joe Johnston. "Assume command of the Army of Tennessee," he dispatched, "and all troops in the Department of South Carolina, Georgia, and Florida. Assign General Beauregard to duty under you as you may select. Concentrate all available forces and drive back Sherman." Johnston responded on the same day, from Lincolnton, North Carolina: "It is too late to expect me to concentrate troops capable of driving back Sherman."[11] The desertions in the Army of Northern Virginia itself were now reaching appalling numbers. "I regret to be obliged to call your attention to the alarming number of desertions that are now occurring in this army," Lee wrote Secretary of War John C. Breckinridge on 24 February. "Since the 12th instant they amount in two divisions of Hill's corps, those of Wilcox and Heth, to about four hundred.

There are a good many from other commands. . . . These desertions have a very bad effect upon the troops who remain and give rise to painful apprehension. . . ."[12]

All hope looked to Lee, but there was now little he could do. "People are almost in a state of desperation," wrote Josiah Gorgas on 2 March. "Lee is about all we have & what public confidence is left rallies around him, and he it seems to me fights without much heart in the cause."[13] The 57,000 Confederates faced 125,000 Yankees. The General did concoct a plan by which he could crush Grant's line by a surprise attack, move south and unite with Joe Johnston, now opposing Sherman in the Carolinas, and together strike Sherman. An unrealistic idea, it was all that was left to try. "General Lee held with me a long and free conference [in March]," wrote Jefferson Davis. "He stated that the circumstances had forced on him the conclusion that the evacuation of Petersburg was but a question of time. [He further stated that] if we had to retreat, it should be in a southwardly direction toward the country from which we were drawing supplies."[14] On 25 March a vicious assault led by Maj. Gen. John B. Gordon hit the Union line south of Petersburg at Fort Stedman. The attack succeeded briefly before falling back after a Union counterattack. With it went the last hope of the plan to break Grant's lines.

Sheridan now joined the Petersburg lines and a large-scale movement began on 29 March along White Oak Road and Boydton Plank Road, lasting three days. "General Lee says to the men who shirk duty," wrote Mary Boykin Chesnut on this day, "'This is the people's war. When they tire, I stop.'"[15] Sheridan arrived at Dinwiddie Court House southwest of Petersburg and, after cavalry actions, was supported by Warren. Confederate infantry under Maj. Gen.

On 25 March 1865 Lee made a final offensive stab at the Petersburg Union line at Fort Stedman, now marked by a stand of trees. Maj. Gen. John B. Gordon briefly penetrated the position before a murderous Federal counterattack forced a retreat.
David J. Eicher

An amateur militarist, John Brown Gordon (1832–1904) nonetheless rose to major general in the Confederate army and led half the infantry during the Army of Northern Virginia's last days. Gordon presented the formal surrender of the army at Appomattox. Gordon was Lee's fifth cousin-in-law, by an adoption.
Library of Congress

A tiny junction called Five Forks, crucial to Confederate control of the Southside Railroad, witnessed a sharp action on 1 April 1865. The skill of Union Maj. Gen. Philip Sheridan and poor performances of Pickett and Fitzhugh Lee forced a Confederate withdrawal, and necessitated abandoning Richmond and Petersburg.

David J. Eicher

George E. Pickett fell back to Five Forks, a road junction, where on 1 April Sheridan and Warren—after a confused start—struck Pickett and drove him northward. Pickett and Fitzhugh Lee were surprised and shaken by the attack. About 4,500 Confederate troops were captured. More devastating for Lee was the loss of the Southside Railroad, which sealed the fate of Petersburg. "I had a verbal conference with General Lee," wrote Bryan Grimes on 1 April, "and afterwards officially reported my inability to hold this point against any vigorous attack . . . on an average throughout, the space from man to man was at least eight feet in the line of trenches."[16] Lee fully understood the seriousness of the strategic blow when he wrote Davis on 1 April: "The movement of Gen Grant to Dinwiddie C.H. seriously threatens our position, and diminishes our ability to maintain our present lines in front of Richmond and Petersburg. . . . I should like very much to have the views of your Excellency upon this matter as well as counsel. . . ."[17]

But time had run out. The General slept on the night of 1–2 April at the Turnbull House, his headquarters in the final stages of the Petersburg siege. "I at once went to General Lee's headquarters [at about 4 A.M. on the 2d]," wrote James Longstreet. "I found him in bed in his tent. While I was sitting upon the side of his couch,

On 2 April 1865 Lee telegraphed Jefferson Davis, "I think it is absolutely necessary that we should abandon our position tonight." A stunned Davis, who received the message while in a Richmond church, undertook to evacuate the city. A fire set in the Shockoe Warehouse to destroy Confederate military stores spread to destroy about one-third of the city, as this April 1865 view by Alexander Gardner shows.

Library of Congress

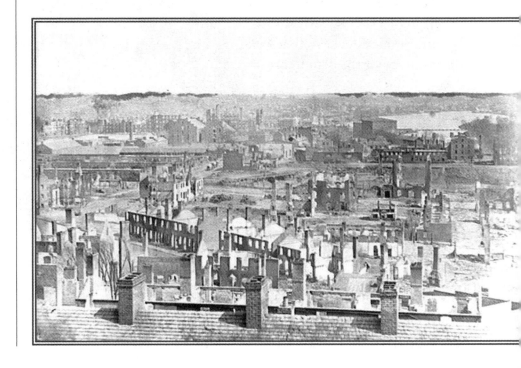

discussing my line of march and receiving my orders for the future—this involving a march on the Five Forks—a courier came in and announced our line was being broken in front of the house in which General Lee had slept. I hurried to the front, and as fast as my troops came up they were thrown into action to check the advance of the Federals. . . ."[18] The Yankees were striking hard at the Confederate right flank—if successful it would necessitate abandoning Petersburg. Although the war was coming to a rapid close, it took many more casualties on that day, including one of the General's favorite subordinates. "I soon joined General Lee," wrote Walter Taylor, "whom I found in company with General A. P. Hill, investigating the movements of a body of troops of whose identity they were uncertain. General Hill rode forward to ascertain what troops they were, accompanied only by his trusted courier, Sergeant George W. Tucker . . . coming suddenly upon two Federal soldiers, Sergeant Tucker [ordered] them to surrender. They raised their muskets . . . General Hill fell from his horse, dead."[19]

The Army of Northern Virginia retreated westward, hoping to regain supplies and ultimately to turn south and link up with Joseph E. Johnston's forces in North Carolina. On 6 April 1865 a portion of the exhausted army clashed with Federals at Sayler's Creek, losing most of the Second Corps, including six generals, among them Custis Lee, who was captured.

David J. Eicher

Lee's eldest son Custis graduated at the top of his West Point class and was a stellar engineer. During much of the war he acted as an aide to Jefferson Davis; the war's last months saw Custis applying his skill to a defense of Richmond.

Library of Congress

As the day progressed it became clear that Petersburg and Richmond would have to be evacuated. "I see no prospect of doing more than holding our position here till night," Lee telegraphed the War Secretary Breckinridge. "I am not certain that I can do that."[20] Confederate officials in Richmond, led by Davis, assembled archives, gold and other valuables, and their families and fled southward by train. An evacuation fire, meant to burn military stores and cotton to prevent their capture, raged out of control from the Shockoe Warehouse and ultimately burned one-third of the city. The following day Yankees entered Richmond and finally

As the broken remnants of the Army of Northern Virginia fled westward, they were about to be encircled. The game would be over at a little crossroads town called Appomattox Court House, a pastoral scene with a few houses, a tavern, the Court House, and residents who little suspected the war would visit them.

David J. Eicher

While the disaster unfolded at Sayler's Creek, Lee ordered the 60-foot high trestles at High Bridge burned to delay the pursuing Federals. The bridge, partially destroyed on 7 April during the engagement at Farmville, was photographed in April 1865 by Timothy O'Sullivan.

Library of Congress

captured the Confederate capital. "[An aide] was hailed by a servant in front of a house, toward which the fire seemed to be moving," wrote Thomas Thatcher Graves, an aide of Union Maj. Gen. Godfrey Weitzel, on the entrance to Richmond on 3 April. "He was met by a lady, who stated that her mother was an invalid, confined to her bed, and as the fire seemed to be approaching she asked for assistance. The subsequent conversation developed the fact that the invalid was no other than the wife of General R. E. Lee, and the lady who addressed the aide was her daughter . . . two men guarded them until all danger was past."[21]

The pursuit of the Army of Northern Virginia continued as it fled westward. Lee hoped to move toward Lynchburg and then turn south to link up with Johnston. Exhausted from poor supplies and lack of sleep, the approximately 50,000 men converged on Amelia Court House by 5 April. Supplies would greet the tattered army there and it would continue south. But Grant planned to intercept the possible retreat routes and did so; the much-needed supplies did not show up. Turning south, the army was blocked by Federal cavalry and infantry and swiftly marched west toward

Since 7 April Lee and U. S. Grant had been exchanging letters, exploring the possibilities of ending the war. On 9 April Lee wrote Grant, "I now request an interview in accordance with the offer contained in your letter of yesterday. . . ."

National Archives and Records Administration

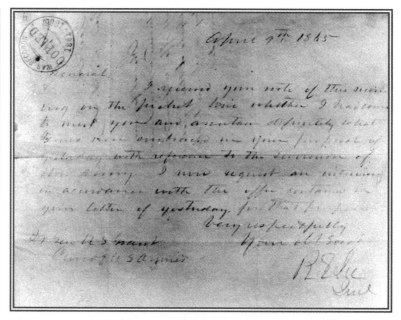

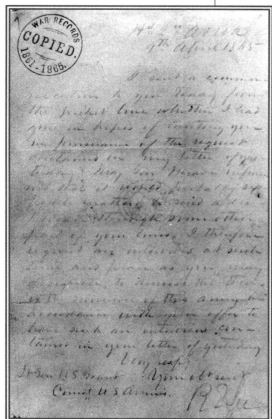

Later on 9 April, Lee more forcefully wrote, "I therefore request an interview . . . to discuss the terms of the surrender of this army. . . ."

National Archives and Records Administration

Farmville and, more importantly, rations, necessitating a night march. Harassed by cavalry to his rear and on his left flank, and staggered by men falling out of the ranks and leaving for home, the weak army blundered on. At Sayler's Creek on 6 April the Yankees caught up with Lee's rear guard and captured 8,000 prisoners including six general officers, among them Custis Lee and Dick Ewell. On this same day, the kernel of what would become the Lee legend was expressed clearly by Brig. Gen. Henry A. Wise, a former governor of Virginia: "[There] has been no country, general, for a year or more," he wrote. "You are the country to these men. They have fought for you."[22]

The next day the Confederates reached Farmville and burned most of the bridges in their rear save for High Bridge, an enormous railroad span and site of a rear guard action on this day. Lee formed a battle line but was flanked by the mixed infantry force under Maj. Gen. Edward O. C. Ord and Sheridan's cavalry, who raced ahead to the vicinity of Appomattox Court House. There the Confederate army was stopped on 9 April, and on that morning Lee sent a force under Gordon and Fitzhugh Lee to break Sheridan's line. This they did until encountering the deep masses of blue uniforms of Ord's two army corps. The Southern force was trapped and capitulation was the only answer. At 9 A.M. Lee asked Walter Taylor, "Well, colonel, what are we to do?" Taylor suggested that if they abandoned the trains they could make an escape. Lee

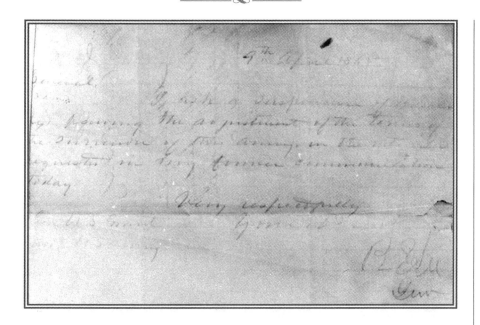

And finally, Lee wrote his nemesis, "I ask a suspension of hostilities pending the adjustment of the terms of the surrender of this army. . . ."

National Archives and Records Administration

responded: "Yes, perhaps we could; but I have had a conference with these gentlemen around me, and they agree that the time has come for capitulation." Lee went on and then said, "It would be useless and therefore cruel to provoke the further effusion of blood, and I have arranged to meet with General Grant."[23]

A correspondence had opened between Grant and Lee on 7 April with a note from Grant suggesting surrender. "I did not intend to propose the surrender of the Army of Northern Virginia," wrote Lee on 8 April, "but to ask the terms of your proposition. To be frank, I do not think the emergency has arisen to call for the surrender of this army; but as the restoration of peace should be the object of all, I desired to know whether your proposals would lead to that end."[24] The next morning, he again

Accompanied by Charles Marshall, Lee met Grant in the front parlor of the Wilmer McLean House at about 1 P.M. on 9 April 1865. Lee and Marshall had waited in the room for half an hour. Grant's terms were generous. Lee's alternatives were gone. This view by Timothy O'Sullivan was made during the same month.

Library of Congress

The reconstructed front parlor of the McLean House today. Built in 1848, the house was dismantled in 1893 in hopes of using it as a war museum in Washington. The pile of debris was never moved, however, and the McLean House was ultimately rebuilt on-site.

David J. Eicher

The McLean House parlor furniture, left to right: Lee sat in this wicker chair, and Grant used the table and the low-back chair during their meeting.

National Museum of American History, Smithsonian Institution

wrote Grant: "I now request an interview in accordance with the offer contained in your letter of yesterday for that purpose."[25] Later in the day, he wrote, "I ask suspension of hostilities pending the adjustment of the terms of surrender of this army, in the interview requested in my former communication today."[26] Still later, he wrote, "I have received your letter of this date containing the terms of surrender of the Army of Northern Virginia as proposed by you. As they are substantially the same as those expressed in your letter of the 8th instant, they are accepted. I will proceed to designate the proper officers to carry the stipulations into effect."[27]

The famous meeting took place about 1 P.M. in the Wilmer McLean House, the most suitable dwelling in the tiny village of Appomattox Court House. Ironically, McLean had moved west to avoid the war after Beauregard used his kitchen as a temporary headquarters during the first battle of Bull Run. Now, despite Johnston in North Carolina and Dick Taylor and Edmund Kirby Smith out west, the war would effectively come to a close in his

Lee's sword carried at Appomattox Court House now resides in the Museum of the Confederacy in Richmond.

The Museum of the Confederacy; photograph by Katherine Wetzel

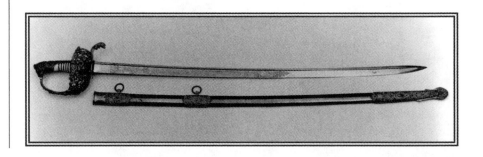

front parlor. Lee, mounted on Traveller and accompanied by Charles Marshall and Yankee Col. Orville E. Babcock of Grant's staff, rode to the house and arrived first, waiting for Grant and his remaining staff. The celebrated Union general officer Joshua L. Chamberlain described his first vision of the General. "Disquieted," he wrote, "I turned about, and there behind me, riding in between my two lines, appeared a commanding form, superbly mounted, richly accoutered, of imposing bearing, noble countenance, with expression of deep sadness overmastered by deeper strength. It is no other than Robert E. Lee! And seen by me for the first time within my own lines. I sat immovable, with a certain awe and admiration."[28]

Grant finally arrived toward 1:30 P.M. and the surrender interview lasted until about 3:45 P.M. Grant attempted a casual conversation based on an old encounter between the two during the Mexican War, and Lee recalled it but could not remember how Grant appeared. Finally, the Southern commander redirected the conversation toward the present situation and they discussed all aspects of the surrender, drawing up copies of documents, and discussing details. The Federal commander offered generous terms, allowing all Confederates to be paroled and return home, keeping their horses, sidearms, and baggage.

Above left: Thomas Nast's rough sketch *Peace — the Sole Object of All* shows Lee in despair in the McLean parlor on 9 April 1865. Nast may have made the sketch in the early 1890s for his master painting *Peace in Union* (see color photograph section). He then used the study for the next illustration. . . .
Eleanor S. Brockenbrough Library, The Museum of the Confederacy, Richmond

Above right: An unfinished painting by Thomas Nast created for H. H. Kohlsaat depicts Lee waiting in agony in the McLean parlor. At left is Orville Babcock, awaiting Grant; to the right of Lee stands Charles Marshall. Nast's death in 1902 ensured the painting would never be completed.
Library of Congress

Above left: Stationed at the McLean House, field artist Alfred R. Waud sketched Lee and Charles Marshall on horseback leaving the building following the meeting with Grant.
Library of Congress

Above right: More than twenty years later, for the massive project *Battles and Leaders of the Civil War*, Waud's sketch served as the basis for this engraving. Relatively speaking, the scene is remarkably true to the original.
Author's Collection

Later, Grant's aide Horace Porter described Lee's appearance during the interview. "Lee . . . was fully six feet in height, and quite erect for one of his age, for he was Grant's senior by sixteen years," he wrote. "His hair and full beard were a silver-gray, and quite thick, except that the hair had become a little thin in front. He wore a new uniform of Confederate gray, buttoned up to the throat, and at his side he carried a long sword of exceedingly fine workmanship, the hilt studded with jewels. . . . His top-boots were comparatively new, and seemed to have on them some ornamental stitching of red silk. . . . A felt hat, which in color matched pret-

W. L. Sheppard's engraving employed in *Battles and Leaders of the Civil War* shows Lee returning to his lines following the McLean House meeting. It was allegedly based on a wartime sketch.
Author's Collection

ty closely that of the uniform, and a pair of long buckskin gauntlets lay beside him on the table."[29]

Following the meeting, word of the surrender formalities spread among the armies. The artillerist William T. Poague asked members of John B. Gordon's staff what was happening: "'Surrender!' was the sententious reply. 'Surrender of what?' I asked. . . . 'General Lee's army' was the only reply I got. All at once my heart got to my throat and everything around me became dim and obscure."[30] Carlton McCarthy, another Southern soldier, recalled, "Many of the men were sobbing and crying, like children recovering from convulsions of grief after a severe whipping. . . . Not a man was heard to blame General Lee. On the contrary, all expressed the greatest sympathy for him and declared their willing-

Hastily printed on a field press, the first parole issued at Appomattox, dated 9 April 1865, released Lee and his remaining staff. The signers were Lee, Walter H. Taylor, Charles Venable, Charles Marshall, Henry E. Peyton, Giles B. Cooke, and Henry E. Young.
National Archives and Records Administration

Lee's most celebrated document, his General Orders No. 9, constituted a farewell to his troops on the surrender at Appomattox. Although many copies were made to circulate to the corps commanders and even as souvenirs— and the original was penned by Charles Marshall—this copy is unique in that it was written entirely in Lee's hand.
Leyburn Library, Washington and Lee University

Lee did not witness the surrender ceremonies, which were too far away from his camp. Instead, he left for Richmond and arrived at the house on Franklin Street, reuniting with family and awaiting his fate as a vanquished hero. This view shows the house in late spring 1865.

Library of Congress

Surrender Triangle at Appomattox Court House witnessed the final stacking of the arms of the Army of Northern Virginia on 12 April 1865. Some 26,765 men surrendered and stacked their arms for the final time.

David J. Eicher

ness to submit at once, or fight to the last man, as he ordered."[31] Bryan Grimes recalled informing one of his soldiers: "Upon answering I feared it was a fact that we had been surrendered, [a soldier] cast away his musket, and holding his hands aloft, cried in an agonized voice, 'Blow, Gabriel, blow! My God, let him blow, I am ready to die!'"[32]

Lee's parole and that of his staff was effected on this day. "We, the undersigned prisoners of war belonging to the Army of Northern Virginia," it read, "having been this day surrendered by General Robert E. Lee, C. S. Army, commanding said army, to Lieut. Gen. U. S. Grant, commanding Armies of the United States, do hereby give our solemn parole of honor that we will not hereafter serve in the armies of the Confederate States, or in any military capacity whatever, against the United States of America, or render aid to the enemies of the latter, until properly exchanged, in such manner as shall be mutually approved by the respective authorities. Done at Appomattox Court-House, Va. this 9th day of April, 1865. R. E. Lee, General; W. H. Taylor, Lieutenant-Colonel and Assistant Adjutant-General; Charles S. Venable,

One of the extraordinary photographs of Lee shows him on the porch of the Richmond House on Franklin Street several days after the surrender. Mathew Brady made the picture. Lee wears a Confederate uniform, despite the parole he had signed. The look on his careworn face is stern.

Library of Congress

Another left-side image of Lee adds his son Custis Lee at left and Walter H. Taylor at right. The two dedicated officers spent days with Lee following the surrender.

Library of Congress

A sharper, more straight-on pose with Lee, Custis, and Taylor on the Lee porch following the surrender.

Library of Congress

A rare print of the commander on the Lee porch shows his hand on the ornate chair.

Author's Collection

Another Brady pose depicts in crisp detail the surrendered leader's left side, seated on his Richmond porch. In their last years the Lees used a custom enlargement of this pose as a fire screen in their home.

Library of Congress

The implication of Lee's surrender was monstrous—during the final year of the war he and his army had come to represent the whole of the Confederate cause. Wilmer McLean, who had moved west because his house near Manassas was damaged during the war's first large action, could later tell visitors "the war began in my back yard and ended in my front parlor."

David J. Eicher

Lieutenant-Colonel and Assistant Adjutant-General; Charles Marshall, Lieutenant-Colonel and Assistant Adjutant-General; H. E. Peyton, Lieutenant-Colonel and Inspector General; Giles B. Cooke, Major and Assistant Adjutant and Inspector General; H. E. Young, Major and Assistant Adjutant-General and Judge-Advocate-General."[33]

When it was done, the General spoke to some of his men as he rode back to the Confederate lines. "I have done what I thought was best for you," he told one group as recorded by John Esten Cooke, "My heart is too full to speak, but I wish you all health and happiness."[34] Charles Marshall remembered a scene from the following evening. "That night [Apr. 9] the general sat with several of us at a fire in front of his tent, and after some conversation about the army, and the events of the day, in which his feelings toward his men were strongly expressed, he told me to prepare an order to his troops. . . . The next day it was raining, and many persons were coming and going. . . . I sat in the ambulance until I had written the order, the first draft of which (in pencil) contained an entire paragraph that was omitted by General Lee's direction. He made one or two verbal changes, and I then made a copy of the order as corrected. . . ."[35]

The resulting order, the famous General Orders No. 9, was read to the troops (but not by Lee) the following day. "After four years of arduous service," it began, "marked by unsurpassed courage and fortitude, the Army of Northern Virginia has been compelled to yield to overwhelming numbers and resources.

"I need not tell the brave survivors of so many hard-fought

battles, who have remained steadfast to the last, that I have consented to the result from no distrust of them. But, feeling that valor and devotion could accomplish nothing that could compensate for the loss that must have attended the continuance of the contest, I determined to avoid the useless sacrifice of those whose past services have endeared them to their countrymen.

"By the terms of the agreement officers and men can return to their homes and remain there until exchanged. You will take with you the satisfaction that proceeds from the consciousness of duty faithfully performed; and I earnestly pray that a merciful God will extend to you His blessing and protection.

"With an increasing admiration of your constancy and devotion to your country, and a grateful remembrance of your kind and generous considerations for myself, I bid you an affectionate farewell. R. E. Lee, General."[36]

Wild emotions packed that day. "When [the soldiers] saw the well-known figure of General Lee approaching," wrote William W. Blackford, "there was a general rush from each side to the road to greet him as he passed, and two solid walls of men were formed along the whole distance. . . . As soon as he entered this avenue of these old soldiers, the flower of his army, the men who had stood to their duty through thick and thin in so many battles, wild heartfelt cheers arose which so touched General Lee that tears filled his

ROBERTO LEE.

Roberto Lee used as a vague basis the prewar Brady image and embellished it for the Madrid publisher, N. Gonzalez, *ca.* 1865. The engraver was García. The officer clearly has adopted Spanish-looking features.

Anne S. K. Brown Military Collection, Brown University

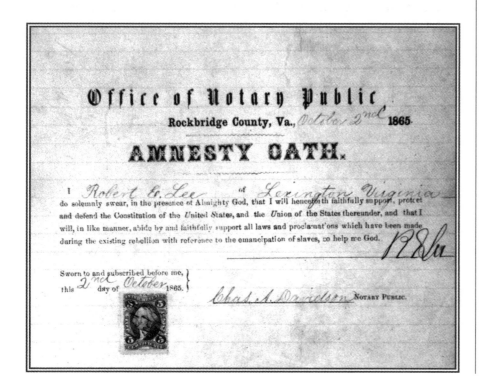

Lee signed this amnesty oath at Lexington on 2 October 1865, once again swearing to support and protect the U.S. Constitution. It was countersigned by Charles A. Davidson, a Lexington attorney and former Confederate soldier.

National Archives and Records Administration

General Robert E. Lee by Nathaniel Currier and James Merritt Ives, published in New York in 1865, is an engraving based on the well-known 1863 Minnis and Cowell photograph.
Library of Congress

eyes and trickled down his cheeks as he rode his splendid charger, hat in hand, bowing his acknowledgements."[37]

The reaction on the Confederate home front was stunning despite the realization of the desperate military situation. Moreover, it seemed immediately apparent that the Confederate war was over despite the fact that Lee surrendered but one army. "How can I write it?" penned Catherine Ann Devereaux Edmondston. "How find words to tell what has befallen us? *Gen Lee has surrendered! . . .* We stand appalled at our disaster! . . . [That] *Lee,* Lee upon whom hung the hopes of the whole country, should be a prisoner seems almost too dreadful to be realized!"[38]

The remnants of the Army of Northern Virginia stacked their arms for the final time. "What visions thronged us as we looked into each other's eyes!" wrote Joshua Chamberlain, the Federal officer appointed to receive the surrender. "Here pass the men of Antietam, the Bloody Lane, the Sunken Road, the Cornfield, the Burnside-Bridge; the men whom Stonewall Jackson on the second night at Fredericksburg begged Lee to let him take and crush the two corps of the Army of the Potomac huddled in the streets in darkness and confusion; the men who swept away the Eleventh Corps at Chancellorsville; who left six thousand of their companions around the bases of Culp's and Cemetery Hills at Gettysburg; these survivors of the terrible Wilderness, the Bloody-Angle at Spottsylvania, the slaughter pen of Cold Harbor, the whirlpool of Bethesda Church!"[39]

Lee had cordial and even friendly conversations with his now ex-adversaries Grant, George G. Meade, and Henry J. Hunt on 10 April. He left for Richmond two days later, accompanied by Walter Taylor, Charles Marshall, and Giles Cooke. His newfound country and cause now gone, ahead of him lay a completely clean slate.

CHAPTER NINE

※

When the War's Over...

APPEARING MARKEDLY AGED BY THE WAR, EXHAUSTED, frequently ill, and beaten, Lee returned to Richmond a paroled prisoner of war about 12 April. On the way, as he rode Traveller, he encountered many of his former soldiers, as evidenced by a single anecdote from Carlton McCarthy. "Looking up the survivors saw, with surprise, General Lee approaching," he wrote. "Having caught sight of the occupants of the log, he kept his eyes fixed on them, and as he passed, turned slightly, saluted, and said in the most gentle manner: 'Good morning, gentlemen; taking your breakfast?' The soldiers had only time to rise, salute, and say 'Yes, sir!' and he was gone."[1] He went to the house on Franklin Street, which was guarded by a single Federal soldier, and awaited what looked like a bleak future for the South. Several days later, Thomas Thatcher Graves, an aide of Maj. Gen. Godfrey Weitzel's, recorded a scene in the Lee home. Weitzel ordered him to "'go to General Lee's house, find Fitzhugh Lee, and say that his old West Point chum Godfrey Weitzel wishes to know if he needs anything, and urge him to take what he may need from that pocketbook.'" he wrote. "I knocked, and Fitzhugh Lee came to the door. He was dressed in a Confederate uniform. . . . He excused himself, and passed into the inner room, where I saw General R. E. Lee sitting, with a tired, worn expression upon his face. Fitzhugh Lee knelt beside his general, as he sat leaning over, and placed a hand upon his knee."[2]

This outstanding photograph was made by Michael Miley about 10 January 1870, and was one of the last images taken of the fabled commander.
Virginia Historical Society, Richmond

153

This superb postwar portrait by Alexander Gardner was made about 17–19 February 1866 when Lee visited Washington and Gardner's gallery.
Library of Congress

This somewhat austere steel engraving by William Edgar Marshall was based on one of the 1864 "blockade" portraits by Julian Vannerson.
Author's Collection

Not only did the Lees lack money, but the Richmond economy was in complete shambles, supplies were practically nonexistent, and, in a calamity as great for the South as for the North, President Lincoln was assassinated on 14 April and died the following morning. Andrew Johnson was sworn in as president. Like other intelligent Southerners, Lee was stunned and saddened by Lincoln's death. A few days after his return the celebrated Yankee photographer Mathew Brady convinced the General to pose for a series of photographs on the rear porch of the Lee House, these photographs now among the most recognized images of the war. Four show Lee alone; two more depict him with son Custis and Walter Taylor. Curiously, they all wore Confederate uniforms in violation of their paroles. Custis and Taylor, along with Rob Lee and others, kept a watch over the activities of their former commander and the mountain of requests aimed at him during this chaotic period. The reunion with family, and particularly with Mary, gave Lee renewed faith as he faced a dark and uncertain future. "At all events, for the defence of Virginia," wrote Edmund Ruffin on 12 April, "there is no longer a hope remaining. Her people are now slaves to the Yankee power, & at the mercy of the Yankee soldiers, & of the civilian Yankee immigrants who will speedily overrun our country & prey upon its wretched inhabitants."[3]

The whole of the Confederacy was indeed winding down. In North Carolina on 26 April, Joe Johnston capitulated to Sherman. On that day too John Wilkes Booth, Lincoln's assassin, was cornered and fatally shot in a Virginia barn. On 4 May Lt. Gen. Richard Taylor's sizable Confederate force surrendered in Citronelle, Alabama. Six days later Jefferson Davis and his party, representing the final nucleus of the Confederate government, were captured as they fled southward near Irwinville, Georgia. In Macon, Davis told Federal soldiers that of all his officers, "Lee was the ablest, most courageous, and most aggressive; in short, the most worthy of all his lieutenants."[4] On 12 May a skirmish at Palmito Ranch, Texas, became the final engagement of the war— ironically, Confederates were victorious. And on 26 May the final Southern force of any size, that of Gen. Edmund Kirby Smith, surrendered at Galveston. Some feared that a guerrilla war could continue for years unabated, and former Confederate leaders including Lee spoke out vigorously in favor of dropping all resis-

The President's House at Washington College, built in 1842, served as the Lee family home from 1865–1869. Stonewall Jackson and his family had inhabited the house from 1853–1857. By the last year of Lee's life, the Lee family moved next door to a more spacious house they had designed.

David J. Eicher

John A. O'Neill created this steel engraving in 1865 and based it on the 1864 photograph by J. W. Davies. The engraving was published in *Southern Generals: Who They Are, and What They Have Done*, by William P. Snow, later republished as *Lee and His Generals*.

Author's Collection

tance for the common good of what was now a single, reunited country. However, he did not sign an oath of allegiance to the United States, wishing to have a clarification of his status as a paroled prisoner first.

On 29 May, Johnson offered amnesty and a pardon for most ex-Confederates who would sign the oath. As he contemplated his status in June, a Federal grand jury at Norfolk indicted Lee and others on charges of treason. He applied for a pardon on the condition that the charges be dropped. The majority of

Grant and Lee by Otto Boetticher, a watercolor painted in 1866, shows the meeting that did occur at Appomattox between the two commanders the day following the McLean House conference.

Lincoln Museum, Fort Wayne, Ind.

Boude and Miley made this fine right
profile view of the aging commander
sometime in the early-mid postwar
period.
The Valentine Museum, Richmond

Lee autographed this copy of the previ-
ous pose on 12 April 1868.
*Leyburn Library, Washington and Lee
University*

ex-Confederate soldiers followed his lead, but many unreconstructed rebels were angered bitterly over this act. Some abandoned
their adoration of their former commander during this month.
Grant interceded and derailed the pending trial, agreeing with Lee's
logic over the surrender terms. The treason charges would never be
pursued, but neither would Lee receive a pardon. Despite this, he
preached reconciliation. "The duty of [Southern] citizens, then,
appears to me too plain to admit of doubt," he wrote John Letcher.
"All should unite in honest efforts to obliterate the effects of the
war and to restore the blessings of peace."[5]

Meanwhile, the ex-leader searched inwardly for a new purpose. "Dr. [Lafayette] G[uild] found Gen. Lee in a little 8 by 10
room on the third story of his home on Franklin St.," wrote Josiah
Gorgas on 22 June, "with a pile of letters, chiefly from Yankee
women, asking after things which belong to dead relatives, which
he was himself laboriously answering, all of his Staff having left
him. Yankee soldiers covered the sidewalk opposite scanning the
windows to get sight of the redoubted General whom they had at
last conquered."[6]

At first the fabled man wished simply to acquire a tract of
land and settle in with his family, tending a farm. He also entertained thoughts of writing a history of the campaigns in Virginia
or of the whole Civil War, but most of his papers and those of the
army were destroyed, lost, or scattered. "I am anxious to collect the
necessary data for the history of the campaigns in Virginia," he
wrote Walter Taylor on 31 July, one of a good many letters to
Confederate officers asking for material or simply seeding a plan
for the mid term future.[7] On 26 August he wrote Joseph Topham, a
Cincinnati publisher, responding to a request for a general history
of the war. "I cannot, at present, undertake such a work," he wrote,
"but am endeavouring to collect certain material to enable me to
write a history of the campaigns in Virginia."[8]

But another big change was poised to enter Lee's life—the
final one. Approached with many opportunities and offers in the
early Reconstruction South, he had turned them all down. The
Board of Trustees at a little school named Washington College in
Lexington, Virginia, near the top of the Shenandoah Valley, began
to court him with an offer of the college presidency. After they
elected him president on 4 August, Lee responded on 24 August.
"Fully impressed with the responsibilities of the office," he wrote, "I
have feared that I should be unable to discharge its duties to the

satisfaction of the trustees or to the benefit of the country. . . ."[9] He reversed his decision, however, accepting in early September, and planned to move his family to the charming little town of Lexington, where Stonewall Jackson lay buried. The school had begun as the Augusta Academy in Greenville in 1749. It endured several site and name changes before arriving in Lexington in 1802 and experiencing a recharter as Washington College in 1813.

This period marked an upturn in Lee's outlook on life. "We have certainly not found [in] our form of government all that was anticipated by its original founders," he wrote Matthew Fontaine Maury on 8 September, "but that may be partly our fault in expecting too much and partly in the absence of virtue in the people. . . . I cannot, however, despair of it yet. I look forward to better days."[10] The method by which the General looked for better days to come was through educating the young people of the

Meeting of Generals Grant and Lee Preparatory to The Surrender of General Lee and His Entire Army to Lieut. General U. S. Grant, April 9th 1865 is a lithograph by Pierre S. Duval and Son. Published by Joseph Hoover in Philadelphia in 1866, the piece wrongly depicts the imagined meeting of Lee and Grant in an apple orchard near the town of Appomattox Court House.
Lincoln Museum, Fort Wayne, Ind.

This cartes-de-visite image made in 1866 shows Lee and his faculty from Washington College.
Leyburn Library, Washington and Lee University

THE HEROES OF THE SOUTH.

The Heroes of the South by Am. Harcq., a fanciful lithograph published in New York in 1866. Aside from Lee, who holds his hat and dominates the scene on Traveller, left of the battle flag are, left to right: Early, Polk, Longstreet, Kirby Smith, Cheatham, Stonewall Jackson, Ewell, A. S. Johnston, J. E. Johnston, Stuart, Hardee, A. P. Hill, Magruder, Pickett, Beauregard, Price, Breckinridge, Bragg, Gardner, Hampton, Taylor, J. H. Morgan, S. D. Lee, Hood, and Wheeler.
Library of Congress

Above left: This remarkably sharp view of Lee's right profile was made about 17–19 February 1866 by Alexander Gardner in Washington.
Virginia Historical Society, Richmond

Above right: A slightly less-sharp version of the Gardner portrait was signed by Lee.
Virginia Historical Society, Richmond

This exceptionally crisp copy of the Gardner profile appears on an over-sized, oval card.
Leyburn Library, Washington and Lee University

South. It was perhaps the most significant decision of his life, and one that added the most humanistic element of his legacy.

On 18 September Lee rode Traveller up Lexington's Main Street, having traveled four days from Cumberland County. His resulting position at the college, which he held until his death, worked superbly well and was mutually beneficial. He was an excellent administrator, initiating an elective system rather than a prescribed course and vigorously promoting journalism, agriculture, and engineering. He came to know many students by name and was loved by all of them. Reacting to an oratorical exercise that included compliments of Lee, nasty shots taken at the Yankees, and oblique references to Lexington's maidens, the former General responded as follows: "You young men speak too long and you make three other mistakes. What you say about me is distasteful to me, and what you say about the North tends to promote ill feeling, and your compliments to the ladies would be more appreciated if paid in private."[11]

The new president prepared to move into the president's house, a structure lived in by Stonewall Jackson from 1853–1857 after he married the daughter of George Junkin, then the president. Now Lee began to ready the house for his family, who would join him later, with a battery of repairs. "I engaged some carpenters last week to repair the roof, fences, stable, etc., but for want of material they could not make a commencement," he wrote Mary in early October. "There is no lumber here at hand. Everything has to be prepared."[12] About this time he seemed to make a complete peace with the restoration of the Union. On 2 October—the day he started at Washington College—an oath of amnesty was sworn but not acted on; an amnesty bill for Robert E. Lee was signed by President Gerald Ford in 1976. "After the surrender of the Southern armies in April," Lee wrote G. T. Beauregard on 3 October, "the revolution in the opinions and feelings of the people seemed so complete, and the return of the Southern States into the union of all the States so inevitable, that it became in my opinion the duty of every citizen, the contest being virtually ended, to cease opposition, and place himself in a position to serve the country."[13] The following month, on 6 November, the CSS *Shenandoah* struck its flag at Liverpool, England, marking the final act of the Confederate States of America.

The old General seemed to be evolving into his role as educator splendidly. He drew a modest wage relative to some ex-Confederate generals who capitalized on their fame. "Gen Lee's salary he says is $1500 per annum," wrote Josiah Gorgas on 17 December. "Compare this with Gen. Johnston's salary of $10,000 as Presdt. of the New National Express Co."[14] Fully supporting the continued restoration of Federal authority—at least publicly—his thoughts still hovered about the war. He answered an unidentified correspondent who had described losing relatives in the war: "I am a poor genealogist and my family records have been destroyed or are beyond my reach. . . . I am led . . . to grieve with you at the death of your brave nephews who fell in the recent war. May their loss be sanctified by you and your country."[15] He autographed many photographs for admirers, as evidenced by letters to Mary. "[I] return the photographs with my signatures," he wrote her on 21 November.[16] And still he contemplated writing a history of the Virginia campaigns as he worked at the slow restoration of the president's house on the Washington College campus. Custis moved in with his father at a Lexington hotel and accepted a teach-

Gen. Robert E. Lee, an engraving by John C. McRae, was published by Thomas Kelly in New York in 1867. The influence is clearly the 1863 Minnis and Cowell photo, although the facial features are derived from an earlier effort by Minnis and Cowell. The outdoor setting makes the print particularly unusual.

Library of Congress

Lee and His Generals, a colored lithograph by Charles and Augustus Tholey, was published by John Calvin Smith in Philadelphia in 1867. Details of the assemblage of commanders draw on a battery of individual photographs. Lee and Stonewall Jackson dominate the scene; also prominent on horseback are G. T. Beauregard, Joseph E. Johnston, and James Longstreet.

Library of Congress

During the summer of 1866 while Lee was at the Rockbridge Baths, ten miles north of Lexington, the photographer A. H. Plecker recorded two photographs of the General with Traveller.
Leyburn Library, Washington and Lee University

The second Plecker photograph is an image made from a tinted copy of the original, which did not survive.
Leyburn Library, Washington and Lee University

ing position at the Virginia Military Institute, adjacent to the college. Finally, on 2 December, the house was ready and the Lee family arrived in town.

With the New Year Lee traveled to Richmond to appeal to the Virginia legislature for funds for his small college on behalf of its 100 students, arriving on 11 January 1866. The appeal succeeded, and help came from other sources, some private—the General himself later loaned $6,000 to the school. He also had the unpleasant task of being summoned to Washington to testify to the joint committee investigating the "so-called Confederate States." He arrived on 16 February, entering Washington for the first time since his meeting at the Blair House on 18 April 1861. On the 17th he testified before Congress and was questioned by Senator Jacob M. Howard of Michigan, revealing little startling information. After his return, on 23 February, he wrote Varina Davis, whose husband was still imprisoned at Fort Monroe and was becoming the chief villain of the rebellion. "I have thought, from the time of the cessation of hostilities, that silence and patience on the part of the South was the true course," he wrote, "and I think so still."[17]

Yet he planned to speak out on paper. The General continued to amass reports and documents in hopes of writing a history of the Virginia campaigns. In March he wrote Jubal Early, asking for copies of reports. "It will be difficult to get the world to understand the odds against which we fought and the destruction or loss of all returns of the army embarrasses me," he wrote.[18] "Can you not occupy your leisure time in preparing memoirs of the war," he wrote James Longstreet. "Every officer whose position and character would give weight to his statements, ought to do so. It is the only way in which we can hope that fragments of truth will reach posterity."[19]

And he continued to teach the South's young. Late in April the college's trustees revised the course of study, introducing an elective system, including chemistry, Greek, Latin, mathematics, modern languages, moral philosophy, natural philosophy, and practical chemistry. Interest from bonds and an endowment and gifts from Cyrus McCormick and others helped the institution to regain its momentum for the school year 1866–1867. The summer passed quietly save for the fluctuations in health of Mary's, which caused Lee to send her frequently to Rockbridge Baths, 11 miles north of Lexington, for recuperation. On 28 July he wrote Rob Lee from this place: "I was very glad to see from your letter . . . the progress you are making on your farm. . . . I am here with your mother, waiting to see the effects of these waters upon her disease, before proceeding to the Warm Springs. She is pleased with the bath, which she finds very agreeable. . . ."[20] Early in August Mary had a fall which impeded her improvements in health. "I am very sorry that you received such a fall, and fear it must have been a heavy shock to you. . . . Love to the girls," the General wrote her on 10 August.[21]

Michael Miley's famous photograph of Lee on Traveller was made in Lexington in November 1866. One of the primary symbols of the Lost Cause imagery, it served as the basis for numerous engravings and artwork that during the Reconstruction period adorned the parlors of homes all across the South.

Library of Congress

With the new academic year, the school was booming—nearly 400 students had enrolled. Lee vigorously undertook his duties with the same dedication he had applied at West Point. He also spent a great deal of time and energy answering correspondence from admirers. During this period Andrew Johnson and the Congress in Washington divided bitterly over the Reconstruction acts, plunging the South and the nation into a prolonged darkness. Meanwhile, in November, Michael Miley and Andrew H. Plecker, photographers, traveled to Rockbridge Baths and made the first photographs of Lee taken in Rockbridge County. Miley was a former Confederate soldier in the Stonewall Brigade, who had been captured at Chancellorsville. Plecker was a transient photographer. In partnership with wartime friends James L. McCown and John C. Boude, who supplied the capital, Miley opened a photographic gallery in Lexington called Boude & Miley that would be instrumental in promoting images of Lee. The studio opened in January 1867. Miley was a twenty-six-year-old artist who was quite shy, and Lee came several times to his studio for sittings, attracted by the young ex-Confederate.[22]

A popular lithograph by A. Hoen and Company in Richmond used the Miley photo and slightly embellished the background. Widely distributed, it was first published in 1876.

Library of Congress

At this time the General's name was raised as a possible governor of Virginia, providing that the radicals in Congress might permit a civilian governor. He declined the invitation from Virginia supporters, and as it turned out such an outcome was made impossible by Congress. On 13 March the First Reconstruction Act passed and Virginia was declared a military district; Maj. Gen. John M. Schofield was placed in command.

In 1866 Lee requested that a chapel be built at Washington College. The building was completed in time for graduation ceremonies in 1868, and thereafter Lee worshipped in the building daily. He used a basement room as his office, and left it for the last time on 28 September 1870. Lee was buried beneath the chapel and in 1883, reentombed in the Lee family crypt inside what is now named Lee Chapel.

David J. Eicher

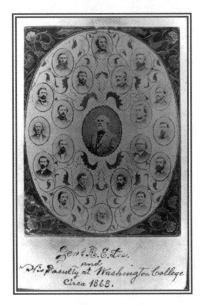

This cartes-de-visite shows Lee and his Washington College faculty about 1868. The outermost ring shows, clockwise from top, J. L. Kirkpatrick, Alexander L. Nelson, William Allan, Edward A. Moore, Rodes Massie, Milton W. Humpheys, John Fuller, Thomas T. Eaton, Charles S. Dod, Richard S. McCulloh, and James J. White. The inner ring, clockwise from top right, shows John L. Campbell, Edward S. Joynes, John W. Brockenbrough, C. Powell Grady, Frank Preston, Harry Estill, William P. Johnston, and Carter J. Harris.

Leyburn Library, Washington and Lee University

During this month five students traveled to a black church and attacked a black parishioner with a pistol. Lee expelled the guilty student and harshly reprimanded the other four.

On 13 May the long imprisonment of Jefferson Davis finally ended, as bail was accepted and the ex-Confederate president was released from Fort Monroe. "You can conceive better than I can express the misery which your friends have suffered from your long imprisonment and the other afflictions incident thereto," Lee wrote his old chief on 1 June. "To none has this been more painful than to me, and the impossibility of affording relief has added to my distress."[23] On 8 June he wrote Rooney, thinking of the future. "Let us all so live that we may be united in that world where there is no separation," he penned, "and where sorrow and pain never come. I think after next year I will have done all the good I can for the college, and I should then like, if peace is restored to the country, to retire to some quiet spot, east of the mountains, where I might prepare a home for your mother and sisters after my death."[24]

Thoughts of his or the family's demise were not without foundation. That autumn he suffered a severe cold complicated by rheumatism, which confined him to bed for about two weeks. By September he could again ride a horse and arrived back in Lexington on the 17th.[25] Mary continued to be quite ill and spent much time healing at Rockbridge Baths, Warm Springs, or White Sulphur Springs. The family spent much of the summer of 1867 at White Sulphur Springs and its large wooden frame hotel. His

A rare image of the General by Pollock of Baltimore was taken about 1869. This cartes-de-visite copy was signed by Lee, probably in Lexington in the last few months of his life.

Eleanor S. Brockenbrough Library, The Museum of the Confederacy, Richmond

An unusual bow tie and peculiar rounded lapels mark this Boude and Miley photo taken about 1869.

The Valentine Museum, Richmond

Edward V. Valentine marked the reverse of this photo from the last two or three years of Lee's life, but definitive photographic data remains elusive.

The Valentine Museum, Richmond

This well-known pose by Boude and Miley was taken in Lexington about 1868–69. The General's careworn appearance shows the burden of the postwar years.

The Valentine Museum, Richmond

This cartes-de-visite copy of the standing Boude and Miley pose was signed by Lee during the last year or two of his life. He signed in dark brown ink; note the matching partial finger or thumbprint at the lower right corner of the card, presumably that of the General.

The Valentine Museum, Richmond

Presumably made on the same day as the previous image, this Boude and Miley image shows a finely detailed left side.

The Valentine Museum, Richmond

In May 1869 Lee returned to Washington to meet with President Grant and posed in Mathew Brady's studio. This view shows the General's left profile crisply and reveals how starkly aged he appeared from several years before.

Library of Congress

This marvelous cartes-de-visite print of the previous Brady pose was signed by Lee. The copyright date of 1865 shows that Brady used an old card.

Leyburn Library, Washington and Lee University

In another pose from the Brady sitting in May 1869, Lee's careworn appearance is plain, particularly the lack of spark in his eyes.

Library of Congress

A third pose from the May 1869 Brady sitting shows Lee with the famous props of Mathew Brady's studio, the Brady chair and the Brady clock.

National Archives and Records Administration

A well-circulated engraving by A. Robin of the third Brady pose was published in *Harper's Weekly* in 1869. Lee's facial features are somewhat embellished, as is the bookshelf setting.

Author's Collection

Another engraving based on the third Brady photo appeared in the popular work *Battles and Leaders of the Civil War* in 1887, first serialized in the *Century* magazine. The engraving was uncredited.

Author's Collection

In August 1869 Lee traveled to White Sulphur Springs, West Virginia, for rest and improved health. He met with luminaries from the philanthropic world as well as ex-Confederate officers to discuss the possibilities of fundraising for Washington College and for care for orphaned children of deceased Confederate soldiers. Seated, left to right, are Blacque Bey, Lee, George Peabody, W. W. Corcoran, and James Lyons. Standing, left to right, are James Conner, Martin W. Gary, John B. Magruder, Robert D. Lilley, G. T. Beauregard, Alexander R. Lawton, Henry A. Wise, and Joseph L. Brent.

National Archives and Records Administration

A large copy print mounted on card stock of the same pose was signed by Beauregard, Lawton, Wise, Peabody, and Lyons.

Leyburn Library, Washington and Lee University

A slight variation in pose was taken a few moments before or after the previous photograph.

Leyburn Library, Washington and Lee University

In still another exposure, Lee has dropped his hat down to near the ground.

Author's Collection

Ill and crippled by rheumatism and arthritis, Mary Custis Lee made the best of her years in Lexington despite being confined to her chair. This photo was made by Michael Miley.

The Valentine Museum, Richmond

thoughts for the future of his family and a trust in God's will were reflected more frequently thereafter in family letters. "Your letter . . . did not give me a very favourable account of yourself or your prospects," he wrote Rob Lee on 26 October. "We must not, however, yield to difficulties, but strive the harder to overcome them. I am sorry for the failure of your crops, your loneliness and uncomfortableness, and wish it were in my power to visit with you and advise with you. . . . God bless you my son, and may He guard, guide, and direct you in all you do."[26]

On his return to Lexington the Lees received joyous news that Rooney, whose wife had died during the war, was courting another young lady, Mary Tabb Bolling of Petersburg. The wedding date was set for 28 November, and on the way to Petersburg the General stopped in Richmond to appear before a Federal grand jury again considering charges against Jefferson Davis. That done, he traveled on to Petersburg and stayed with an old subordinate, William Mahone. He renewed many friendships there and again in Richmond before returning to Lexington by 7 December.

In the New Year of 1868, Lee's thoughts again frequently turned back to the war. On 15 February the General held a conversation with former Confederate officer William Allan, who recorded the passages. Commenting on inaccuracies in D. H. Hill's published account of the Maryland campaign, Lee stated that he

In the spring of 1869 Lee and his family moved into the new President's House, complete with three verandahs that enabled Mary Custis Lee mobility in her wheelchair on three sides of the structure. Lee also had a brick stable built beside the house for Traveller.

David J. Eicher

This steel engraving of Lee was executed by John A. O'Neill in 1869 to accompany a new edition of Light-Horse Harry Lee's *Memoirs of the War in the Southern Department of the United States*. It is based on one of the 1864 photographs by Julian Vannerson.

Author's Collection

This image was made in the last year or two of the 1860s by Boude and Miley in Lexington, and this cartes-de-visite copy was signed by Lee.

The Valentine Museum, Richmond

This unusual postwar cartes-de-visite, signed by Lee, appears not to have been published before in the Lee literature. It is reproduced from a copy furnished by Maj. Edward C. Betts.

National Archives and Records Administration

This Boude and Miley photo was made in the final year or two of Lee's life and formed the basis for much artwork produced after his death. On the verso of this cartes-de-visite copy, which was signed by the General, is an inscription by Edward V. Valentine: "This autograph is written by General Lee at Lexington 14 June 1870."

The Valentine Museum, Richmond

Another cartes-de-visite copy of the Boude and Miley photo was also signed by Lee, suggesting this image's popularity with the General himself in the final months of his life.

The Valentine Museum, Richmond

In the late 1860s Boude and Miley created this image in Lexington, which influenced a host of lithographs and engravings following Lee's death. Some students of Lee's photography have claimed this to be the final image of Lee from life.

National Archives and Records Administration

Right: To improve his health, Lee traveled to Savannah in the spring of 1870. On behalf of their benevolent fund, the Ladies Memorial Association persuaded Lee and Joseph E. Johnston to pose together at D. Ryan's Gallery in April.
Library of Congress

Far right: A second image from the Ryan studio sitting shows the old general officers having switched sides at the table.
Virginia Historical Society, Richmond

The Swiss artist Frank Buchser painted this handsome portrait of Lee late in 1869, the General sitting for the work in Lexington. The work spanned the period 25 September–18 October.
Leyburn Library, Washington and Lee University

A wood engraving by D. J. Ryan based on the Lee–Johnston sitting appeared in the *Century* magazine and subsequently in *Battles and Leaders of the Civil War* in 1887. It became an icon in Lost Cause imagery.
Author's Collection

initiated the campaign to "relieve Va. from both armies" and "to live for a time on the abundant supplies in Maryland." He said he intended to attack McClellan had the order not been lost, if he had his men reconcentrated on the Maryland side, his stragglers up, and his men rested. The loss of the dispatch, he felt, changed the character of the campaign.

Of Chancellorsville, the General said that Jackson preferred at first to attack Sedgwick at Fredericksburg. But it was hard to get

at the enemy down by the river. The next day, Lee found Jackson attacking at Chancellorsville. He wanted to attack the right flank, cutting off Hooker from the river, and thereby the plan to take the furnace road around the right developed.[27] In another conversation on 15 April, he told Allan that he never intended to give general battle in Pennsylvania. The South was too weak to carry on a war of invasion, he said before chastising his critics, and stated that he "fought honestly and earnestly to the best of his knowledge and ability for the 'Cause' and had *never allowed* his own advantage or reputation to come under consideration."[28] On 7 May he had a conversation with William Preston Johnston, son of Albert Sidney Johnston. "Stay-at-home critics may censure my army," he said, "but I believe I got out of them all that they could do or all that any men could do."[29]

And the country at large was coming to respect the Confederate general. The New York *Herald* proposed that Lee be named a Democratic candidate for president. But even had he desired such a thing, the General was in no health for it. By the summer of 1868 he could not travel considerable distances by horseback. The Lexington doctors recommended drinking copious amounts of the waters at White Sulphur Springs. He had occasional, painful episodes of rheumatism.[30] Mary continued in poor health. "Your mother, I presume, has told you of home affairs," Lee wrote Rooney on 1 July. "She has become nervous of late, and broods over her troubles that I fear it increases her sufferings."[31]

Above left: This image was made by Boude and Miley sometime around 1867. This cartes-de-visite print was signed by Lee on 3 October 1867.
Leyburn Library, Washington and Lee University

Above center: A poorer cartes-de-visite copy of the Boude and Miley image was signed by Lee on 10 January 1870.
Leyburn Library, Washington and Lee University

Above right: This is a heavily retouched version of the photograph taken by Boude and Miley sometime around 1867. It considerably softens the aged facial features relative to the original photo.
National Archives and Records Administration

Genl. Robert E. Lee was published by Bradley and Co. of Philadelphia in 1870. The engraving by Adam B. Walter is based on the J. W. Davies "floppy tie" portrait made in 1864.

Library of Congress

About 1870–1871 Mary Custis Lee hand-tinted this image of George Washington. On the verso of the cartes-de-visite she wrote, "George Washington from an original portrait in the provincial uniform that hung first at Mount Vernon and then at Arlington, Mary Custis Lee."

Leyburn Library, Washington and Lee University

Mary Custis Lee hand-tinted this image of Martha Washington about 1870–1871. On the verso she wrote, "Martha Washington from an original portrait of Woollaston [sic], Mary Custis Lee."

Leyburn Library, Washington and Lee University

Mary Custis Lee hand-tinted this image of her husband, based on the Vannerson profile, about the end of 1870–1871. On the verso she wrote, "A memorial picture of General R. E. Lee, retouched for the benefit of the Memorial Church at Lexington, Va., by Mary Custis Lee."

Leyburn Library, Washington and Lee University

Mary Custis Lee hand-tinted this image of herself about 1870–1871. On the verso she wrote, "Tinted for the benefit of the Memorial Church at Lexington by Mary Custis Lee."

Leyburn Library, Washington and Lee University

Mary Custis Lee hand-tinted this image made by Michael Miley in the late 1860s. She also pasted a clipped signature of her husband's onto the cartes-de-visite, taken from a letter or document.

Leyburn Library, Washington and Lee University

The academic year 1868–1869 began without fanfare and saw the General staying put in Lexington more than during any previous autumn and winter. A chapel he requested be built on the campus was finished and he established an office in the building's basement and worshipped upstairs daily. The politics of retribution dissolved in large part that winter when the Fourteenth Amendment was adopted and the potential trials against Davis and others, possibly including Lee, were nullified by a general amnesty proclamation.

Michael Miley also took this photograph of the aging commander sometime late in the 1860s.

Leyburn Library, Washington and Lee University

A popular lithograph represented Lee visiting the grave of Stonewall Jackson. This one shows the commander visiting his fallen comrade in Confederate uniform, no less. The details of Lee are based on the Brady photographs in Richmond following Appomattox.

Library of Congress

The biggest fallout for the Lees from this act came in writing a Congressman to attempt to reclaim the property seized by the Federal government at Arlington. "From what I have learned," Lee wrote on 12 February, "a great many things formerly belonging to General Washington, bequeathed to [Mary Custis Lee] by her father, in the shape of books, furniture, camp equipage, etc., were carried away by individuals and are now scattered over the land."[32] Congress declared the request to return them "an insult" and denied it, but the items were finally sent back to the Lee family by an order of President McKinley in 1903.[33]

The General traveled to Baltimore during part of the spring of 1869 and enjoyed a brief engagement convincing railroad executives to stretch a line to Lexington. About this time his old nemesis and more recently friendly acquaintance Ulysses S. Grant was inaugurated president. On 1 May he traveled to Washington to visit Grant, and on 3–7 May he visited his boyhood city of Alexandria, doubtless reliving many memories of his youth and spending ample time with his brother Sidney Smith Lee. When he finally arrived home in Lexington on 1 June the family experienced quite an uplift with the finish of their new home, a new president's house, that featured a first-floor bedroom and contained a porch on three sides for Mary, so that she could enjoy great mobility with her chair. "Your mother

The Grave of Stonewall Jackson, Lexington, Virginia, is a hand-colored lithograph published by Nathaniel Currier and James Merritt Ives in New York in 1870. Lee appears after the war visiting his fallen comrade, dressed in ordinary attire and with a weeping willow tree in the background.

Lincoln Museum, Fort Wayne, Ind.

A large crowd assembled at the college chapel on 15 October for Lee's funeral.
Leyburn Library, Washington and Lee University

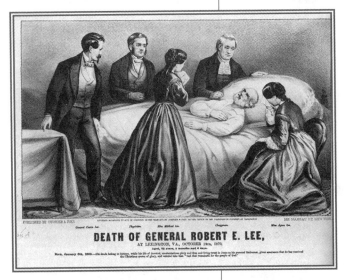

DEATH OF GENERAL ROBERT E. LEE,
AT LEXINGTON, VA., OCTOBER 12th, 1870,
Aged, 62 years, 8 months and 6 days.

Death of General Robert E. Lee at Lexington, Va., October 12th, 1870, aged 62 years, 8 months, and 6 days, by Nathaniel Currier and James Merritt Ives, a lithograph published in New York in 1870. Depicted around Lee's bed are George W. C. Lee, a physician, Mildred Lee, a clergyman, and Agnes Lee.

Library of Congress

is becoming interested in her painting again," the General wrote Rooney on 22 May, "and is employing her brush for the benefit of our little church, which is very poor. She yet awhile confines herself to colouring photographs, and principally to those of General and Mrs. Washington, which are sold very readily."[34] A handsome brick stable for Traveller stood adjacent to the house.

During the summer of 1869 the General labored on editing a new edition of his father's book, *Memoirs of the War in the Southern Department of the United States.* He added, among other things, a biographical sketch of Light-Horse Harry, the longest document ever composed by Lee. He compared Light-Horse Harry to "the vast and matchless character of Washington," granting him "the veneration of remotest posterity."[35] He then took Mary to Rockbridge Baths and on arriving received the news that his brother, Smith Lee, had died. "I arrived [in Alexandria] last evening, too late to attend the burial of my dear brother," he wrote Mary on 25 July, "an account of which I have clipped from the Alexandria *Gazette* and inclose to you. I wish you would preserve it. . . . May God bless us all and preserve us for the time when we, too, must part, the one from the other, which is now close at hand."[36]

He was correct. In October the General had an attack of pericarditis accompanied by muscular pain on the back and the right side, which later extended to his arms.[37] "I have had a wretched cold," he wrote Rooney on 2 December, "the effects of which have not left me, but I am better. The doctors still have me in hand, but I fear can do no good. . . . Traveller's trot is harder to me than it used to be and fatigues me. We are all as usual—the women of the family very fierce and the men very mild."[38]

In early 1870 he "could not walk much more than 150 yards without stopping to rest."[39] He saw Virginia reenter the Union with the new decade, when on 26 January President Grant signed a bill readmitting the commonwealth. During March he became

more feeble, his rheumatism more bothersome, and he was con-
tinually sad and depressed.[40] His health alarming, he took a leave
from the college and traveled south with Agnes, hoping his condition would improve. He desired to visit the grave of Annie Lee in
Warren White Sulphur Springs, North Carolina. Agnes and her
father departed on 24 March. In Richmond they saw John Mosby.
"The general was pale and haggard, and did not look like the
Apollo I had known in the army," wrote Mosby. After leaving the
room, Mosby encountered George Pickett and returned to see Lee
with him. It was "cold and formal, and evidently embarrassing to
both. It was their only meeting after the war." Mosby reported that
Pickett later called Lee "that old man" and said "he had my division massacred at Gettysburg."[41]

In Savannah the General and his daughter were greeted by
enthusiastic crowds, and Lee posed for two photographs with Joe
Johnston at D. Ryan's gallery. He also visited his father's grave at
"Dungeness" on Cumberland Island on 12 April. Still, he suffered
much in the Southern climate. When he attempted to walk moder-
ately quickly, chest pains restricted his movement. Rather than the
sometimes suggested angina due to arteriosclerotic heart disease,
the recurrent rheumatism and pericarditis suggest rheumatic heart
disease.[42] He spent time in Charleston and on 28 April left for
Wilmington, then to Portsmouth, where he again saw Walter
Taylor. Then he traveled by ferry to Norfolk and continued on to
visit the old family home of Shirley on the James. On 12 May he
was reunited at the White House with Rooney, then spent time in
Richmond, and returned to Lexington on 28 May.

Despite his ill health, Lee kept on the move. He went to Baltimore and then south to Alexandria, where he again saw John Mosby. "Colonel, I hope we shall have no more wars," he told the former partisan ranger.[43] He spent time at Warm Springs, hoping that "thermal treatments" would improve his suffering. At the outset of the 1870–1871 academic year, the General began his duties, but he was weak, his gait slow, and his shoulders drooping. On 28 September he returned to the new president's house from the chapel and that evening mostly lost his ability to speak. He experienced sporadic consciousness, and his pulse was slightly rapid and weak. He was soaked in rain as he walked home very slowly, and as he sat at the table for supper felt weak and discovered he couldn't speak. The last full sentence his doctors, R. L. Madison and Howard T. Barton, remembered, was "you hurt my arm," as he pointed with his right hand to his left arm.[44]

The General improved only very slightly over the following week, and all around him were drawn together by great concern. He stayed in the house and talked little, sleeping much of the time. Most of the Lee literature promotes an apocryphal story of his last hours, claiming he uttered the phrases "Tell Hill he *must* come up" and "strike the tent."[45] A recent, systematic evaluation of his illness strips away the legend, however. Lee suffered from atherosclerosis involving coronary and cerebral arteries, producing abulia

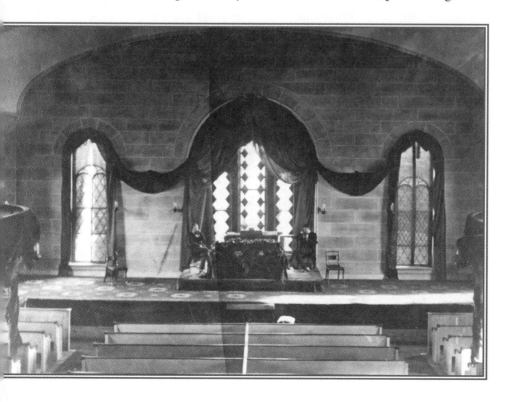

Inside the chapel, Lee's coffin lay in state, guarded by two ex-Confederate soldiers.

Virginia Historical Society, Richmond

Lee's death mask was created in 1870 by the renowned sculptor Clark Mills. The plaster cast resides in the Museum of the Confederacy in Richmond.

The Museum of the Confederacy, Richmond

(loss of will, lethargy) and also some aphasia (loss of speech). In short, he suffered a stroke, at the time believed to be "congestion of the brain," and because of this, deathbed speeches almost certainly did not take place.[46]

He talked very little, occasionally nodding in response to questions. Once, offered medicine, he said with difficulty, "It is no use." On 10 October he spoke the last phrase recorded by the doctors, "I . . . feel . . . better," only with great difficulty.[47] Near midnight on 11–12 October the doctors felt his condition worsened and warned the family of the impending end. He again refused medicine and food and he seemed confused when semiconscious. Surrounded by his wife Mary, son Custis, and daughters Agnes and Mildred, the great commander died at 9:30 A.M. on 12 October, leaving the Lee family, his students, and the veterans of his beloved Army of Northern Virginia behind.

CHAPTER TEN

Lee, the Lost Cause, and Southern Memory

Lee at West Point appears in this superb portrait accomplished by Ernest L. Ipsen in 1931. The work depicts him about 1855, as superintendent of the Military Academy, in the uniform of a brevet colonel of engineers.

Virginia Historical Society, Richmond

ON LEE'S DEATH, THE REVERED COMMANDER transformed in quick order from human being to legend. The postwar period had been rocky for Southerners. Reconstruction policies driven by the radical Republican Congress were often brutal, the economy was still in a shambles, and few true heroes had emerged from the Confederate side of the war. Certainly Jefferson Davis received squarely much of the blame from Southerners for losing the war. For the many reasons we have seen, the focus on a supreme Confederate military hero in the field first struck Stonewall Jackson and then shifted toward Lee. Now, with the General gone, Virginians would accelerate the Lee legend-making in a variety of ways, particularly in the pages of the *Southern Historical Society Papers*, published in Richmond. On the day of Lee's death, a group of former Confederate soldiers met in Lexington and organized a memorial association to preserve his grave and build a monument for it. They included William N. Pendleton, J. William Jones, William Allan, and William P. Johnston.[1]

Many former associates of the General contributed reports to the *Papers*, adding to the superhuman luster of the Lee story, and these were coordinated by the chief unreconstructed rebel, Jubal A. Early, the society's first president. Lee's "bad old man"

The three Lee boys as mature adults, Rob, Custis, and Rooney. Much of their activity centered on reflecting on their legendary father.
Virginia Historical Society, Richmond

One of the busts of Lee produced by Edward V. Valentine, which now resides in the Lee Chapel Museum at Washington and Lee University.
David J. Eicher

Edward V. Valentine completed this magnificent bronze bust of Lee in the summer of 1870, less than four months before the General's death.
National Portrait Gallery

and many others, under the uncomfortable period of the Reconstruction 1870s, were determined to continue to fight the war on paper. In doing so, they recorded much of historical value but also interjected a great deal of revisionist history in the attempt to "clarify" Confederate war aims, strategy, tactics, and the reasons for various actions. In doing so they revealed much about Lee's performance during the war but also created a Lee mythology that sometimes strayed far from reality. The historian Gary W. Gallagher has reminded us that between 1866 and 1872 Early "interpreted five major points on the war: that 1) Robert E. Lee was the best and most admirable general of the war; 2) Confederate armies faced overwhelming odds and mounted a gallant resistance; 3)

Ulysses S. Grant paled in comparison to Lee as a soldier; 4) Stonewall Jackson deserved a place immediately behind Lee in the Confederate pantheon; and 5) Virginia was the most important arena of combat."[2]

The transformation began shortly after Lee's death. "The loss is a public one," wrote Early in a letter to William N. Pendleton, on 13 October 1870, "and there are millions of hearts now torn with anguish at the news that has been flashed over the wires to all quarters of the civilized world."[3] The funeral ceremonies were planned for 15 October, to be held around the chapel where Lee worshipped and had his office, and the procession was described by J. William Jones, former Confederate officer and pastor of the Baptist Church in Lexington. The procession formed in front of the Lees' house and moved through the town, down Washington Street, up Jefferson Street, to Main Street, and to the Virginia Military Institute. It then moved back to the Washington College grounds and halted at the chapel. The Episcopalian burial service was read by William N. Pendleton.

Early and others pressed on with their version of the motives and history of the war—one that deemphasized slavery as a cause and proposed that Confederate victory would have occurred had it not been for unlimited men and supplies in the North. This new view of the Confederate war effort in the pages of books and journals aligned itself in a movement known as the Lost Cause. The

focal point of this view in paper after paper was Lee. By 1865 he was viewed as the supreme Confederate general, having beaten soundly or confused the attempts of McClellan, Pope, Burnside, and Hooker. The Lee mythology, however, was a distinctly postwar phenomenon. Early, J. William Jones, Fitzhugh Lee, Charles Marshall, Walter Taylor, and others actively promoted the legend. In an 1872 address, Early said, "General Lee had not been conquered in battle. . . . [He] surrendered . . . the mere ghost of the Army of Northern Virginia, which had been gradually worn down by the combined agencies of numbers, steam-power, railroads, mechanism, and all the resources of physical science."[4] John B. Gordon wrote, "Lee was never really beaten. Lee could not be beaten."[5] "This Lost Cause mentality took on the proportions of a heroic legend; a southern Götterdämmerung with Robert E. Lee as a latter-day Siegfried," according to James M. McPherson.[6]

Lee was not only looked after in his absence but deified—something that may have appalled him had he been around to see it. Said a Virginia soldier in an 1875 speech: "Lee was the grandest thing in all the world to us, when he loved us like a father and led us like a king, when we trusted him like a providence and obeyed him like a god."[7] The assessments have continued unabated into the present century. According to E. Merton Coulter, "the leader

A fanciful lithograph of an imaginary meeting between Lee, Joseph E. Johnston, and Thomas J. Jackson, was based on three different photographs. Such a meeting might have preceded the Peninsular campaign: the sources of imagery came from a photo of Jackson by Michael Miley, a photo of Johnston taken a year after Jackson's death, and the Vannerson profile of Lee from 1864.

A marble slab in Lee Chapel marks the spot where General Lee's remains rested from 1870 to 1883, before being interred in the family vault nearby in the same building.

David J. Eicher

An especially fine engraving based on the 1862 Minnis and Cowell photograph was published *ca.* 1870 by Goupil et cie., Paris, and M. Knoedler, New York. The engraver was P. Girardet. The artists took careful measures to delicately animate Lee's expression.

Anne S. K. Brown Military Collection, Brown University

This portrait, executed by John Adams Elder, is based on a Boude and Miley photo taken between 1866–1869. The painting hangs in the Corcoran Gallery in Washington.

Library of Congress

that [sic] was to typify the embattled Confederacy, sacrosanct from the time he took command in Virginia in 1862 throughout the rest of the war and ever thereafter, was Robert E. Lee. . . . his name alone kept his armies together for the last six months of the war."[8]

Early biographies of the General cast him as a saint, or even compared his life with that of Jesus. One compared his decision to resign from the U.S. Army to the Last Supper. Coming after the war, this religious symbolism suggests that for some Southerners, Lee took on the aspect of a sacrificial lamb, having died for the three great sins of the South—slavery, secession, and war.[9] Lee's failure at Gettysburg, however, threatened this Christ imagery. Hence, a scapegoat was needed to explain the failure and the Virginia contingent wasted no time in finding one.[10] In 1867, James Longstreet published a letter in the New Orleans *Times* advocating acceptance of the radical Republican measures in Congress. This ruptured relations between Longstreet and most of his wartime comrades. Second, Longstreet supposedly disobeyed orders at Gettysburg, failing to attack early on the morning of 2 July. Finally, Longstreet committed the cardinal sin of criticizing Lee in print, in letters, magazines, and ultimately in his memoirs.[11]

This combination was irresistible to Early and the other Virginians—Longstreet would be blamed for the loss at Gettysburg and therefore would exonerate their beloved Lee. Such sentiments were bolstered by other statements: "I once heard General Lee say," recalled J. William Jones, "with far more feeling than he was accustomed to exhibit: 'If I had had Jackson at Gettysburg, I should have won that battle, and a complete victory there would have resulted in the establishment of the independence of the South.'"[12]

Early delivered an address in 1872 in the chapel where his commander was now entombed, on Lee's birthday, 19 January. The whole institution had been renamed Washington and Lee University the previous year, and in 1870, following in his father's footsteps, Custis became president of the college, a position he would hold until 1897.[13] "We have a sacred duty to discharge," Early said. "It is . . . proper that the tomb of our beloved Commander, in this chapel, shall be suitably decorated and honored. Let it be our especial charge to see that the pious work is accomplished."14

A revised engraving by John A. O'Neill grew out of the project to publish Light-Horse Harry's *Memoirs of the War in the Southern Department of the United States*, completed in 1870. It draws influence from the Julian Vannerson photographs.
Author's Collection

Not only were the General's physical remains looked after, but care was given to the raw materials of the Lee legacy. Fortunately for the photographic record, the young Lexington photographer Michael Miley befriended Edward Valentine, who had come to Lexington in May 1870 to work on a bust of Lee. Miley and Valentine cooperated on more photographs in an attempt to aid Valentine's sculpture project. Also in 1870, Miley bought out his partner Boude's share and then owned his own operation. During the final year or two of Lee's life, Miley not only photographed the General but copied many previous photographs associated with the Lee, Custis, and Washington families.

Meanwhile, the Virginia contingent from the Lee Memorial Association studied the problem of erecting a suitable permanent tomb and monument for their fallen commander. Mary Custis Lee suggested the young sculptor Edward V. Valentine be hired for the assignment, the man who had created the Lee statuette. She preferred the kind of design like the recumbent figure of Queen

This handsome portrait by Hattie E. Burdette shows a considerable influence from the Miley photographs.
Leyburn Library, Washington and Lee University

Lee and Jackson at Cold Harbor by Alfred R. Waud captures a scene from the Peninsular campaign of 1862. The engraving was published in John Esten Cooke's *A Life of Gen. Robert E. Lee*, New York, 1871.
Author's Collection

Fredericksburg, an engraving also produced by Alfred R. Waud for Cooke's book, depicts Lee, Longstreet, and other officers on Marye's Heights during the battle of 13 December 1862.
Author's Collection

Chancellorsville by Alfred R. Waud shows Lee in front of the burning Chancellor Tavern, in a pose remarkably similar to the earlier work by Adalbert J. Volck.
Author's Collection

Louise of Prussia, made in 1813 for her tomb in Charlottenburg. By the autumn of 1872 models had been made and the $15,000 cost for a larger-than-life figure authorized, and by 1875 the project was completed and the statue, showing Lee asleep on the battlefield, was placed into storage. By 1883 the mausoleum was finished and the whole project ready to be dedicated.

On 28 June 1883 nearly 10,000 people gathered on the campus of Washington and Lee University to

Alfred R. Waud's *Lee at Gettysburg*, also produced for Cooke's *Life of Gen. Robert E. Lee*, depicts Lee riding through the survivors of Pickett's Charge on the afternoon of 3 July 1863.
Author's Collection

witness the unveiling of the Lee recumbent statue. Joseph E. Johnston, president of the Lee Memorial Association, was sick, so Jubal Early presided. John W. Daniel delivered a lengthy address on Lee's life. Unveiling the statue marked the passage of the first wave of memorialization. Not only would Southerners mourn the losses and lament the war's outcome, but now positive aspects of the war would emerge as they began to celebrate the past glories of the Confederacy.[15]

Following the unveiling, Lee's image soared, linking with the Lost Cause imagery itself. According to Jefferson Davis, his life "was a high model for the imitation of generations yet unborn." Senator Benjamin Hill of Georgia said Lee was "a public officer without vices; a private citizen without wrong . . . a man without guile."[16] Even Northern officers began to sing the praises of the old commander. "Lee's position was unique," wrote John C. Ropes. "No army commander on either side was so universally believed in, so absolutely trusted. Nor was there ever a commander who better deserved the support of his Government and the affection of his soldiers."[17] William Mahone once told Lee, "General, you are the state."[18]

More recently, historian Joseph T. Glatthaar pointed out that Lee succeeded so well because "he imposed his will upon the enemy. By seizing and maintaining the initiative, he determined how and where his army fought battles."[19] The question may then be asked, as it has been by James M. McPherson, "If Marse Robert was such a genius and his legions so invincible, why did they lose?" The historian points to several critical points during the war that acted as hinges, when the situation might have swayed significantly in one direction or the other. The first came in the summer of 1862, when counteroffensives of Jackson and Lee in the east and Bragg in the west stifled Union momentum. The second took place in the autumn of 1862, when Antietam and Perryville threw back Confederate invasions, stalled potential European involvement, aided Lincoln's party in the 1862 elections, and established a basis for the Emancipation Proclamation. The third occurred in the summer and autumn of 1863, when Gettysburg, Vicksburg, and Chattanooga suggested the eventuality of Federal victory. The fourth took place in the summer of 1864, when on the brink of Democratic political victory and peace negotiations, the North was transformed by the Georgia and Shenandoah Valley campaigns.[20]

During the antebellum period, McPherson has reminded us, Lee described slavery as a "political and moral evil." But he also owned slaves, probably sold some, and recaptured two who had escaped. He denounced abolitionists and said during the war that the Confederacy fought to save "our social system." Many writers have described the General's opposition to slavery, included those who penned the enormously popular PBS television

A variant of E. B. D. Julio's famous portrait *The Last Meeting of Lee and Jackson* resides in this colored engraving by Frederick Halpin, accomplished in New York in 1872. Published widely throughout the early period of Lee memorialization, the image recalls one of the high moments of promise for the young Confederacy, when Stonewall was alive and the Army of Northern Virginia, at Chancellorsville, seemed invincible.

Anne S. K. Brown Military Collection, Brown University

The Wilderness, Lee to the Rear by Alfred R. Waud presents Lee during the thick of the morning fight on 6 May 1864.

Author's Collection

A widely circulated chromolithograph by Charles or Augustus Tholey follows Adalbert J. Volck's *General Lee's Last Visit to Stonewall Jackson's Grave*. Published by Louis Eckhardt and Bros., Philadelphia, in 1872, the print was powerful Lost Cause imagery.
Library of Congress

Adalbert Johann Volck's *Robert E. Lee in His Study at Washington College* was finished in Lexington and Baltimore *ca.* 1872. This lithograph from one year later depicts the details of Lee's office—located in the basement of the college chapel—as it was when he died and as it remains today.
Library of Congress

Battle of Chancellorsville, a crude engraving by Adalbert J. Volck, was created for Emily V. Mason's *Popular Life of Gen. Robert Edward Lee*, published in Baltimore in 1872. Lee is shown on 3 May 1863 with the Chancellor Tavern ablaze in the background.
Author's Collection

General Lee Entering Richmond after the Surrender by Adalbert J. Volck accompanied other engravings for Mason's 1872 *Popular Life*. This fanciful scene captures the flavor of Lee returning to the city after Appomattox.
Author's Collection

This version of *The Last Meeting of Lee and Jackson*, published by the Turnbull Brothers, after J. G. Fay, differs significantly from E. B. D. Julio's more famous work and its derivatives. The chromolithograph was published in 1879, at the end of Reconstruction.
Library of Congress

series "The Civil War." The producer Ken Burns described this aspect of the General, which is correct "only if one applies the most expansive definition of "antislavery.""[21] Much has been made by recent writers about an even more sinister side of Lee: did he fight on for a year or more without purpose, having realized by 1864 that defeat was inevitable? "Not guilty," says McPherson. The hopelessness of the Confederate cause came after Lincoln's reelection in November 1864 and not earlier.

Another engraving from Mason's *Popular Life* is *Lee to the Rear*, in which Adalbert J. Volck shows a crude rendering of Lee waving a tattered flag at the Widow Tapp farm on 6 May 1864.
Author's Collection

"Ironically," McPherson concluded, "Lee's victories helped to prolong the war to the point where it destroyed precisely what the Confederacy was fighting for—slavery, state rights, the plantation economy, and political influence."[22]

To be sure, the General did not have opportunities for helping armies in the field during the whole of the war. "Lee was held in peripheral commands or at a desk in Richmond until 14 of the 27 months during which the South had striking power had elapsed," wrote historian David M. Potter.[23] His inward vision toward Virginia and Virginians also hurt him and the Confederacy, as he withheld support for the West or even for other armies as opposed to his own. "Because [Lee] would think and work in a corner, taking no notice of the whole, taking no interest in forming policy or in the economic side of the war, he was ultimately cornered and his cause lost," wrote the British analyst John F. C. Fuller.[24]

"Like other ex-Confederates, Robert Lee denied betraying

Surrender of Genl. Lee, at Appomattox C. H. Va. April 9th, 1865, is a rather primitive hand-colored lithograph by Nathaniel Currier and James Merritt Ives, published in New York in 1873. It is based on a cruder, vertical version published in 1865. The wallpaper includes an olive-branch design.
Lincoln Museum, Fort Wayne, Ind.

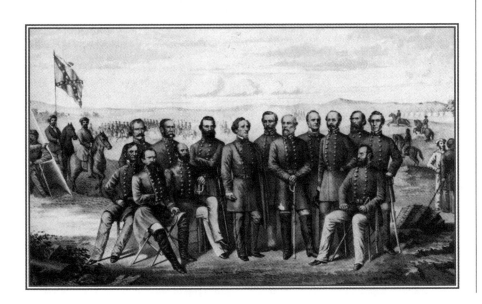

The Generals of the Confederate Army by Frederick Bourquin, after Shlaginlaufin, was published by the National Publishing Co. in Philadelphia in 1879. Jefferson Davis and Lee are central; also pictured, left to right, are Morgan, Forrest, Polk, A. S. Johnston, Gordon, Hampton, Ewell, Stuart, Beauregard, Price, Joseph E. Johnston, A. P. Hill, Stonewall Jackson, and Bragg.
Library of Congress

The recumbent statue of Lee in Lee Chapel is one of the most powerful symbols of the Lost Cause. Located directly above the Lee family crypt in the statue chamber, the statue was executed by Edward V. Valentine based on a meticulous series of measurements and plaster casts. The work, dedicated in 1883 by Stonewall Jackson's daughter Julia, depicts Lee asleep on the field of battle.

David J. Eicher

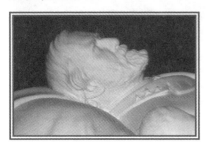

An engraving from the 1880s by A. B. Hall was based on the J. W. Davies photograph from 1864 and widely circulated during the expansive Lost Cause period.

Author's Collection

the American Revolution either in seceding or in losing a revolutionary war to secede," as Charles Royster reminds us. He lacked "a revolutionary vision like his father's that made the victory of ideals essential to happiness and made defeat fatal."[25] His battlefield decisions were also sometimes driven by, occasionally clouded by, religion. "Lee, as an Episcopalian, believed in the God-man relationship," wrote historians Thomas Connelly and Barbara Bellows, "in man's striving for salvation beyond a transient earthly existence, and in the daily intercession of Jehovah in man's affairs."[26] In the end, perhaps Lee was not the saint painted by the Southern Historical Society but he was a superbly skilled military commander whose ideals formulated an outstanding and remarkable life. As the historian T. Harry Williams recalled, "[Lee] was not all that his admirers have said of him, but he was a large part of it."[27]

Connelly and Bellows offered a career summary of Lee that outlines many of the General's personality traits. He experienced an early, dutiful attendance to a sickly mother. He amassed a model record at the Military Academy. He demonstrated a pattern of abstemious habits formed early in life. He showed signifi-

This embellished, hand-colored lithograph by Arnold Vic closely followed photographs by Julian Vannerson. Published by A. S. Seer in New York in 1882, the pose resulted from a combination of two models produced by Julian Vannerson. The engraver added a hat.

Anne S. K. Brown Military Collection, Brown University

cant devotion to a sickly wife. He displayed skill and courage from Vera Cruz to Mexico City, and beamed with admiration of Winfield Scott. He stayed with the army despite its slow promotion, low pay, and dusty frontier duty. Much of his existence was tedious and lonely, as evidenced by numerous letters to his family. He uttered daily prayers and performed Christian rituals. Everything he did was marked by a sense of duty, humility, self-denial, and self-control. "Those who loved Lee most knew him least," they wrote. "That's the irony of Lee's adoption as the central figure of the Confederacy."[28]

The deification of Lee continued throughout the 1880s and moved toward a new phase by about 1890, marked by the unveiling and dedication of the Lee Statue on Monument Avenue in

The Lee family crypt in Lee Chapel contains the graves of Lee, Mary Custis Lee, their children, Lee's mother, and several descendants. Additionally, the remains of Lee's father, Light-Horse Harry, were moved to the crypt in 1913.
David J. Eicher

Above: Jefferson Davis and the Confederate Generals by F. Gutekunst, after Faas, Jr., was published by Dr. J. Olney Banning and Son, Philadelphia, in 1890. Lee is shown centrally. Others are (left to right): A. P. Hill, Hood, Davis, Stuart, Jackson, Longstreet, J. E. Johnston, Beauregard, and Early. The portrait depicts Robert Toombs.
Author's Collection

Left: Engraved by Walton Taber after Benjamin West Clinedinst, this fanciful depiction of the McLean House surrender was produced about 1887 for *Battles and Leaders of the Civil War*. Aside from Lee and Grant, other officers appear (left to right): Porter, Marshall, Merritt, Sheridan, Parker, Ingalls, Babcock, and Custer.
Author's Collection

Right: The Lee Monument on Monument Avenue in Richmond, the most celebrated of all Lee statuary. Dedicated on 29 May 1890 to crowds of survivors from Lee's army, it is the work of Marius Jean Antonin Mercié. An eighty-three-year-old Joseph E. Johnston pulled the rope that unveiled the monument.

David J. Eicher

Far right: Charles Shober's *Gen. Robert E. Lee* presents an image of Lee on Traveller in the thick of battle. The lithograph was published by Shober and Carqueville, Chicago, in 1891.

Library of Congress

Lee at Fredericksburg by Henry A. Ogden depicts a calm, grandfatherly Lee watching over the Fredericksburg field. The work was produced in the 1890s.

Author's Collection

Richmond. The equestrian figure of Lee on Traveller was the joint effort of the Lee Monument Association and the Ladies' Lee Monument Association. On 28 June 1887 they engaged Marius Jean Antonin Mercié, a French sculptor, to create the statue, which would be the outstanding example of a series on Monument Avenue also honoring Jefferson Davis, Stonewall Jackson, Matthew Fontaine Maury, and James E. B. Stuart. On 29 May a huge crowd assembled at the Lee Monument and listened to a dedicatory address by Charles Marshall. Active at the ceremonies was an impressive grouping of former Confederate officers including Fitzhugh Lee, Porter Alexander, Harry Heth, Wade Hampton, Joe Johnston, Jubal Early, and James Longstreet.

The event was a milestone. The significant wartime personalities were passing on with increased frequency, and a new generation of Southerners was coming of age. Four Southern states

declared Lee's birthday, 19 January, a legal holiday.
He began to be seen as a national hero, as respect
for the commander grew in Northern states. And
the General's postwar, educational activities, perhaps the noblest endeavors of his life, allowed
people to accept him as a more common figure
than the aristocratic activities of his antebellum
life did.[29] By 1890, when the Northern people
reached out to the Lee legend, a writer stated in
Harper's Weekly that the General "personified
what was best in a bad cause. His individual
virtues gave the southern people . . . something
substantial and unquestionably creditable to rally
around."[30] Little more than a decade later, in
1904, Rob Lee's *Recollections and Letters of General
Robert E. Lee* was published and became critically
important in fashioning the new understanding of
the traits of his father.[31]

The new generation of Lees solidified their
activities about this time and looked forward into
the new century. Mary Custis Lee had died three
years after her husband, leaving Custis as the family leader. Never marrying, he lived until 1913 after many good
years as president at Washington and Lee and a retirement at
Ravensworth. Rooney recovered from his Civil War wounds and

*General Lee Leading the Troops at
Chancellorsville* by Warren B. Davis was
published in *Frank Leslie's Popular
Magazine* in June 1896. Again Lee
appears set against the blazing
Chancellor Tavern.
Author's Collection

Lee and His Generals, a peculiar lithograph, was executed by Americus
Patterson in Gainesville, Texas, in 1904,
and features rebel generals in blue uniforms. Lee stands just left of center.
Library of Congress

A widely seen engraving of Lee at the turn of the century was this uncredited work published in *The Confederate Soldier in the Civil War* in 1895. It is based on one of the Julian Vannerson photos of 1864.

Author's Collection

The Lees of Virginia, Generals C.S.A. 1861–1865, a hand-colored etching by Charles B. Hall, was published in New York in 1898. A view of Lee based on the 1864 Julian Vannerson profile photograph dominates the center. Clockwise from upper left are Lee's nephew Fitzhugh Lee; Edwin Gray Lee, Lee's first cousin once removed; Lee's eldest son, Custis; and Lee's second son Rooney.

Lincoln Museum, Fort Wayne, Ind.

Our Heroes and Our Flags, a lithograph with a chromolithographed central portrait group, was published by the Southern Lithographic Company in New York in 1896. Stonewall Jackson, G. T. Beauregard, and Lee dominate the center. Small portraits depict, clockwise from top center, Davis, Stephens, Stonewall Jackson, Price, Polk, Holmes, Stuart, J. E. Johnston, Kirby Smith, J. H. Morgan, A. S. Johnston, Hampton, Gordon, Longstreet, Hood, Bragg, and Beauregard.

Lincoln Museum, Fort Wayne, Ind.

Robert Edward Lee, 1807–1870, an etching produced by the John A. Lowell Bank Note Co., Boston, 1906, depicts Lee accompanied by the family coat of arms. Created for the Confederate Memorial Literary Society, the pose was adapted from the Brady post-Appomattox session in Richmond.

Author's Collection

The most elegant monument incorporating Lee on a Civil War battlefield is that on Seminary Ridge at Gettysburg. The sculptor, F. William Sievers, incorporated a bronze equestrian statue of Lee atop a granite monument and seven bronze figures at the base. Dedicated in 1917, the Virginia Monument marks the position from which some troops engaged in Pickett's charge embarked.

David J. Eicher

Near the spot where Lee accepted command of the Virginia militia on 23 April 1861, in Virginia's Capitol, stands Rudulph Evans's heroic statue of the General, which errs by depicting Lee on that day with a beard. Positioned in 1931, the statue graces the old House Chamber.

David J. Eicher

Edward V. Valentine's masterful statue of Lee that graces the National Statuary Hall in the U.S. Capitol. Placed in 1934, the monument adorns the Old House Chamber, where many debates that led to Civil War occurred.

Library of Congress

The final resting place of Traveller, Lee's beloved war horse, is merely a few feet away from Lee Chapel, where the Lee family members themselves rest. Tourists regularly adorn the grave with coins and, occasionally, apples.

David J. Eicher

On 29 May 1890 the magnificent Lee Statue, an equestrian monument on Richmond's luxurious Monument Avenue, was unveiled. The sculptor was Jean Antoine Mercié. Thousands of Confederate veterans were present; the dedicatory oration was delivered by Charles Marshall. Among those present were Fitzhugh Lee, Edward Porter Alexander, Jubal A. Early, John B. Gordon, Henry Heth, Joseph E. Johnston, and James Longstreet. As the remaining Confederate leaders were now aging, the event activated a new era in celebrating the South and in remembering its greatest hero.

The Valentine Museum, Richmond

This wood engraving by G. Kruell, executed in 1898, stood as a favorite depiction of Lee for years after the turn of the century.

Author's Collection

capture and served as president of the Virginia Agricultural Society after the war. In 1887 he was elected to Congress, serving until his death at Ravensworth in 1891. His remains were reinterred in the chapel at Washington and Lee, now called Lee Chapel, in 1922. Rob died in 1914. None of the four Lee daughters married, Annie dying in 1862 and Agnes in 1873. Mildred lived until 1905, and Mary Custis Lee until 1918.

By the era of World War I, the curtain had fallen on the Civil War Lees. Interest was shifting away from those heady days as the spotlight on the "war to end all wars" cast a new interpretation of American society in a global sense. Some years later Douglas Southall Freeman, the distinguished Virginia historian, would expend a mammoth effort on his four-volume *R. E. Lee*, a work that won a Pulitzer Prize and reawakened the world to the Lee legend if it glamorized and exaggerated the story occasionally along the way. In recent times scholars and talented writers have explored the Lee story again, finding a more complex and interesting path than the one put forth earlier this century. It shows the General to have been a great commander but imperfect, to indeed have made questionable and sometimes poor decisions, to have been simply a man with lofty aspirations and high ideals cast into an extraordinary situation. In short, it shows that Robert Edward Lee was quintessentially American, and someone whose humanity allows us to understand and admire the man even today.

APPENDIX I

∞

Robert E. Lee's Military Record

Adapted from *Civil War High Commands*, a work in progress by John H. Eicher and David J. Eicher.

Robert Edward Lee

Born at "Stratford," Westmoreland County, Va., 19 Jan. 1807. *(Great-grandson-in-law of George Washington, son of Henry "Light-Horse Harry" Lee, cousin of Richard L. Page, second cousin of Edwin G. Lee, third cousin of Samuel P. Lee, uncle of Fitzhugh Lee, father of George W. C. Lee and of William H. F. Lee.)* Cadet 1 July 1825; USMA (2/46) 1 July 1829; Bvt. 2d Lt. U.S.A. 1 July 1829; 2d Lt. U.S.A. Eng. 1 July 1829; 1st Lt. U.S.A. 21 Sept. 1836; Capt. U.S.A. 7 July 1838; staff of John E. Wool; Bvt. Maj. U.S.A. for Cerro Gordo, Mex. 18 Apr. 1847; staff of Winfield Scott; Bvt. Lt. Col. U.S.A. for Contreras and Churubusco, Mex. 20 Aug. 1847; wounded at Chapultepec, Mex. 13 Sept. 1847; Bvt. Col. U.S.A. for Chapultepec, Mex. 13 Sept. 1847; supt. USMA 1 Sept. 1852–31 Mar. 1855; Lt. Col. U.S.A. 2 Cav. 3 Mar. 1855.

Col. U.S.A. 1 Cav. 16 Mar. 1861; res. 25 Apr. 1861; Maj. Gen. and C. in C. Va. Provisional Army 22 Apr. 1861–8 June 1861; Brig. Gen. A.C.S.A. 14 May 1861; Gen. A.C.S.A. 14 June 1861; conducted operations of the Army of the Kanawha and forces in western Va. 21 Sept. 1861; Dept. of S.C., Ga., and E. Fla. 5 Nov. 1861–4 Mar. 1862; military advisor to the pres. C.S.A. 13 Mar. 1862–31 May 1862; Dept. and Army of Northern Virginia 1 June 1862–9 Apr. 1865. Robert E. Lee and his command were tendered the Thanks of Congress on 8 Jan. 1864 "for the great and signal victory they have won over the vast hosts of the enemy and for the inestimable services they have rendered in defense of the liberty and independence of our country." General-in-Chief C.S.A. 31 Jan. 1865; paroled Appomattox Court House, Va. 9 Apr. 1865; pres. Washington College, Va. 1865–1870. An oath of amnesty was sworn on 2 Oct. 1865 but not acted on; an amnesty bill for Robert E. Lee was signed by Pres. Gerald Ford in 1976.

Died at Lexington, Va. 12 Oct. 1870; interred at Lee Chapel, Washington and Lee University, Lexington.

A Selected Lee Surname Genealogy

Compiled by John H. Eicher; x means no issue and = denotes a marriage. Indented letters are the children of the preceding line. Patriarchy and primogeniture predominate. Some dates are in the old calendar system, with the New Year on 25 March, while those after 1752 are based on the new calendar (New Year, 1 January). Some dates are uncertain due to "educated guesses." Parentheses around identification letters (generations) and numbers (unique designations within a generation) are repeated identifications. The numbers are assigned arbitrarily for each generation. Thus, Robert Edward Lee (1807–1870) is R96, named under the generation denoted with the letter R.

Bibliography

A. Lee, Edmund Jennings, Jr. *Lee of Virginia, 1642–1892: Biographical and Genealogical Sketches of the Descendants of Colonel Charles Lee.* E. J. Lee, M.D., Philadelphia, 1895.

B. Hardy, Stella Pickett. *Colonial Families of the Southern States of America.* Genealogical Publishing Co., Baltimore, 1868 (revised to 1911).

C. Malone, Dumas, ed. *Dictionary of American Biography.* Charles Scribner's Sons, New York, 1933.

D. Hendrick, Burton J. *The Lees of Virginia.* Little, Brown and Co., Boston, 1935.

E. Virkus, Frederick A. *The Abridged Compendium of American Genealogy.* Seven vols., Institute of American Genealogy, Chicago, 1925–1942 (reprinted 1987).

F. Lee, Casanove Gardner, Jr. *Lee Chronicle.* New York University Press, New York, 1957.

G. Burt, Nathanial. *First Families.* Little, Brown and Co., Boston, 1970.

H. Nagel, Paul C. *The Lees of Virginia.* Oxford University Press, New York, 1990.

I. Genealogical chart, Washington and Lee University, Lexington, Virginia, 1996 edition.

J. Lee, Robert Edward IV, personal communication.

THE SHROPSHIRE ANTECEDENCE

Considered by most authorities the proper Lee family lineage, including the Lees who worked on genealogy during the 19th century and the authoritative books written by family members Edmund Jennings Lee, Jr. and Casanove Gardner Lee, Jr.

A1 Reyner de Lega (*ca.* 1200) of Shropshire, England
  [Rayner de la Le, Lea, Leigh, Lee; the name meaning on the lee or protected side of a mountain ridge, or, alternatively, a clearing or cultivated field, or meadowland]
=A2 ?
          , son:
  B1 Thomas de la Lee, Sr. (*ca.* 1221–1258)
  = B2 Petronella Corbet (?–?)
          , son:
    C1 Thomas de la Lee, Jr. (?–?)
    = C2 Petronella Stanton (?–?)
          , son:
      D1 John de la Lee (?–?)
      = D2 Matilda Erdington et Roden (*ca.* 1300)
          , son:
        E1 John Lee I (?–?)
        = E2 ?
          , son:
          F1 Roger Lee (*ca.* 1350) of Roden
          = F2 Margaret Astley (?–?) of Coton
          , son:
            G1 John Lee II (?–?) of Coton Hall
            = G2 Joyce Packington (?–?)
          , son:
              H1 John Lee III (?–?)
              = H2 Elizabeth Corbin (?–?)
          , son:

I1 Thomas Lee (?–?)
= I2 Johannah Morton (?–?)   , son:
  J1 Humphrey Lee (?–1589)
  = J2 Catherine Blount (?–?)   , son:
    K1 John Lee IV (1528–1605)
    = K2 Joyce Romney (?–?)   , son:
      L1 Richard Lee (1563–?) of Nordley Regis
      = L2 Elizabeth Bendy
      [parents of M1 Richard Lee I, "The Emigrant"]

THE WORCESTER ANTECEDENCE

This is an alternative ancestry proposed by Paul C. Nagel — see reference H in the bibliography section above.

L13 John Lee, Sr. (?–1630) of Worcester, England
= L14 Jane Hancock (?–1639)   , sons:
  M27 John Lee, Jr. (1616–?)
  M28 Thomas Lee (?–?)
  [another brother was M1 Richard Lee I, "The Emigrant"]

STRATFORD LINE

M1 Richard Lee I (1618–1664) "The Emigrant" of Paradise
= M2 Anne Constable (?–1663) of Dividing Creek
  N2 John Lee v (1645–1673) of Machodoc
  N2 Richard Lee II (1647–1714) "The Scholar" of Paradise and Mt. Pleasant
  = N3 Laetitia Corbin (1657–1706) "Lettice"
    O1 John Lee VI (1677–1678)x
    O2 Richard Lee III (1678–1718) of Machodoc
    = O3 Martha Silk (Moore) (?–1734)
      P1 George Lee (1714–1761)
      1 = P2 Judith Wormeley (1714–1751)
        Q1 Richard Lee IV (1739–?)x
        Q2 Elizabeth Lee (1750–1828)x
      2 = P3 Anne Fairfax (Washington) (1728–1760) of Belvoir *[half sister-in-law of George Washington]*
        Q3 George Fairfax Lee (1754–1809)
        = Q4 — (Travers) (?–?)
        Q5 Lancelot Lee (1756–1812)
        1 = Q6 Mary Bathorst Jones (?–?)
          R1 Lancelot Bathorst Lee (?–?)x
          R2 Sallie Fairfax Lee (?–?)
          = R3 Robert Sangster (?–?)
          R4 Elizabeth Lee (?–?)
          = R5 James Chipley (?–?)
          R6 Nancy Lee (?–?)
          = R7 Richard Cockrell (?–?)
          R8 Thomas Lee (1796–1841)
          = R9 Harriet Hutchinson (?–?) of Pleasant Valley
            S1 Mary Elizabeth Jones Lee (1819–1844)
            = S2 George Washington Millan (1820–1867)
        2 = Q7 — Cockrell (?–?)
          R10 Martha Lee (?–?)
        Q8 William Lee (1758–1838)x
        Q9 Louisa Lee (?–?)x
        = Q10 John Tasker Carter (?–?)x
      P4 Laetitia Lee (1715–1768) "Lettice"
      = P5 John Corbin (1715–?)
      P6 Martha Lee (1716–?)
      1 = P7 George Turberville (?–?) of Hickory Hill
      2 = P8 William Fitzhugh (1721–1798)
    O4 Philip Lee, Sr. (1681–1746) of Blenheim
    1 = O5 Sarah Brooke (?–1724)
      P9 Richard Lee (1708–1789) of Blenheim
      = P10 Grace Ashton (?–1749) *[See also as wife of O4]*
        Q11 Philip Richard Francis Lee (?–1834)x
        Q12 Philip Thomas Lee (?–1778)
        = Q13 — Russell (?–?)
          R11 Russell Lee (1776–1793)x
          R12 Sarah Russell Lee (?–?)
          = R13 Benjamin Contee (1755–1816)
          R14 Margaret Russell Lee (?–?)

```
                        = R15 James Clerk (1758–1819) "Clerklee"
                        R16 Elinor Lee (?–?)
                        = R17 William Dawson (?–?)
                        R18 Ann Lee (?–?)
                        = R19 William Gamble (?–?)
                Q14 Sarah Laetitia Lee (?–?) "Lettice" [See under Q31]
                Q15 Elinor Ann Lee (?–1806)x
                Q16 Alice Lee (?–1789)
                = Q17 John Weems (?–?)
        P11 Francis Lee (?–1749)
        = P12 Elizabeth Hollyday (?–?)
                Q18 Francis Leonard Lee (?–?)
                Q19 Lancelot Richard Thomas Lee (?–?)
                Q20 Amelia Lee (?–?)
        P13 Philip Lee, Jr. (?–1739)
        = P14 Brigit — (?–?)
                Q21 Philip Lee III (?–?)
                Q22 Sarah Lee (?–?)
                Q23 Elizabeth Lee (?–?)
                Q24 Lettice Lee (?–?)
        P15 Thomas Lee I (?–1749)
        = P16 Christia Sim (?–?)
                Q25 Thomas Sim Lee I (1745–1819) of Needwood
                = Q26 Mary Digges (?–?)
                        R20 Ignatius Lee (1772–?)x
                        R21 Thomas Lee II (1774–1826)
                        = R22 Eleanor Cromwell (?–?)
                                S3 Richard Henry Lee (1798–?)x
                                S4 Mary Digges Lee (1800–?)
                                = S5 Charles Carroll (?–?)
                                S6 Georgiana Washington Lee (1802–?)x
                                S7 Thomas Lee III (?–?)
                                = S8 Harriet Carver (?–?)
                                        T1 Charles Lee, Sr. (?–?)
                                        = T2 Rebecca Gran (?–?)
                                                U1 Charles Lee, Jr. (?–?)
                                                = U2 ? (?–?)
                                                        V1 Richard Lee (?–?)
                                        T3 Mary Lee (?–?)
                                        T4 Rebecca Lee (?–?)
                                        T5 Richard Lee (?–?)
                                        T6 Rosa Lee (?–?)
                                        = T7 — Breese (?–?) U.S.N.
                                S9 Eleanor Cromwell Lee (1805–?)
                                = S10 ? (?–?)
                                S11 John Carroll Lee (1807–?)x
                                S12 Henry Pough Lee (1809–?)x
                                S13 William Lee (1811–?)x
                                S14 Sophia Lee (1813–?)x
                                S15 Charles Lancelot Lee (1815–?)x
                                S16 Charles Arthur Lee (1817–?)x
                        R23 William Lee (1775–1845)
                        = R24 Mary Hollyday (?–1818)
                                S17 Mary Digges Lee (1810–?)x
                                = S18 Samuel I. Gouverneur (?–?)x
                                S19 Sarah Brooke Lee (1811–?)x
                                S20 Eliza Horsey Lee (1813–?)x
                                S21 Eleanor Lee (1814–1873)x
                                S22 Anna Gaston Lee (1816–?)x
                                S23 Thomas Sim Lee II (?–?)
                                = S24 Josephine O'Donnell (?–?)
                                        T8 Charles O'Donnell Lee, Sr. (1841–?)
                                        =T9 Matilda Dale Jenkins (?–?)
                                                U3 Joseph Wilcox Jenkins Lee (1870–?)
                                                U4 Thomas Sim Lee III (?–?)
                                                U5 Charles Stewart Lee (?–?)
                                                U6 Matilda Lee (1875–1890)x
                                                U7 Samuel Gouverneur Lee (1877–1891)x
                                                U8 Mary Digges Lee (?–?)
                                                U9 Louisa Carroll Lee (?–?)
                                                U10 Charles O'Donnell Lee, Jr. (?–?)
                                                = U11 Anne McCauley (?–?)
                                                U12 Gertrude Lee (?–?)
```

U13 Adrian Iselin Lee (?–?)
T10 Mary Digges Lee (1842–?)
= T11 Robert Goodlow Harper Carroll (?–?)
T12 William Lee, Sr. (1844–?)
= T13 Mary Frances Matthias (?–?)
    U14 Mary Lee (?–?)
    U15 Josephine O'Donnell Lee (1869–?)x
    U16 Ellen Lynch Lee (?–?)
    U17 William Lee, Jr. (?–?)
    U18 Mildred Lee (?–?)
T14 Columbus O'Donnell Lee, Sr. (?–?)
= T15 Hannah Anne Tyson (?–?)
    U19 James Tyson Lee (1879–1881)x
    U20 Josephine Lee (?–?)
    U21 Hannah Lee (?–?)
    U22 Columbus O'Donnell Lee, Jr. (?–?)
    U23 Philip Francis Lee (?–?)
    U24 Jesse Tyson Lee (?–?)
    U25 Mordecai Lewis Dawson Lee (?–?)
    U26 Frederick Collins Lee (?–?)
    U27 Edward Jackson Lee (?–?)
R25 Mary Christian Lee (1777–1813)
= R26 Tench Ringgold (?–?) *[See also under R42]*
R27 Archibald Lee (1778–1781)x
R28 Archibald Lee (1781–1839)x
R29 Eliza Lee (1783–1862)
= R30 Outerbridge Horsey (?–?)
R31 John Lee (1788–1871)
= R32 Harriet Carroll (?–?)
    S25 Mary Digges Lee (1834–?)
    = S26 Jonathan Letterman (?–1872) U.S.A.
    S27 Harriet Chew Lee (?–?)x
    S28 Charles Carroll Lee, Sr. (1839–1893)
    = S29 Helen Parrish (?–?)
        T16 Sarah Redwood Lee (?–?)
        T17 Richard Henry Lee (1867–1868)x
        T18 Thomas Sim Lee (?–?)
        T19 James Parrish Lee (?–?)
        T20 Charles Carroll Lee, Jr. (1872–1875)x
        T21 Mary Helen Lee (1875–1876)x
        T22 Helen Lee (?–?)
        T23 Mary Digges Lee (?–?)
    S30 Thomas Sim Lee (1842–?)
Q27 Sarah Brooke Lee (?–?)
1 = Q28 Archibald Buchanan (?–?)
2 = Q29 — Turnbull (?–?)
P17 Arthur Lee, Sr. (?–1760)
= P18 Charity Hanson (Howard) (?–?)
    Q30 Arthur Lee, Jr. (?–?)
P19 Sarah Lee (?–?)
= P20 William Potts (?–?)
P21 Anne Lee (?–?)
= P22 James Russell (?–?)
P23 Eleanor Lee (?–?)
= P24 Philip Richard Fendall, Sr. (?–?)
    Q31 Philip Richard Fendall, Jr. (1734–?)
    1 = (Q14) Sarah Laetitia Lee (?–?) "Lettice" *[Daughter of P9 and P10]*
    2 = (P25) Elizabeth Steptoe (Lee) (?–1789) *[Widow of P46]*
    3 = (Q32) Mary Bland Lee (1752–1803) *[Daughter of P68 and P69]*
2 = O6 Mary Elizabeth Sewell (?–?)
P26 Hanna Lee (?–?)
1 = P27 Daniel Bowie (?–?)
2 = P28 Joseph Sprigg (?–?)
P29 Laetitia Lee (?–?) "Lettice"
1 = P30 James Wardropp (?–?)
2 = P31 Adam Thompson (?–?)
3 = P32 Joseph Sims (?–?)
P33 John Lee (?–?)
1 = P34 Mary — (?–?)
    Q33 Edward Lee (?–1821)
    = Q34 Susan Shaw (?–1828)
        R33 Hugh Lee (?–1844)
        = R34 Patsy Holuman/Holliman (?–?)

S31 Addison Green Lee (1831–1887)
= S32 Mary Ann Hinton (1831–1911)
    T24 Edward Hugh Lee (1851–1930)
    = T25 Anne Selby Perkins (?–?)
    T26 Cleophus Ransom Lee (1854–1904)
    = T27 Nannie Tomlinson (?–?)
    T28 Reginal Addison Lee (1858–1917)
    T29 Elizabeth Hinton Lee (1860–?)
    T30 James Madison Lee (1862–1866)x
    T31 Cecil Green Lee (1868–?)
    = T32 Catherine Smith (?–?)
2 = P35 Susannah Smith (?–?)
    Q35 Hancock Lee (?–1792)x
    = Q36 Anne Smith (?–?)x
    Q37 John Pitt Lee (?–?)x
    Q38 Baldwin Matthews Lee (?–1822)x
    Q39 George W. Lee (?–?)x
    Q40 Philip Lee (?–?) of Nomini
    = Q41 Mary Jacqueline Smith (1769–1856)
        R35 Mary Smith Lee (1788–1866)
        = R36 James C. Anthony (?–?)
        R37 Susanna Hancock Lee (?–?)
        R38 Philicia Sally Lee (?–?)
    Q42 Mary Smith (?–?)
    = Q43 Paul Micon (?–?)
    Q44 Lettice Lee (?–?)
    = Q45 John Whiting (?–?)
    Q46 Elizabeth Lee (?–?)
P36 Corbin Lee (?–?)
P37 Elizabeth Lee (1730–1752)x
P38 Alice Lee (?–?)
1 = P39 Thomas Clark (?–?)
2 = P40 Meriwether Smith (?–?)
P41 Margaret Lee (?–?)
P42 Hancock Lee (?–1759)x
P43 George Lee (?–?)
= P44 ? (?–?)
3 = (P10) Grace Ashton (?–1749) *[Probably not a wife according to Casanove Lee, see reference F above; see also under P9]*
O7 Anne Lee (1683–1732)
1 = O8 William Fitzhugh (?–1716)
2 = O9 Daniel McCarty (1679–1724)
O10 Francis Lee (1685–1752)x
O11 Thomas Lee (1690–1750) of Machodoc and The Cliffs; *rebuilt Mt. Pleasant as Stratford*
= O12 Hannah Harrison Ludwell (1701–1749) of Greenspring
P45 Richard Lee (1724–1750)x
P46 Philip Ludwell Lee, Sr. (1726–1775) of Stratford
= P25 Elizabeth Steptoe (?–1789) of Homony Hall *[See under Q31]*
    Q47 Matilda Lee (1763–1790) of Stratford *[Wife of Q94]*
    Q48 Flora Lee (1765–1795) *[Wife of Q61]*
    Q49 Philip Ludwell Lee, Jr. (1775–1775)x *[Posthumous son]*
P47 Hannah Lee (1728–1782)
1 = P48 Gawin Corbin II (1725–1760) of Peckatone
2 = P49 Richard Lingan Hall (?–1774)
P50 John Lee (1729–1729)x
P51 Lucy Lee (1729–1730)x
P52 Thomas Ludwell Lee, Sr. (1730–1778) of Bellview
= P53 Mary Aylett (?–?)
    Q50 Thomas Ludwell Lee, Jr. (?–?)
    = Q51 Fanny Carter (?–?)
        R39 Thomas Ludwell Lee III (?–?)
        R40 Elizabeth Lee (?–?)
        = R41 St. Leger Landon Carter (?–?)
        R42 Mary Aylett Lee (?–?)
        = (R26) Tench Ringgold (?–?) *[See also under R25]*
        R43 Winifred Beale Lee (?–?)
        = R44 William Brent (?–?) *[Son of Q57 and Q58]*
        R45 Fanny Carter Lee (?–?)
        R46 Ann Lucinda Lee (?–?)
        = R47 John M. McCarty (?–?)
        R48 Catherine Lee (?–?)x
        R49 Sydney Lee (?–?)x *[a daughter]*
    Q52 William Aylett Lee (?–?)

Q53 George Lee, Sr. (?–?)
= Q54 Evelyn Byrd (Beverly) (?–?)
    R50 Maria Carter Lee (?–?)
    R51 George Lee, Jr. (1796–1858)
    = R52 Sarah Moore Henderson (?–1888)
        S33 Orra Lee (?–?)
        = S34 John M. Orr (?–?)
        S35 Maria Lee (?–?)x
        S36 Elizabeth Claggett Lee (?–?)x
        S37 Evelyn Byrd Lee (?–?)
        = S38 Thomas Delany (?–?)
        S39 George Lee III (?–?)
        = S40 Laura Frances Rogers (?–?)
            T33 Hugh Douglas Lee (?–?)
            T34 Eleanor Orr Lee (?–?)
            T35 Asa Rogers Lee (?–?)
            T36 Arthur Lee (?–?)
        S41 Archibald Henderson Lee (?–?)
    Q55 Lucinda Lee (?–?)
    = Q56 John Dalrymple Orr (?–?)
    Q57 Anne Fenton Lee (?–?)
    = Q58 Daniel Carroll Brent (1759–?)
    Q59 Rebecca Lee (?–?)x
P54 Richard Henry Lee (1732–1794) "The Signer" of Chantilly
1 = P55 Anne Aylett (1738–1768) of Homony Hall
    Q60 Thomas Lee (1758–1805)
    1 = Q61 Mildred Washington (?–?)
    2 = Q62 Eliza Ashton Brent (?–?)
        R53 Eleanor Lee (1783–1807) "Nellie"
        = R54 Gerard Alexander (1784–1834)
    Q63 Ludwell Lee (1760–1836) of Belmont
    1 = (Q48) Flora Lee (1765–1795) [Daughter of P46 and P25]
        R55 Philip Ludwell Lee (1788–1789)x
        R56 Eliza Matilda Lee (1790–1875)
        = R57 Richard Henry Love (?–1832)
        R58 Cecilia Lee (1792–?)x
        = R59 James L. McKenna (?–?)x
        R60 Richard Henry Lee II (1794–?)
        1 = R61 Mary Duncan Mahone (?–?)
            S42 Mary Ann Lee (1819–1856)x
            = S43 Isaac Winston (?–?)x [See also under S46]
            S44 Flora Lee (1821–1863)x
            S45 Richard Henry Lee III (?–?)x
            S46 Frances Hayne Lee (1823–1885)x
            = (S43) Isaac Winston (?–?)x [See also under S42]
        2 = R62 Anna Eden Jordan (?–?)
            S47 Samuel A. Lee (1829–?)x
            S48 Richard Henry Lee IV (1831–1891)
            = S49 Mary Wilson (?–?)
                T37 Richard Henry Lee V (1859–?)
                = T38 Catherine M. Sheaffer (?–?)
                    U28 Richard Henry Lee VI (1895–?)
                T39 Agnes Wilson Lee (1868–?)
                = T40 Albert Ladd Colby (?–?)
            S50 Philip Ludwell Lee (1835–1889)x U.S.A.
            S51 John Llewellyn Lee (1838–1870)
            S52 Francis Lightfoot Lee (?–?)
            = S53 Mary Duncan Mahone (?–?)
                T41 Agnes Mary Lee (1866–1867)x
                T42 Anna Eden Lee (1868–?)
                = T43 Robert E. Peterson (?–?)
                T44 Mary Lee (1872–?)
                T45 Sophia Mahon Lee (1875–?)
    2 = Q64 Eliza Armistead (1780–1820)
        R63 Mary Ann Lee (1795–?)
        = R64 Robert Blair Campbell (?–?)
        R65 Ellen McMacken Lee (1802–?)
        1 = R66 Thomas Bedford (?–?)
        2 = R67 Nathaniel Phippen Knapp (?–?)
        R68 Eliza Lee (1805–?)
        R69 Emily Lee (?–1875)x
        R70 Francis Lightfoot Lee (?–?)x
        = R71 — Rogers (?–?)x
        R72 Bowles Alexander Lee (?–?)x

Q65 Mary Lee (1764–1793)x
= Q66 William Augustus Washington (?–?) of Bridges Creek
Q67 Hannah Lee (1766–1801)
= Q68 Corbin Washington (1765–1850)
2 = P56 Anne Gaskins (Pinckard) (?–1796)
Q69 Anne Lee (1770–1804) "Nancy" of Chantilly
= Q70 Charles Lee, Sr. (1758–1815) "The Attorney General" *[Son of P68 and P69]*
Q71 Henrietta Lee (1773–1803) "Harriet"
1 = Q72 Richard Lee Turberville (?–?) of Chantilly
2 = Q73 William Maffitt (?–?)
Q74 Sarah Lee (1775–1837) *[Wife of Q101]*
Q75 Cassius Lee (1779–1789)x
Q76 Francis Lightfoot Lee II (1782–1850) of Sully
1 = Q77 Elizabeth Fitzgerald (?–?)
2 = Q78 Jane Digges Fitzgerald (?–?) *[Q77 and Q78 were sisters]*
R73 Jane Elizabeth Lee (1811–1837)
= R74 Henry T. Harrison (?–?)
R75 Samuel Phillips Lee (1812–1887) U.S.N.
= R76 Elizabeth Blair (1818–1906)
S54 Francis Preston Blair Lee (1857–1944)
= S55 Anne Clymer Brooke (?–?)
T46 Edward Brooke Lee (1892–?)
T47 Preston Blair Lee (1893–?)
= T48 ? (?–?)
U29 Brooke Lee (?–?)
R77 John Fitzgerald Lee, Sr. (1813–1884)
= R78 Eleanor Ann Hill (?–1891)
S56 William Hill Lee (1846–?)
= S57 Julia Turner (?–?)
T49 Eleanor Hill Lee (1870–1874)x
T50 Henry Turner Lee (1872–?)
T51 Julia Hunt Lee (1874–?)
T52 Janet Fitzgerald Lee (1877–?)
T53 William Hill Lee (1879–1889)x
T54 Margaret Loretto Lee (1883–?)
T55 Marianne Lee (1884–?)
S58 Arthur Lee (1847–?)
S59 John Fitzgerald Lee, Jr. (1848–?)
S60 Anne Lee (1851–?)
= S61 Henry Harrison (?–?)
S62 Francis Phillips Lee (1856–?)
R79 Arthur Lee (?–1841)x
R80 Frances Ann Lee (1816–1889)
1 = R81 Goldsborough Robinson (1819–1884)
2 = R82 William Frederick Pittit (?–?)
P57 Francis Lightfoot Lee I (1734–1797) "The Signer" of Menckin
= P58 Rebecca Plater Tayloe (1751–1797) "Becky" of Mt. Airy
P59 Alice Lee (1736–1818)
= P60 William Shippen (?–?) "The Surgeon-General"
P61 William Lee (1739–1795)
= P62 Hannah Philippa Ludwell (1737–1784) of Greenspring
Q79 William Ludlow Lee (1775–1803)x
Q80 (son) (1775–1775)x *[Q79 and Q80 were twins]*
Q81 Portia Lee (1778–1840)
= Q82 William Hodgson (?–1820)
Q83 Brutus Lee (1778–1779)x
Q84 Cornelia Lee (1779–1818)
= Q85 John Hopkins (1760–?)
P63 Arthur Lee (1740–1792) "Monitor," "Junius Americus" of Lansdowne
O13 Henry Lee, Sr. (1691–1747) of Machodoc and Lee's Hall
= O14 Mary Randolph Bland (1704–1764)
P64 John Lee (1724–1767)x of Cabin Point
= P65 Mary Smith Ball (?–1802)x
P66 Richard Lee, Sr. (1726–1795) "Squire"
= P67 Sarah Poythress (?–?)
Q86 Richard Lee, Jr. (?–1795)x
Q87 Mary Lee (1790–1848)
= Q88 Thomas Jones (?–?)
Q89 Lettice Lee (1792–1827)
= Q90 John Augustus Smith (?–?)
Q91 Richardia Lee (1795–1852)
= Q92 Presley Cox (?–?)
P68 Henry Lee, Jr. (1728–1787) of Leesylvania

= P69 Lucy Grymes (1734–1792) of Morattico

    Q32 Mary Bland Lee (1752–1803) *[See also under Q31]*

    1 = Q93 Nelson Ankrom (?–?)

    2 = (Q31) Philip Richard Fendall, Jr. (1734–?) *[Son of P23 and P24]*

    Q94 Henry Lee III (1756–1818) "Light–Horse Harry" of Leesylvania

    1 = (Q47) Matilda Lee (1763–1790) of Stratford *[Daughter of P46 and P25]*

        R83 Lucy Grymes Lee (1786–1860)

        = R84 Bernard Moore Carter (1780–1850)

        R85 Henry Lee IV (1787–1837) "Blackhorse Harry"

        = R86 Ann Robinson McCarty (1797–1840) of Popes Creek

            S63 (Dan) Lee (1818–1820)x

        R87 Nathaniel Greene Lee (1788–?)x

        R88 Philip Ludwell Lee (1789–1796)x

    2 = Q95 Anne Hill Carter (1773–1829) of Shirley

        R89 Algernon Sidney Lee (1795–1796)x

        R90 Charles Carter Lee (1798–1871) of Windsor Forest

        = R91 Lucy Penn Taylor (?–?) of Horn Quarter

            S64 George Taylor Lee (1848–?)

            = S65 Ella Marion Goodrum (Fletcher) (1863–?)

                T56 Charles Carter Lee (?–?)

                T57 Lucy Randolph Lee (?–?)

            S66 Henry Lee V (1849–?)

            = S67 Lilian Elizabeth Anderson (?–?)

            S68 William Carter Lee, Sr. (1852–1882)x

            S69 Robert Randolph Lee (?–?)

            = S70 Alice Wilkinson (?–?)

                T58 William Carter Lee, Jr. (?–?)

                T59 Robert Randolph Lee (?–?)

            S71 Mildred Lee (1857–?)

            = S72 John Taylor Francis (?–?)

            S73 Catherine Randolph Lee (1865–?)

            = S74 John Guerrant (?–?)

            S75 John Penn Lee (1867–?)

         R92 Ann Kinloch Lee (1800–1864)

        = R93 William Louis Marshall (1797–1869) of Buckpond

        R94 Sidney Smith Lee, Sr. (1802–1869) C.S.N. of Richland

        = R95 Anna Maria Mason (1802–1860) "Nannie" of Clermont

            S76 Fitzhugh Lee (1835–1905) C.S.A.

            = S77 Ellen Bernard Fowle (?–?)

                T60 Ellen Lee (?–?) *[Mentioned by Edmund Jennings Lee, Jr., but not other sources; see reference A above]*

                T61 Fitzgerald Lee (?–?) *[Mentioned by Edmund Jennings Lee, Jr., but not other sources; see reference A above]*

                T62 George Lee (?–?) *[Mentioned by Edmund Jennings Lee, Jr., but not other sources; see reference A above]*

                T63 Nannie Lee (?–?) *[Mentioned by Edmund Jennings Lee, Jr., but not other sources; see reference A above]*

                T64 Virginia Lee (?–?) *[Mentioned by Edmund Jennings Lee, Jr., but not other sources; see reference A above]*

                T65 Robert Edward Lee (1870–1922)

                = T66 Mary Wilkinson Middleton (?–?)

                T67 George Mason Lee (?–?)

                = T68 ? (?–?)

                    U30 Fitzhugh Lee II (1905–?) U.S.N.

                    = U31 ? (?–?)

            S78 Sidney Smith Lee, Jr. (1837–1888)x

            S79 John Mason Lee (1839–?) C.S.A.

            = S80 Nora Bankhead (?–?)

                T64 Nannie Mason Lee (?–?)

                T65 Dorothea Bankhead Lee (?–?)

                T66 Bessie Winston Lee (?–?)

                T67 John Mason Lee, Jr. (?–?)

                T68 William Bankhead Lee (?–?)

            S81 Daniel Murray Lee, Sr. (?–?) C.S.A.

            = S82 Nannie F. Ficklin (?–?)

                T69 Daniel Murray Lee, Jr. (?–?)

                T70 Joseph Burwell Ficklin Lee (?–?)

                T71 Edmonia Corbitt Lee (?–?)

                T72 Sidney Smith Lee IV (?–?)

                T73 Mary Custis Lee (?–?)

                T74 Henry Fitzhugh Lee (?–?)

            S83 Henry Carter Lee (1842–1889) C.S.A.

            = S84 Sally Buchanan Floyd (?–?)

S85 Robert Carter Lee (1848–?) C.S.A.
S86 Elizabeth Mason Lee (1853–1853)x
R96 **Robert Edward Lee** (Sr.) (1807–1870) C.S.A.
= R97 Mary Anne Randolph Custis (1807–1873) "Molly" of White House and
Arlington
    S87 George Washington Custis Lee (1832–1913)x C.S.A. of Ravensworth
    S88 Mary Custis Lee (1835–1918)x
    S89 William Henry Fitzhugh Lee, Sr. (1837–1891) C.S.A. "Rooney" of White
    House and Ravensworth
    1 = S90 Charlotte Wickham (?–1863) "Chass"
        T75 Robert Edward Lee (1860–?)x *[Mentioned by Edmund Jennings
        Lee, Jr., but not other sources; see reference A above]*
        T76 (child) Lee (?–?)x *[Mentioned by Edmund Jennings Lee, Jr., but
        not other sources; see reference A above]*
    2 = S91 Mary Tabb Bolling (1846–1924)
        T77 Robert Edward Lee III (1869–1922)
        = T78 Mary Middleton Pinckney (?–1959)
        T79 Mary Tabb Lee (1870–1871)x *[Mentioned by Edmund Jennings
        Lee, Jr., but not other sources; see reference A above]*
        T80 George Bolling Lee (1872–1948)
        = T81 Helen Keeney (1895–1968)
            U32 Mary Walker Lee (1921–)
            = U33 A. Smith Bowman (?–?)
            U34 Robert Edward Lee IV (1924–)
            = U35 Marjorie Tracy (1929–)
                V2 Tracy Lee (1959–)
                = V3 William Townsend Crittenberger (1959–)
                V4 Robert Edward Lee v (1963–)
        T82 Anne Agnes Lee (1874–1874)x
        T83 William Henry Fitzhugh Lee, Jr. (1875–1875)x
    S92 Anne Carter Lee (1839–1874)x
    S93 Eleanor Agnes Lee (1841–1873)x
    S94 Robert Edward Lee, Jr. (1843–1914)
    1 = S95 Charlotte Taylor Haxall (1848–1872)x "Lettice"
    2 = S96 Juliet Carter (1860–1915) of Pampatike
        T84 Anne Carter Lee (1897–?)
        = T85 Hanson Ely, Jr. (1896–1938)
        T86 Mary Custis Lee (1900–?)
        = T87 William Hunter deButts (1899–?)
    S97 Mildred Childe Lee (1846–1905)x
  R98 Catherine Mildred Lee (1811–1856)
  = R99 Edward Vernon Childe (?–?)
(Q71) Charles Lee, Sr. (1758–1815) "The Attorney-General" *[See also under Q70]*
1 = (Q69) Anne Lee (1770–1804) "Nancy" of Chantilly *[Daughter of P54 and P56]*
  R100 Charles Lee, Jr. (?–?)x
  R101 Arthur Lee (?–?)x
  R102 Ann Lucinda Lee (1790–1835)
  = R103 Walter Jones, Jr. (1775–1861)
  R104 (son) Lee (1791–1792)x
  R105 Richard Henry Lee (1793–1793)x
  R106 Charles Henry Lee (1794–?)
  R107 William Arthur Lee (1796–?)
  R108 Alfred Lee (1799–1865)x
2 = Q96 Margaret Christian Scott (Peyton) (1783–1843) of Gordonsdale
  R109 Robert Eden Lee (1810–1843)x
  = R110 Margaret Gordon Scott (1817–1866)x
  R111 Elizabeth Gordon Lee (1813–?)
  = R112 Abraham David Pollock (1807–1890)
  R113 Alexander Lee (1815–?)
Q97 Richard Bland Lee, Sr. (1761–1827) of Sully
= Q98 Elizabeth Collins (1768–1858)
  R114 Mary Ann Lee (1795–1796)x
  R115 Richard Bland Lee, Jr. (?–?)
  = R116 Julia Anna Marion Prosser (1806–1882)
    S98 ? Lee (?–?)
    S99 ? Lee (?–?)
    S100 ? Lee (?–?)
    S101 Mary Elizabeth Lee (1827–?)
    = S102 Robert Fleming (?–1871)
    S103 Julia Eustace Lee (?–?)
    S104 Evelina Prosser Lee (1832–?)
    = S105 Edwin Cecil Morgan (1827–1867)
    S106 Richard Bland Lee III (1835–?)

      = S107 Mary Alice Butt (1838–1890)
          T88 Richard Bland Lee IV (1867–?)
          T89 Francis Morris Lee (1869–?)
          T90 Robert McCosky Lee (1871–?)
          T91 Mary Elizabeth Lee (1873–?)
          T92 Philip Henry Lee (1877–?)
          T93 George Allen Lee (1880–?)
    S108 Anna Cornelia Lee (?–?)
    = S109 Robert Stockton Johnston Peebles (1839–1873) C.S.A.
    S110 Julian Prosser Lee, Sr. (1840–?)
    = S111 Meta Wallace Weaver (?–?)
          T94 Janet Henderson Lee (?–?)
          T95 Julia Anna Marion Lee (?–?)
          T96 Arell Weaver Lee (?–?)
          T97 Richard Bland Lee V (?–?)
          T98 Julian Prosser Lee, Jr. (?–?)
    S112 Myra Gaines Lee (1841–?)
    = S113 Charles Napoleon Civalier (1836–?)
    S114 William Augustus Lee (1846–?) C.S.N.
    S115 Robert Fleming Lee (1849–?) C.S.A.
R117 Ann Matilda Lee (1799–1880)
= R118 Bailey Washington (?–?) U.S.N.
R119 Mary Collins Lee (1801–1805)x
R120 Cornelia Lee (1804–1876)
= R121 James W. F. McRae (?–?)
R122 Zaccheus Collins Lee (1805–1859)
= R123 Martha Ann Jenkins (1819–1864)
    S116 Richard Henry Lee, Sr. (1839–1883)
    = S117 Isabella George Wilson (1848–1892)
          T99 Richard Henry Lee, Jr. (?–?)
          = T100 Mary Warner (?–?)
          T101 Elizabeth Collins Lee (?–?)
          T102 Zaccheus Collins Lee II (?–?)
          T103 Robert Edward Lee (1883–1840)x
    S118 Margaret Elizabeth Lee (1840–?)
    1 = S119 William B. Perine (?–1863)
    2 = S120 Bernard John Cooper (?–1884) R.N.
Q99 Theodorick Lee (1766–1840)
= Q100 Catherine Hite (?–?)
    R124 Caroline Hite Lee (?–?)
    = R125 Samuel Purviance Walker (?–?)
    R126 John Hite Lee, Sr. (1797–1832) U.S.N.
    = R127 Elizabeth Prosser (?–?)
        S121 Theodoric Lee (1826–1867) U.S.N.
        = S122 — Grigg (?–?)
          T104 John Grigg Lee (1857–1891)
        S123 Matilda Lee (?–?)
        = S124 John Royall Holcombe (?–?)
        S125 John Hite Lee, Jr.
    R128 Sarah Juliana Lee (?–?)
    = R129 Joseph Gales, Jr. (?–1860)x
    R130 Catherine Hite Lee (?–?)
    = R131 George May (?–?)
Q101 Edmund Jennings Lee, Sr. (1772–1843)
= (Q75) Sarah Lee (1775–1837) *[Daughter of P54 and P56]*
    R132 Edmund Jennings Lee, Jr. (1797–1877)
    1 = R133 Eliza Shepherd (1799–1833)
        S126 Ellen Lee (1824–?)
        = S127 John Sims Powell (?–?)
        S128 Charles Shepherd Lee (1826–?)
        = S129 Margaret H. Page (?–?)
          T105 Eliza Shepherd Lee (?–?)
          T106 Margaret Page Lee (?–?)
          T107 Charles Randolph Lee (?–?)
          T108 Edmonia Louise Lee (?–?)
          T109 Ellen Byrd Lee (?–?)
          T110 Philips Fitzgerald Lee (?–?)
          T111 Edwin Gray Lee (?–?)
          T112 Mann Randolph Page Lee (?–?)
          T113 Eliza Holmes Lee (?–?)
    2 = R134 Henrietta Bedinger (1810–?)
        S130 Edwin Gray Lee I (1836–1870) C.S.A.
        = S131 Susan Pendleton (?–?)
        S132 Ida Lee (1840–?)

= S133 Armistead Thompson Mason Rust (?–?)
S134 Henrietta Bedinger Lee (1844–?)
= S135 Charles Worthington Goldsborough (?–?)
S136 Edmund Jennings Lee III (1845–?)
1 = S137 Rebecca Lawrence Mason (?–1882)
      T114 Lawrence Rust Lee (?–?)
      T115 Edmund Jennings Lee IV (?–?)
      T116 Armistead Mason Lee (?–?)
2 = S138 Bessie Read Neilson (?–?)
S139 Henry Bedinger Lee, Sr. (1849–1921)
= S140 Lucy Johnston Keith (1857–?)
      T117 Frances Ambler Lee (1878–1879)x "Fannie"
      T118 Henry Bedinger Lee, Jr. (1880–?)
      T119 Charles Marshall Lee, Sr. (1882–?)
      = T120 Mary Willoughby Duke Slaughter (1883–?)
         U36 Martha Eskridge Lee (1906–?)
         = U37 Harrison Trueheart Postere (?–?)
         U38 Mary Willoughby Lee (1908–1918)x
         U39 Lucy Ambler Lee (1910–?)
         = U40 John E. Roberts (?–?)
         U41 Claude Marshall Lee, Jr. (1911–?)
         U42 Charlotte Marshall Lee (1913–?)
         = U43 William Jett Lauck, Jr. (?–?)
         U44 Elizabeth Duke Lee (1919–)
         U45 Mary Cary Lee (1926–)
      T121 Rebecca Rust Lee (1884–?)
      T122 Edwin Gray Lee II (1890–?)
      = T123 Estell Marshall Behrendt (?–?)
      T124 James Keith Marshall Lee (1893–?)
      = T125 Arline J. Bird (?–?)
      T126 Richard Henry Lee (1897–?)
      = T127 Susan Glass (?–?)
      T128 Lucy Marshall Lee (1901–?)
      = T129 William Eskridge Duke (?–?)
R135 Anne Harriotte Lee (1799–1863)
= R136 John Lloyd (1775–1854)
R137 Sara Lee (1801–1879)x
R138 William Henry Fitzhugh Lee, Sr. (1804–1837)
= R139 Mary Catherine Simms Chilton (1806–1884)
   S141 William Henry Fitzhugh Lee, Jr. (?–?)
   = S142 Lillie Parran (?–?)
      T130 Laura Morgan Lee (?–?)
      T131 William Augustus Simpson (?–?)
   S143 Mary Morrison Lee (1830–1891)
   = S144 Robert Allen Castleman (1829–1885)
R140 Hannah Lee (1806–1872)
= R141 Kersey Johns Stewart (?–?)
R142 Cassius Francis Lee, Sr. (1808–1890)
1 = R143 Hannah Philippa Ludwell Hopkins (1811–1849)
   S145 Cornelia Lee (1835–1890)x
   S146 William Ludwell Lee (1838–1858)
   S147 Harriotte Hopkins Lee (1840–?)
   = S148 Thomas Seldon Taliaferro (?–?)
   S149 Sara Lee (1842–?)
   S150 Cassius Francis Lee, Jr. (?–?)
   = S151 Mary Henry (1845–?)
      T132 Lucy Lyons Lee (?–?)
      T133 Elizabeth Lloyd Lee (?–?)
2 = R144 Anna Eliza Casenove Gardner (1819–1885)
   S152 Philippa Lee (1847–1853)x
   S153 Constance Gardner Lee (1848–1877)
   = S154 George William Peterkin (?–?)
   S155 Casanove Gardner Lee, Sr. (?–?)
   = S156 Margarite Irénée duPont (?–?)
      T134 Casanove Gardner Lee, Jr. (1882–1945)
      = T135 ? (?–?)
         U46 Richard Henry Lee (?–?)
      T136 Maurice duPont Lee, Sr. (1885–?)
   S157 Francis duPont Lee (?–?)
   = S158 Ann Henderson Taylor (?–?)
      T137 (son) Lee (?–?)
      T138 (son) Lee (?–?)
      T139 Constance C. Lee (?–?)

S159 Edmund Jennings Lee
= S160 Mary Emma Smith (?–?)
    T140 Constance Gardner Lee (?–?)
    T141 Charles Smith Lee (?–?)
    T142 Mildred Washington Lee (?–?)
    T143 Florence Friesen Lee (?–?)
S161 William Gardner Lee (1855–1855)x
S162 Annie Eliza Lee (1861–?)
= S163 John Thompson Cole (?–?)
R145 Susan Meade Lee (1814–1815)x
R146 Charles Henry Lee (1818–?) C.S.A.
= R147 Elizabeth Dunbar (1822–?)
    S164 Laura Dunbar Lee (1846–1883)
    = S165 George Harrison Burwell (?–?)
R148 Richard Henry Lee, Sr. (1820–1902) C.S.A.
= R149 Evelyn Byrd Page (1823–1889)
    S166 William Byrd Lee
    = S167 Sarah Jane Blackburn Kownslar (1853–?)
        T144 Elizabeth Sinclair Blackburn Lee (1879–?)
        T145 Richard Henry Lee, Jr. (1880–1881)x
        T146 Evelyn Byrd Lee (1881–?)
        T147 Mary Page Lee (1881–?) *[T143 and T144 were twins]*
        T148 Ellen Moore Lee (1884–?)
        T149 William Byrd Lee (1888–?)
        T150 Jane Kownslar Lee (?–?)
        T151 Eliza Atkins Lee (?–?)
    S168 Charles Henry Lee (1866–?)
    = S169 Susan Randolph Cooke (?–?)
    S170 Eliza Atkinson Lee (1878–?)
    = S171 James Ridout Winchester (1852–?)
Q102 Lucy Lee (1774–?)
Q103 Anne Lee (1776–1857)
= Q104 William Byrd Page (?–?)
P70 Laetitia Lee (1730–1788) "Lettice"
= P71 William Ball (?–?)
N4 Francis Lee (1648–1714)
N5 William Lee (1650–1696)
= N6 Anne — (?–?)

DITCHLEY LINE

N7 Hancock Lee, Sr. (1653–1709) of Ditchley
1 = N8 Mary Kendall (1661–1694) of Newport House
    O15 William Lee (1680–?)
    O16 Anne Lee (1682–1759)
    1 = O17 William Armistead (1671–1711)
    2 = O18 William Eustace (?–1740)
    O19 Kendall Lee (?–?)
    O20 Richard Lee (1691–1740) of Ditchley
    = O21 Judith Steptoe (1695–1780)
        P72 Elizabeth Lee (?–?)
        = P73 Peter Conway (?–?)
        P74 Mary Lee (?–1774) *[See also under O28]*
        = P75 Charles Lee III (1722–1749) of Cobbs Hall *[Son of O28 and O29]*
        P76 Kendall Lee (?–1780) of Ditchley
        = P77 Elizabeth Heale (?–?) "Betty"
            Q105 William Lee (?–?)
            = Q106 Jane Payne (?–?)
            Q107 Arthur Lee (?–?)x
            Q108 George Lee, Sr. (?–?)
            = Q109 Frances Ball (?–?)
                R150 Alice Lee (?–?)x
                = R151 Joseph Bull (?–?)x
                R152 Arthur Lee, Sr. (?–1883)
                = R153 Sarah Haggeman (?–?)
                    S172 William Kendall Lee (?–?)
                    = S173 — Henderson (?–?)
                        T152 William Henderson Lee (?–?)
                        T153 Arthur Lee II (?–?)
                    S174 Arthur Lee, Jr. (?–1891)x
                    S175 Mary Lee (?–?)
                    = S176 — Locke (?–?)

        S177 Joseph Haggeman Lee (?–1886)x
        S178 Joseph Ball Lee (?–?)x
        S179 George Kendall Lee, Sr. (?–?)
        = S180 Ellen Bruce (?–?)
            T154 Arthur Lee (1864–1925)
            = T155 Grace Thomas Davis (1870–?)
            T156 William Howson Clark Lee (1866–?)
            = T157 Lilah L. Peck (?–?)
            T158 Ellen Bruce Lee (?–?)
            T159 George Kendall Lee, Jr. (1868–1924)
        S181 James Ball Lee (?–?)x
        S182 Richard Henry Lee (?–?)x
      R154 George Lee, Jr. (?–?)
      = R155 Mary Edwards (?–?)
        S183 (daughter) Lee (?–?)
      R156 Betty Lee (?–?)
      R157 Frances Lee (?–?)
      = R158 — Seward (?–?)
    Q110 Elizabeth Lee (?–?)
    = Q111 Thomas Edwards (1752–1798)
    Q112 Kendall Lee (1763–1811)
    1 = Q113 — Nutt (?–?)
      R159 George Kendall Lee (1789–1859)x
      R160 Thomas Lee (1791–1849)
      = R161 Mary Pearson (?–?)
        S184 Elizabeth Kendall Lee (1820–1854)x
        = S185 William P. Hahn (?–?)x
        S186 George Thomas Lee (1824–1827)x?)
        S187 Mary Virginia Lee (1826–1855)
        = S188 William B. Scott (?–?)
        S189 Judith Lee (1828–?)
        = S190 John Gargan (?–?)
        S191 Richard Henry Lee (1831–1861) C.S.A.
      R162 Richard Henry Lee (1792–1816)x
      R163 Elizabeth Kendall Lee (1794–1863)x
      R164 Martha Kendall Lee (?–?)
      = R165 Joseph Ball (1788–?)
      R166 William Lee (1795–1874)
      1 = R167 Eliza Warmack (?–?)
      2 = R168 Hannah Saunders (?–?)
        S192 William Thomas Lee (1830–1865) C.S.A.
        = S193 Susan Blanton (?–?)
            T160 Elisha Kendall Lee (?–?)
        S194 James Hancock Lee (1844–1865) C.S.A.
    2 = Q114 Sarah Gordon (1764–?)x
    3 = Q115 Judith Barton Payne (1769–1850)
      R169 Hancock Lee (1797–1860)
      1 = R170 Mary Henderson (1802–1844)
        S195 Mary Henderson Lee (1825–1826)x
        S196 Virginia Payne Lee (1826–1839)x
        S197 Frances Elizabeth Lee (1827–1828)x
        S198 James Kendall Lee (1829–1861) C.S.A.
        S199 Ellen Lee (1831–1841)x
        S200 William Hancock Lee (1834–1835)x
        S201 Charlotte Lee (1836–?)
        S202 Margaret Henderson Lee (1838–?)
        S203 Judith Burton Lee (1839–1839)x
        S204 Jane Barclay Lee (1841–1843)x
      2 = R171 Martha Bickerton Drew (1818–1892)
        S205 Juliet Lee (1853–?)
        S206 Mary Rutherford Lee (1855–1880)x
        = S207 Robert Somerville (?–?)x
        S208 (son) Lee (1857–1857)x
        S209 Carter Henry Lee (1859–1859)x
      R172 Virginia Payne Lee (1799–?)
      = R173 Howell Lewis (?–?)
    Q116 Richard Lancelot Lee (?–1790)x
    Q117 Hancock Lee (?–?)
    = Q118 Sinah Ellen Chichester (?–?)
      R174 Richard Kendall Lee (?–?)
      R175 Betty Lee (?–?)
      R176 Sarah McCarty Lee (?–?)
      = R177 James Wren (?–?)

R178 Mary Kendall Lee (?–?)
= R179 Edward Sangster (?–?)
R180 Ann McCarty Lee (?–?)
= R181 John R. Ratcliff (?–?)
R182 Catherine Ann Lee (?–?)
= R183 George W. Wren (?–?)
R184 Sinah Ellen Chichester Lee (?–?)
= R185 — Fitzhugh (?–?)
R186 Dodridge C. Lee (?–?)
R187 Hancock Lee, Jr. (?–?)
R188 William I. Lee (?–?)
R189 Daniel C. Lee (?–?)
Q119 Mary Lee (?–?)
= Q120 Archibald Campbell (?–?)
Q121 Judith Lee (?–?) "Judy"
1 = Q122 — Pierce (?–?)
2 = Q123 —Peachy (?–?)
3 = Q124 John Blackwell (?–?)
Q125 Priscilla Lee (1770–1834)
= Q126 Griffin Edwards (1768–?)
P78 Thomas Lee (1729–?) *[Probably not a son according to Casenove Gardner Lee, Jr.; see reference F above]*
= P79 Mary Bryan (1745–1821)
Q127 John Lee (1763–?)
= Q128 — Stephens (?–?)
R190 Needham Lee (1786–1852)
= R191 Lydia Pryor (?–?)
S210 Lovred Lee (1817–1896)
= S211 Susan Emmeline Lovelace (1823–1877)
T161 Alto Velo Lee, Sr. (1843–1911)
= T162 Ildegerte Lawrence (1845–1909)
U47 Lawrence Haywood Lee (1867–?)
U48 Lillie Vela Lee (1869–?)
= U49 George W. Peach (?–?)
U50 William Lovred Lee (1873–?)
= U51 Nettie Passmore (?–?)
U52 Henry Fitzhugh Lee (?–?)
= U53 Wyllane Pruett (?–?)
U54 Alto Velo Lee, Jr. (1876–?)
= U55 Eloise Frost (?–?)
U56 Tennant Lee (1883–?)
= U57 Norma Lawrence (?–?)
Q129 Needham Lee (1770–1820)
= Q130 Susan Bailey (1774–1830)
R192 William Carroll Lee (1796–1884) C.S.A.
1 = R193 Pollie Mary Bailey (?–1825)
S212 Teresa Lee (1819–1860)
= S213 William Orr (1813–1871)
S214 Tabitha Dorcas Lee (1839–1898)
= S215 Henry F. Lafayette Taylor (1837–1862) C.S.A.
2 = R194 Dorcas Littlefield (?–1863)
R195 Needham Lee, Jr. (1808–1896)
= R196 Nancy Wharton (1809–1869)
S216 Helen Lee (1847–?)
= S217 Bartholomew Boyle (1827–1875)
P80 Laetitia Lee (1731–1811) "Lettice"
= P81 James Ball (1718–1789) of Bewdley
P82 Judith Steptoe Lee (1739–1791)
= P83 David Galloway, Sr. (?–?)
P84 Anne Lee (?–?)
= P85 Edward Kerr (?–?)
P86 Stephen Lee (?–?)
2 = N9 Sarah Elizabeth Allerton (1660–1720)
O22 Isaac Lee (1707–1727)
O23 John Lee (1708–1789)x
O24 Elizabeth Lee (1709–?)
= O25 Zachary Taylor, Sr. (1707–1768)
O26 Hancock Lee, Jr. (1709–1762) of Greenview
= O27 Mary Willis (?–1798)
P87 Willis Lee (?–1776)x
P88 Mary Willis Lee (?–1798)
= P89 Ambrose Madison (?–?) *[Brother of Pres. James Madison]*
P90 John Lee (1743–1802)

1 = P91 Laetitia Atwell (?–1775)
    Q131 Willis Atwell Lee (?–?)
    = Q132 Mary McAfee (?–?)
        R197 Laetitia Atwell Lee (?–?)
        = R198 Alexander Hueston Rennick (?–?)
2 = P92 Elizabeth Bell (?–?) *[Granddaughter of N7]*
    Q133 John Hancock Lee (?–?)x *[See also under P95]*
    = Q134 Anne Lee (?–?)x *[Daughter of P95 and P96]*
    Q135 Lewis Lee (?–?)x
    Q136 Sarah O. Lee (?–1824)
    = Q137 John Jordan Crittenden (1787–1863)
    Q138 Matilda A. Lee (?–?)
    = Q139 Samuel McDowell Wallace (?–?)
    Q140 Elizabeth Lee (?–?)x
    = Q141 — Wilkinson (?–?)x
    Q142 Lucinda Lee (?–?)
    = Q143 R. H. Call (?–?)
    Q144 Anne Lee (?–?)
    = Q145 — Price (?–?)
P93 Hancock Lee III (1748–1819) of Greenview
= P94 Winifred Eustace Beale (?–?)
Q146 Hancock Lee IV (1794–1842)
= Q147 Susan Richards (?–?)
    R199 Anne Lee (1820–1862)
    = R200 John Howison (?–?)
    R201 Frances Lee (1822–?)
    = R202 Robert Willis (?–?)
    R203 Mary Lee (1823–1860)x
    R204 Virginia Lee (1824–?)
    1 = R205 Smith Rixey (?–?)
    2 = R206 A. Richards (?–?)
    R207 Ludwell Lee (1826–?)x
    R208 Susan Lee (1830–?)
    = R209 Horace Dodd (?–?)
    R210 Louisa Lee (1832–?)x
    R211 Thomas Lee (1834–?)
    R212 Henry Hancock Lee, Sr. (1837–?)
    = R213 Olivia Nutt (?–?)
        S218 Henry Hancock Lee, Jr. (1862–?)
        = S219 Maud Paine (?–?)
            T163 Mary Olivia Lee (1893–?)
            T164 Norma Lee (1894–?)
        S220 Annie Lee (1864–?)
        S221 Robert Edward Lee (1866–?)
        = S222 Meta Shumate (?–?)
            T165 Mary Downman Lee (1893–?)
        S223 Mary Lee (1867–?)
        S224 Lucy Lee (1870–?)
        S225 Olivia Lee (1872–?)
        S226 Frances Lee (1874–?)
        S227 Ludwell Lee (1876–?)
        S228 Francis Lee (1879–?)
        S229 Alice Lee (1882–?)
    R214 William Lee (1840–1863)x
Q148 Willis Lee (?–?)
= Q149 Mary Richards (?–?)
    R215 John Hancock Lee (1805–1873)
    1 = R216 Mary Willis (?–?)
    2 = R217 Fannie Willis (?–?)
    3 = R218 Mary Jones (?–?)
        S230 Laetitia Lee (?–?)
        = S231 Robert Madison (?–?)
        S232 Nellie Conway Lee (1826–1875)
        S233 Lewis Herman Lee (1849–1878)
        = S234 Georgia Garland Hansborough (?–?)
            T166 Mary Madison Lee (1877–?)
        S235 Lizzie Madison Lee (?–?)
        = S236 William Albert Bragg (?–?)
        S237 Norma Overton Lee (?–?)
        = S238 John Brockenbrough Woodward (?–?)
    R219 Mary Willis Lee (?–?)
    = R220 Thomas Scott Ashton (1803–1873)
Q150 Elizabeth Lee (?–?)

          = Q151 — Sangster (?–?)
          Q152 Mary Frances Lee (?–1868)
          Q153 Thomas Ludwell Lee (?–1860)
          = Q154 — Bell (?–?)
               R221 Matilda Lee (?–?)
               = R222 Thomas T. Gaskins (?–?)
               R223 Thomas Lee (?–?)
               R224 Jennie Lee (?–?)
               = R225 Charles N. Beale (?–?)
               R226 Mary Lee (?–?)
               = R227 William T. Anderson (?–?)
               R228 Elizabeth Lee (?–?)
               = R229 John N. Carter (?–?)
               R230 Edwin G. Lee (?–?)
               = R231 Ann — (?–?)
               R232 Jane Lee (?–?)x
          Q155 Emeline Lee (?–?)x
          = Q156 — Richards (?–?)
          Q157 Arthur Lee (?–?)
          Q158 Pamela Lee (?–?)
          Q159 Anne Lee (?–?)
      P95 Henry Lee (?–?)
      = P96 Mary Willis (?–?)
          Q160 Willis Lee (?–?)x
          Q161 Hancock Lee (?–?)x
          Q162 John Lee (?–?)x
          Q163 — Lee (?–?)
          = Q164 — Davis (?–?)
          (Q134) Anne Lee (?–?)x *[See also under Q133]*
          = (Q133) John Hancock Lee (?–?)x *[Son of P90 and P92]*
      P97 Richard Lee (?–?)x
      P98 Sarah Alexander Lee (?–?)
      = P99 John Gillison (?–?)
N10 ? (?–?)
N11 ? (?–?) *[N10 and N11 were twins]*
N12 Elizabeth Lee (1653–?) "Betsy"
= N13 Leonard Howson (?–?)
N14 Anne Lee (1655–?)
1 = N15 John Leland (?–?)
2 = N16 Thomas Ewell (1656–?)

COBB LINE

N17 Charles Lee, Sr. (1656–1701) of Cobbs Hall
= N18 Elizabeth Metstand (?–?)
    O28 Charles Lee, Jr. (1684–1740) of Cobbs Hall
    = O29 Elizabeth Pinckard (?–?)
        (P75) Charles Lee III (1722–1747) *[See also under P74]*
        1 = (P74) Mary Lee (?–1774) *[Daughter of O20 and O21]*
            Q165 Ann Lee (1742–?)
            Q166 Charles Lee IV (1744–1785)
            1 = Q167 Sarah Hull (?–?)
            2 = Q168 Susan Hall (?–?)
                R233 Charles Lee V (?–?)x of Cobbs Hall
                = R234 Elizabeth Edwards (?–?)x
                R235 Sarah Lee (?–1813)x
                R236 Edwin Lee, Sr. (?–?)
                = R237 Ann Livingston Cox (?–?)
                    S239 Susan Virginia Lee (1817–1895)
                    = R238 William Spann Wright (1815–?)
                    S240 Edwin Lee, Jr. (?–?)
                R239 Richard Lee (1768–1824) of Cobbs Hall
                = R240 Elizabeth Hurst (?–?)
                    S241 Sarah Lee (?–?)x
                    S242 Charles Lee VI (?–?)x
                    S243 Hurst (?–?)x
                    S244 Jane Lee (?–?)x
                    S245 Martha Lee (1803–1876)
                    = S246 Lewis G. Harvey (?–?)
                    S247 Mary Lee (?–?)x *[See also under R240]*
                    = S248 Edwin Lee (?–?)x *[Son of R240 and R241]*
                    S249 Susan Lee (?–?)

= S250 William Harvey (?–?)
S251 Elizabeth Lee (?–?) "Betsy"
= S252 — Hughlett (?–?)
R241 Kendall Lee (?–1815)
= R242 Mary Nutt (?–?)
S253 Mary Leland Lee (?–?)x
S254 Sarah Elizabeth Lee (?–?)x
= S255 — Garlington (?–?)x
S256 Martha Kendall Lee (?–?)
= S257 Joseph Ball (?–?)
S258 George G. Lee (?–?)
1 = S259 — Carpenter (?–?)
T166 George Lee (?–?)
T167 Leroy Lee (?–?)
2 = S260 — Sprigg (?–?)
T168 Anne Lee (?–?)
T169 Henry Lee (?–?)
S261 John I. Lee (?–?)
= S262 Elizabeth Ball (?–?)
T170 Mary Jane Lee (1835–?)
1 = T171 Joseph W. Brent (?–1861) C.S.A.
2 = T172 Walter Shay (?–?) C.S.A.
T173 Sally Ann Lee (1838–?)
= T174 John D. Kemm (?–?) C.S.A.
T175 Richardette Lee (?–?)
S263 William Henry Lee (?–?)
= S264 Henrietta R. S. Ball (?–?)
T176 David Ball Lee (?–?)
T177 John Edward Lee (?–?)
(S248) Edwin Lee (?–?)x *[See under R238]*
= (S247) Mary Lee (?–?)x *[Daughter of R238 and R239]*
R243 John Lee (?–?)
R244 Elizabeth Lee (?–?)
= R245 Thomas Broun (?–?)
R246 Judith Lee (?–?)
R247 Mary Lee (?–?)
2 = P100 Leanna Lee Jones (?–?) *[Daughter of O30 and O31]*
Q169 Thomas Lee (1745–?)
Q170 (son) Lee (?–?)
P101 Elizabeth Lee (1724–?)
P102 Margaret Lee (1726–?)
P103 Ann Lee (1728–?)
P104 Lucy Lee (1730–?)
P105 Judith Lee (1732–?)
= P106 John Wilkinson (1730–?)
O30 Leanna Lee (?–?)
= O31 William Jones (?–1741)
O32 Elizabeth Lee (?–1714)
= O33 Jonathan Howson (?–?)
O34 Thomas Lee, Sr. (1679–1735)
= O35 ? (?–?)
P107 Leanna Lee (1728–?)
= P108 John Fearn (1717–?)
P109 Thomas Lee, Jr. (?–?)
= P110 Lucy — (?–?)
Q171 Mary Lee (?–?)
Q172 George Lee (?–?)
P111 Charles Lee (?–?)
= P112 Johanna Morgan (?–?)
Q173 Thomas Lee, Sr. (?–?)
= Q174 ? (?–?)
R248 Thomas Lee, Jr. (1795–1851)
= R249 Margaret Ormond (?–?)
S265 James Ormond Lee (?–?)
S266 Elizabeth Lee (?–?)
S267 Ann Lee (?–?)
S268 Elizabeth Ormond Lee (?–?)
S269 Sarah Ann Lee (?–?)
Q175 Richard Lee (?–?)
= Q176 Lucy Druly (?–?)
Q177 Elizabeth Lee (?–?)
= Q178 John Eustace Beale (?–?)
Q179 Sarah Lee (?–?)

Q180 Ann Lee (?–?)
P113 John Lee (?–?)
P114 Elizabeth Lee (1733–1770)
1 = P115 Jean Antoine Dibrell (1728–1800) "Anthony" of New Store
2 = P116 Mathew Rodham (?–?)
P117 William Lee (?–1770)
= P118 Rachel — (?–?)
    Q181 John Lee (?–1804)
    = Q182 Jane — (?–?)
        R250 Ambrose Lee (?–1795)
        = R251 Elizabeth White (?–?)
            S270 Henderson Lee (1793–1862)
            = S271 Susan Lewis Lamkin (?–?)
                T177 Petronella Lee (1838–1924)
                = T178 Edward Henry Turpin (1836–1867)
    Q183 Ambrose Lee (?–1764)
    = Q184 Frances Penn (1735–1812)
        R252 George Lee, Sr. (1750–1825)
        = R253 Elizabeth Sheldon (1754–1813)
            S272 Pamela Lee (1774–1812)
            = S273 John Welsh (1768–1832)
            S274 George Lee, Jr. (1792–1879)
            = S275 Lucy Ann Thompson (?–?)
                T179 George Francis Lee (1829–1896)
                = T180 Susan Jane Miller (1823–1900)
                    U58 Eugene Wallace Lee (1847–1905)
                    = U59 Clara Louise Warren (1850–1890)
                        V5 Hortense Lee (1875–?)
                        V6 Virginia Lee (1877–?)
                        = V7 Louis Edwards Bryant (1868–?)
                        V8 George Francis Lee (1887–?)
                        = V9 Florence Keller (?–?)
        R254 Frank Lee (1764–1791)
        = R255 Frances Penn (1766–1791)
            S276 Sophia Lee (1788–1828)
            = S277 Richard Pollard Harrison (1785–1840)

Robert E. Lee's Famous Relatives

Richard Lee Turberville Beale (1819–1893), C.S.A. brigadier general, was a third cousin-in-law, twice removed.

Francis Preston Blair, Jr. (1821–1875), U.S.A. major general, was a third cousin-in-law.

Francis Preston Blair, Sr. (1791–1876), U.S. politician, was a third cousin-in-law, once removed.

Montgomery Blair (1813–1883), U.S. postmaster general, was a third cousin-in-law.

John Cabell Breckinridge (1821–1875), U.S. vice president , C.S. major general, and C.S. secretary of war, was a grandnephew of Robert Carter Harrison, who was a first cousin-in-law, twice removed, of the great-granduncle of Lee.

Stephen Grover Cleveland (1837–1908), 22d and 24th President of the United States, was a third cousin-in-law, four times removed, of Susannah Delano, who was a first cousin-in-law, three times removed, of James Roosevelt II, who was a fourth cousin-in-law, once removed, of Douglas Robinson, Jr., who was a third cousin-in-law, twice removed, of Mary Conway Mason Fitzhugh, who was a third cousin-in-law.

Samuel Cooper (1798–1876), ranking Gen. C.S.A., adjutant and inspector general, was a brother-in-law.

George Bibb Crittenden (1812–1880), C.S.A. major general, was a fourth cousin.

John Jordan Crittenden (1787–1863), U.S. politician, was a fourth cousin-in-law, once removed.

Thomas Leonidas Crittenden (1819–1893), U.S.A. major general, was a fourth cousin.

Thomas Turpin Crittenden (1825–1905), U.S.A. brigadier general, was a fourth cousin-in-law.

George Davis (1820–1896), C.S. attorney general, was a fourth cousin-in-law, once removed, of Mary Townsend Polk, who was a third cousin-in-law of Mary Conway Mason Fitzhugh, who was a third cousin-in-law, by an adoption.

Jefferson Finis Davis (1808–1889), C.S. President, was a fourth cousin-in-law.

William McKee Dunn (1814–1887), U.S.A. brevet brigadier general, was a seventh cousin-in-law, once removed, by an adoption.

Elizabeth II, Alexandra Mary Windsor (1926–   ), Queen of England, is a fifth cousin-in-law, four times removed, by an adoption.

John Buchanan Floyd (1806–1863), U.S. secretary of war and C.S.A. brigadier general, was a first cousin-in-law, once removed, of John Breckinridge, whose brother-in-law was Robert Carter Harrison, whose first cousin-in-law, once removed, was Thomas Lee, whose great-grandnephew was Lee.

John Brown Gordon (1832–1904), C.S.A. major general, was a fifth cousin-in-law, by an adoption.

Ulysses S. Grant (1822–1885), 18th President of the United States, ranking general officer of the U.S. armies, U.S.A. lieutenant general, was a fourth cousin-in-law of James Roosevelt II, who was a fourth cousin-in-law, once removed, of Douglas

Robinson, Jr., who was a third cousin-in-law, twice removed, of Mary Conway Mason Fitzhugh, who was a third cousin-in-law.

John Breckinridge Grayson (1806–1861), C.S.A. brigadier general, was a grandnephew of Robert Carter Harrison, who was a first cousin-in-law, twice removed, of the great-granduncle of Lee.

Wade Hampton III (1818–1902), C.S.A. lieutenant general, was a first cousin, once removed, of John Breckinridge, whose brother-in-law was Robert Carter Harrison, whose first cousin-in-law, once removed, was Thomas Lee, whose great-grandnephew was Lee.

Benjamin Harrison VI (1833–1901), 23d President of the United States and U.S.A. brevet brigadier general, was the first cousin-in-law, four times removed, of Lee's great-granduncle.

William Henry Harrison (1773–1841), 9th President of the United States, was the first cousin-in-law, twice removed, of Lee's great-granduncle.

Patrick Henry (1736–1799), U.S. politician, was an uncle-in-law of Francis Preston, who was a first cousin-in-law of John Breckinridge, whose brother-in-law was Robert Carter Harrison, whose first cousin-in-law, once removed, was Thomas Lee, whose great-grandnephew was Lee.

Eppa Hunton, Sr. (1822–1908), C.S.A. brigadier general, was a third cousin-in-law, once removed, by an adoption.

Thomas Jonathan Jackson (1824–1863), C.S.A. lieutenant general, was a brother-in-law of Anne Aylett Anderson, who was a fourth cousin-in-law, once removed.

Thomas Jefferson (1743–1826), 3d President of the United States, was a second cousin-in-law, twice removed.

Albert Sidney Johnston (1802–1862), C.S.A. general, was a first cousin-in-law, once removed, of John Breckinridge, whose brother-in-law was Robert Carter Harrison, whose first cousin-in-law, once removed, was Thomas Lee, whose great-grandnephew was Lee.

Joseph Eggleston Johnston (1807–1891), C.S.A. general, was a first cousin, once removed, of Francis Preston, whose first cousin-in-law was John Breckinridge, whose brother-in-law was Robert Carter Harrison, whose first cousin-in-law, once removed, was Thomas Lee, whose great-grandnephew was Lee.

Robert Garlick Hill Kean (1828–1898), head of the C.S. bureau of war, was a fourth cousin-in-law, once removed.

Charles Lee (1758–1815), U.S. attorney general, was an uncle.

Edwin Gray Lee (1836–1870), C.S.A. colonel, was a first cousin, once removed.

Fitzhugh Lee, Sr. (1835–1905), C.S.A. major general, was a nephew.

Francis Lightfoot Lee (1734–1797), U.S. politician, was a first cousin, twice removed.

Richard Henry Lee (1732–1794), U.S. politician, was a first cousin, twice removed.

Samuel Phillips Lee (1812–1887), U.S.N. acting rear admiral, was a third cousin.

John Love (1820–1881), Ind. militia major general, was a third cousin, once removed.

James Madison, Jr. (1751–1836), 4th President of the United States, was a first cousin-in-law, twice removed, by an adoption.

John Marshall (1755–1835), U.S. jurist, was a third cousin-in-law, once removed.

Christopher Gustavus Memminger (1807–1888), C.S. secretary of the treasury, was the grandfather of a grandnephew-in-law.

James Monroe (1758–1831), 5th President of the United States, was a second cousin, once removed, of Arthur Alexander Morgan Payne, who was a third cousin-in-law, by an adoption.

Richard Lucian Page (1807–1901), C.S.A. brigadier general and C.S.N. captain, was a first cousin.

William Henry Fitzhugh Payne (1830–1904), C.S.A. brigadier general, was a third cousin-in-law, once removed, by an adoption.

William Nelson Pendleton (1809–1883), C.S.A. brigadier general, was the father of a first cousin-in-law, once removed.

James Knox Polk (1795–1849), 11th President of the United States, was a third cousin of Mary Townsend Polk, who was a third cousin-in-law of Mary Conway Mason Fitzhugh, who was a third cousin-in-law, by an adoption.

Leonidas Polk (1806–1864), C.S.A. lieutenant general, was a fourth cousin of Mary Townsend Polk, who was a third cousin-in-law of Mary Conway Mason Fitzhugh, who was a third cousin-in-law, by an adoption.

William Preston III (1816–1887), brigadier general, was a first cousin-in-law, once removed, of John Breckinridge, whose brother-in-law was Robert Carter Harrison, whose first cousin-in-law, once removed, was Thomas Lee, whose great-grandnephew was Lee.

George Wythe Randolph (1813–1867), C.S.A. brigadier general and C.S. secretary of war, was a fourth cousin-in-law.

Franklin Delano Roosevelt (1882–1945), 32d President of the United States, was a fifth cousin-in-law of Corinne Roosevelt, who was a third cousin-in-law, twice removed, of Mary Conway Mason Fitzhugh, who was a third cousin-in-law.

Theodore Roosevelt, Jr. (1858–1919), 26th President of the United States, was a brother of Corinne Roosevelt, who was a third cousin-in-law, twice removed, of Mary Conway Mason Fitzhugh, who was a third cousin-in-law.

James Edwin Slaughter (1827–1901), brigadier general, was a third cousin-in-law, once removed, by an adoption.

Edmund Kirby Smith (1824–1883), C.S.A. general, was a fourth cousin-in-law, three times removed.

James Ewell Brown Stuart (1833–1864), C.S.A. major general, was a third cousin-in-law, once removed.

Joseph Pannell Taylor (1796–1864), U.S.A. brigadier general, was a third cousin, once removed.

Richard Taylor II (1826–1879), C.S.A. lieutenant general, was a fourth cousin.

Zachary Taylor, Jr. (1784–1850), 12th President of the United States, was a third cousin, once removed.

Allen Thomas (1830–1907), C.S.A. brigadier general, was the brother-in-law of a fourth cousin.

Daniel Tyler (1799–1882), U.S.A. brigadier general, was a grandfather of Edith Kermit Carow, whose sister-in-law Corinne Roosevelt was a third cousin-in-law, twice removed, of Mary Conway Mason Fitzhugh, who was a third cousin-in-law.

Martin Van Buren (1782–1862), 8th President of the United States, was a third cousin-in-law, twice removed, of Douglas Robinson, Jr., who was a third cousin-in-law, twice removed, of Mary Conway Mason Fitzhugh, who was a third cousin-in-law.

George Washington (1732–1799), 1st President of the United States, was a great grandfather-in-law, by an adoption.

Frank Wheaton (1833–1903), U.S.A. brigadier general, was a nephew-in-law.

John Henry Winder (1800–1865), C.S.A. brigadier general, was a first cousin-in-law of Victor Monroe, who was a third cousin of Arthur Alexander Morgan Payne, who was a third cousin-in-law, by an adoption.

Robert Crooke Wood, Jr. (1832–1900), C.S.A. "acting" brigadier general, was a fourth cousin-in-law, once removed.

Robert Crooke Wood, Sr. (1801–1869), U.S.A. brevet brigadier general, was a fourth cousin-in-law.

APPENDIX 4

Members of
Robert E. Lee's Staff

Many officers served on the staff of General Lee during his Confederate service. The following lists all those known by the present writer and is adapted from data by ex-Confederate general officer Marcus Wright. Appointment dates, grades at appointment, and duration of service are provided if available.

† Alexander, Edward Porter, Lt. Col., chief of ordnance, June–November 1862; resigned 4 December 1862.

Allen, John M., Capt., Asst. Q.M.

Anderson, Clifford, Capt., Asst. Adj. Gen., 2 November 1863.

Baldwin, Briscoe G., Lt. Col., chief of ordnance, 4 December 1862–April 1865.

Bell, R. S., Capt., Asst. Q.M.

Bemiss, Samuel M., Surg.

Bernard, J. T., Capt., ord.

Bolling, Henry, Capt., Asst. Adj. Gen., 2 November 1863.

Breckinridge, F. J., Surg, Med. Insp.

Brooke, John M., Lt., Virginia Provisional Navy, Addnl. ADC, 4 May 1861.

Brown, William, Capt., Asst. Adj. Gen. and Asst. Insp. Gen., July 1863

Cameron, W. E., Capt., Asst. Adj. Gen., 2 November 1863.

Cary, Wilson Miles, Capt., Asst. Q.M., 1864

† Chilton, Robert H., Col., Brig. Gen., Asst. Adj. Gen., 4 June 1862; Asst. Adj. Gen. and Asst. Insp. Gen., 6 March, 31 July, and 31 August 1863, resigned 1 April 1864.

Claggett, Joseph E., Surg.

Cleary, Reuben, Capt. Asst. Adj. Gen., 2 November 1863.

Cole, Robert G., Lt. Col., Sub., 6 March, 31 July, and 31 August 1863; Comm. Sub. June–July 1864.

Cooke, Giles B., Maj., Asst. Insp. Gen., 4 November 1864.

Corley, James L., Lt. Col., Q.M., June 1862; 1 March, 31 July, and 31 August 1863; 1865.

Coughenour, William C., Capt., Asst. Adj. Gen. and Asst. Insp. Gen., 2 November 1863.

Cox, F. C., Capt., Asst. Adj. Gen., 27 November 1863.

Crenshaw, Joseph R., Maj., Acting Comm. Sub., 29 April 1861; Lt. Col., Asst. Adj. Gen., June 1861.

Cunningham, E., Capt., Adj. Gen. and Insp. Gen.

Dabney, Chriswell, Capt., Asst. Adj. Gen., 2 November 1863.

Deas, George, Maj., Asst. Adj. Gen., April 1861; Lt. Col., Chief of Staff, 15 June 1861; Asst. Adj. Gen., 22 June–4 July 1861.

Eyster, George, Capt., Asst. Adj. Gen., 2 November 1863.

Fitzhugh, E. C., Capt., Asst. Adj. Gen., 2 November 1863.

Galize, John, Capt., Q.M.

Garber, A. M., Capt., Asst. Q.M.

† Garnett, Robert Selden, Col., Asst. Adj. Gen., 26 April–7 May 1861.

Gill, W. S., Lt. Col., ord., 8 November 1861.

Gilmer, Jeremy Francis, Lt. Col., Col., Chief Engr., 4 August 1862–4 October 1862.

Gorham, W. J., Capt., Asst. Adj. Gen., 2 November 1863.

Guild, Lafayette, Surg., 6 March–31 August 1863; April 1865.

Harman, John A., Maj., Q.M.

Harvie, E. J., Lt. Col., Asst. Insp. Gen., June 1862.

Hays, James, Capt., Asst. Adj. Gen., 2 November 1863.

Herndon, James C., Surg.

† Heth, Henry, Lt. Col., Acting Q.M. Gen., 26 April 1861; relieved 31 May 1861.

Hullehen, Walter F., Capt., Asst. Adj. Gen., 2 November 1863.

Hunter, R. W., Maj., Asst. Adj. Gen., 2 November 1863.

Ives, Joseph C., Capt., Chief Engr., 8 November 1861.

Janney, E. H., Maj., Q.M.

Johnson, T. K., Capt., Engr., November 1863.

Johnston, Elliott, Capt., Asst. Adj. Gen., 2 November 1863; ret. 14 December 1864.

Johnston, Samuel R., Capt., Engr., 31 July–31 August 1863; Maj., 17 March 1864.

Kennon, R. B., Capt., Asst. Adj. Gen., 2 November 1863.

Land, A. L., Maj., Asst. Chief Q.M.

Lay, George W., Col., Asst. Insp. Gen., 6 March 1863.

Lee, John M., Capt., Asst. Adj. Gen., 2 November 1863.

† Long, Armistead Lindsay, Col., military secretary, 21 April 1862–31 August 1863.

Maffitt, John M., Capt., Vol. ADC, 1861.

Manigault, Joseph, Lt., Vol. ADC, 8 November 1861.

Mannagault, Charles, Maj., ADC, November 1861.

Marrow, N. C., Capt., Prov. M.

Marshall, Charles, Maj., ADC, 22 March, 21 April 1862–31 August 1863; Lt. Col., Asst. Adj. Gen., 25 February–4 November 1864.

Mason, A. P., Lt. Col., Asst. Adj. Gen., August 1862; 6 March 1863.

McClellan, Henry B., ADC, 1864.

Memminger, R. W., Capt., Asst. Adj. Gen., 1861.

Muller, Samuel, Asst. Surg., 1861.

Murray, Edward, Lt. Col., Asst. Adj. Gen. and Asst. Insp. Gen., September 1863–4 November 1863.

Myers, A. C., Col., Q.M., 31 May 1861.

Newton, E. D., Surg.

Page, Thomas J., Lt. Virginia Provisional Navy, Addnl. ADC, 3 May 1861.

† Pendleton, William Nelson, Brig. Gen., Chief of Art., June 1862.

Peyton, Henry E., Maj., Asst. Adj. Gen., 31 July 1863–4 November 1864; Lt. Col., Insp. Gen.

Pleasants, J. A., Surg., 8 January 1862.

Richardson, J. M., Capt., Asst. Adj. Gen., 2 November 1863.

Richardson, W. H., Capt., Adj. Gen., 11 May 1861.

Riddick, James W., Capt., Asst. Adj. Gen., 2 November 1863.

Rondot, St. Jules, Capt., Asst. Adj. Gen., 17 February 1863.

Scott, Fred R., Maj., Asst. Comm. Sub.

Seldon, John A., Maj., Asst. Q.M.

Shell, G. W., Capt., Q.M.

Smith, Francis W., Capt., military secretary, 27 May 1861.

† Smith, Martin Luther, Maj. Gen., Chief Engr., 16 April 1864–20 July 1864.

Smith, William Proctor, Lt. Col., Chief Engr., 31 July–31 August 1863.

Somers, S. M., Capt., Q.M.

Spann, Ranson D., Capt., Asst. Adj. Gen., 2 November 1863.

† Stevens, Walter Husted, Col., Chief Engr., June 1862–July 1862 and August 1864–April 1865.

† Stuart, James Ewell Brown, Brig. Gen., Maj. Gen., Chief of Cav., June 1862.

Talcott, Thomas M. R., Maj., ADC, 21 April 1862; 6 March, 31 July, and 31 August 1863; resigned 4 April 1864.

Tatnall, J. R. F., Capt., Vol. ADC, 1861.

Taylor, Walter Herron, Capt., Asst. Adj. Gen., 8 November–10 December 1861; Maj., ADC, 21 April, August 1862; Asst. Adj. Gen., 24 November 1862; Asst. Adj. Gen., 6 March 1863; ADC 3 July–31 August 1863; Lt. Col., Asst. Adj. Gen., 7 October 1863–4 November 1864; 1865.

Thomas, W. F., Capt., Q.M.

Treanor, George, Maj., Asst. Adj. Gen., 2 November 1863.

Venable, Charles S., Maj., ADC, 21 April 1862; Lt. Col., Asst. Adj. Gen., 25 February–4 November 1864; 1865.

Walker, James, Capt., Asst. Adj. Gen., 2 November 1863.

Washington, John A., Lt. Col., ADC, 6 May 1861; *killed in action* at Cheat Mountain, Virginia, 13 September 1861.

Washington, Thornton A., Capt., Adj. Gen. and Insp. Gen., 6 November 1861; Lt. Col., Asst. Adj. Gen.

Williamson, George, Capt., Asst. Adj. Gen., 2 November 1863; *killed in action.*

Wingfield, T. H., Surg.

Winthrop, Stephen, Capt., Asst. Adj. Gen., 30 April 1863–1865.

Woodville, Latham, Capt., ADC, September 1862.

Young, Henry E., Capt., Asst. Adj. Gen., 31 July–31 August 1863; Maj., Asst. Adj. Gen., 20 September, 4 November 1864; Judge Adv. Gen., to April 1865.

Young, Louis G., Capt., Asst. Adj. Gen., 2 November 1863.

† Denotes an officer who became a Confederate general.

APPENDIX 5

∞

Robert E. Lee's Mounts

During the Civil War Lee used five horses. Their brief histories follow.

Richmond was a bay stallion given to him in the spring of 1861, and he used the horse to inspect the Richmond defenses. "He is a troublesome fellow and dislikes to associate with strange horses," Lee wrote. The horse died following the battle of Malvern Hill.

The Roan, also called Brown-Roan, was purchased by Lee in western Virginia during the war's first summer. The Roan began to go blind during the Seven Days, and was left with a farmer.

Traveller, first called Jeff Davis and then Greenbrier, was the General's favorite horse and the one used by him throughout most of the war. He bought Traveller, a gray, from Capt. Joseph M. Broun for $200 during his stay in South Carolina toward the end of 1861. Traveller served his commander well, outlived him, and was buried beside the Lee Chapel. His skeleton was disinterred in 1907 and displayed at the chapel for some time before being reburied.

Lucy Long, a quiet mare, was obtained for the General after the Second Bull Run campaign by James E. B. Stuart. This horse served Lee as the primary backup to Traveller until near the end of the war, when it was sent to the rear, lost, and recovered. Lucy Long went to Lexington after the war and outlived the General.

Ajax, a sorrel horse that was effectively too large for Lee to ride comfortably, was used infrequently by him. Ajax went to Lexington after the war and during the mid-1860s killed himself by running into an iron gate.

Notes

The Uneven Start of a Legend

[1] Jones, *Life and Letters of Robert E. Lee.*
[2] Lee, *Memoirs of the War in the Southern Department of the United States.*
[3] *ibid.*
[4] Royster, *Light-Horse Harry Lee.*
[5] Long and Wright, *Memoirs of Robert E. Lee.*
[6] Royster, *Light-Horse Harry Lee.*
[7] Morrison, *"The Best School in the World."*

A Man's Life in the Army

[1] Freeman, *R. E. Lee.*
[2] Lee, *Recollections and Letters of General Robert E. Lee.*
[3] *ibid.*
[4] Freeman, *R. E. Lee.*
[5] *ibid.*
[6] *ibid.*
[7] *ibid.*
[8] *ibid.*
[9] *ibid.*
[10] *ibid.*
[11] Coffman, *The Old Army.*
[12] Freeman, *R. E. Lee.*
[13] *ibid.*
[14] *ibid.*
[15] Jones, *Life and Letters of Robert E. Lee.*
[16] Freeman, *R. E. Lee.*
[17] Long and Wright, *Memoirs of Robert E. Lee.*
[18] Lee, *General Lee.*
[19] Freeman, *R. E. Lee.*
[20] Long and Wright, *Memoirs of Robert E. Lee.*
[21] Lee, *Recollections and Letters of General Robert E. Lee.*
[22] Jones, *Life and Letters of Robert E. Lee.*
[23] Elliott, *Winfield Scott.*
[24] Esposito, *The West Point Atlas of American Wars.*
[25] Hitchcock, *Fifty Years in Camp and Field.*
[26] *ibid.*
[27] Scott, *Memoirs of Lieut.-Gen. Scott.*

[28] Lee, *General Lee.*
[29] Scott, *Memoirs of Lieut.-Gen. Scott.*
[30] Hitchcock, *Fifty Years in Camp and Field.*
[31] *ibid.*
[32] *ibid.*
[33] *ibid.*
[34] Elliott, *Winfield Scott.*
[35] Scott, *Memoirs of Lieut.-Gen. Scott.*
[36] Welsh, *Medical Histories of Confederate Generals.*
[37] Scott, *Memoirs of Lieut.-Gen. Scott.*
[38] Lee, *General Lee.*
[39] Chambers, *Stonewall Jackson.*
[40] Lee, *Recollections and Letters of General Robert E. Lee.*

The Coming of the War

[1] Freeman, *R. E. Lee.*
[2] Welsh, *Medical Histories of Confederate Generals.*
[3] Davis, *The Papers of Jefferson Davis.*
[4] Jones, *Life and Letters of Robert Edward Lee.*
[5] *ibid.*
[6] Lee, *Recollections and Letters of General Robert E. Lee.*
[7] *ibid.*
[8] *ibid.*
[9] deButts, *Growing Up in the 1850s.*
[10] Davis, *The Papers of Jefferson Davis.*
[11] Freeman, *R. E. Lee.*
[12] Davis, *The Papers of Jefferson Davis.*
[13] Freeman, *R. E. Lee.*
[14] Morrison, *"The Best School in the World."*
[15] deButts, *Growing Up in the 1850s.*
[16] Davis, *The Papers of Jefferson Davis.*
[17] Chambers, *Stonewall Jackson.*
[18] Davis, *The Papers of Jefferson Davis*; Morrison, *"The Best School in the World."*
[19] deButts, *Growing Up in the 1850s.*
[20] Long and Wright, *Memoirs of Robert E. Lee.*
[21] Hood, *Advance and Retreat.*
[22] deButts, *Growing Up in the 1850s.*
[23] Jones, *Life and Letters of Robert Edward Lee.*

[24] Hancock, *Reminiscences of Winfield Scott Hancock*.

[25] Freeman, *R. E. Lee*.

[26] Lee, *General Lee*; Taylor, *General Lee*.

[27] Jones, *Life and Letters of Robert Edward Lee*.

[28] *ibid*.

[29] McClellan, *The Life and Campaigns of Major-General J. E. B. Stuart*.

[30] Lee, *Recollections and Letters of General Robert E. Lee*.

[31] Jones, *Life and Letters of Robert Edward Lee*.

An Uneventful Year for Granny Lee

[1] Jones, *Life and Letters of Robert Edward Lee*.

[2] Freeman, *R. E. Lee*.

[3] Long and Wright, *Memoirs of Robert E. Lee*.

[4] U.S. War Department, *The War of the Rebellion*.

[5] Freeman, *R. E. Lee*.

[6] Johnson and Buel, *Battles and Leaders of the Civil War*.

[7] U.S. War Department, *The War of the Rebellion*.

[8] Mosby, *The Memoirs of Colonel John S. Mosby*.

[9] Jones, *Life and Letters of Robert Edward Lee*.

[10] Lee, *Recollections and Letters of General Robert E. Lee*.

[11] *ibid*.

[12] Mosby, *The Memoirs of Colonel John S. Mosby*.

[13] Royster, *Light-Horse Harry Lee*.

[14] U.S. War Department, *The War of the Rebellion*.

[15] Jackson, *Life and Letters of General Thomas J. Jackson*.

[16] Chesnut, *Mary Chesnut's Civil War*.

[17] Jones, *A Rebel War Clerk's Diary*.

[18] Lee, *Recollections and Letters of General Robert E. Lee*.

[19] Freeman, *R. E. Lee*.

[20] Blackford, *War Years with Jeb Stuart*.

[21] Hood, *Advance and Retreat*.

[22] Taylor, *General Lee*.

[23] Lee, *General Lee*.

[24] Lee, *Recollections and Letters of General Robert E. Lee*.

[25] Andrews, *The South Reports the Civil War*.

[26] Davis, *The Papers of Jefferson Davis*.

[27] Taylor, *General Lee*.

[28] Davis, *The Rise and Fall of the Confederate Government*.

[29] Lee, *Recollections and Letters of General Robert E. Lee*.

[30] Jones, *Life and Letters of Robert Edward Lee*.

[31] Lee, *Recollections and Letters of General Robert E. Lee*.

[32] Freeman, *R. E. Lee*.

[33] Longstreet, *From Manassas to Appomattox*.

[34] Lee, *Recollections and Letters of General Robert E. Lee*.

[35] Lee, *The Wartime Papers of R. E. Lee*.

[36] Andrews, *The South Reports the Civil War*.

[37] Worsham, *One of Jackson's Foot Cavalry*.

[38] Lee, *Recollections and Letters of General Robert E. Lee*.

[39] Jackson, *Life and Letters of General Thomas J. Jackson*.

[40] Lee, *Recollections and Letters of General Robert E. Lee*.

[41] *ibid*.

[42] Goree, *Longstreet's Aide*.

[43] Andrews, *The South Reports the Civil War*.

[44] Lee, *Recollections and Letters of General Robert E. Lee*.

[45] Davis, *The Papers of Jefferson Davis*.

[46] Davis, *The Rise and Fall of the Confederate Government*.

[47] Taylor, *General Lee*.

[48] Lee, *General Lee*.

[49] Jones, *Life and Letters of Robert Edward Lee*.

[50] *ibid*.

The Emergence of Military Genius

[1] Lee, *Recollections and Letters of General Robert E. Lee*.

[2] *ibid*.

[3] *ibid*.

[4] *ibid*.

[5] Chambers, *Stonewall Jackson*.

[6] Lee, *Recollections and Letters of General Robert E. Lee*.

[7] Lee, *General Lee*.

[8] Johnston, *Narrative of Military Operations*.

[9] Alexander, *Fighting for the Confederacy*.

[10] Ruffin, *The Diary of Edmund Ruffin*.

[11] U.S. War Department, *The War of the Rebellion*.

[12] Davis, *The Papers of Jefferson Davis*.

[13] Marshall, *An Aide-de-Camp of Lee*.

[14] Sorrel, *Recollections of a Confederate Staff Officer*.

[15] Chambers, *Stonewall Jackson*.

[16] Haskell, *Alexander Cheves Haskell*.

[17] Jones, *A Rebel War Clerk's Diary*.

[18] Alexander, *Fighting for the Confederacy*.

[19] Lee, *Lee's Dispatches*.

[20] *ibid*.

[21] Chambers, *Stonewall Jackson*.

[22] Chesnut, *Mary Chesnut's Civil War*.

[23] Stiles, *Four Years Under Marse Robert*.

[24] Jones, *Life and Letters of Robert Edward Lee*.

[25] Beringer, *Why the South Lost the Civil War*.

[26] Poague, *Gunner with Stonewall*.

[27] Hood, *Advance and Retreat*.

[28] Stiles, *Four Years Under Marse Robert*.

[29] U.S. War Department, *The War of the Rebellion*.

[30] Longstreet, *From Manassas to Appomattox*.

[31] Alexander, *Fighting for the Confederacy*; Johnson and Buel, *Battles and Leaders of the Civil War*.

[32] Andrews, *The South Reports the Civil War*.

[33] *ibid*.

[34] Sorrel, *Recollections of a Confederate Staff Officer*.

[35] Welsh, *Medical Histories of Confederate Generals*.

[36] Longstreet, *From Manassas to Appomattox*.

[37] Beringer, *Why the South Lost the Civil War*.

[38] Lee, *Lee's Dispatches*.

[39] *ibid*.

[40] Hood, *Advance and Retreat*.

[41] Welsh, *Medical Histories of Confederate Generals*.

[42] Johnson and Buel, *Battles and Leaders of the Civil War*.

[43] Beringer, *Why the South Lost the Civil War*.

[44] U.S. War Department, *The War of the Rebellion*.

[45] Davis, *The Papers of Jefferson Davis.*

[46] Longstreet, *From Manassas to Appomattox.*

[47] Glatthaar, *Partners in Command.*

[48] Johnson and Buel, *Battles and Leaders of the Civil War.*

[49] *ibid.*

[50] Lee, *Recollections and Letters of General Robert E. Lee.*

[51] Poague, *Gunner with Stonewall.*

[52] Sorrel, *Recollections of a Confederate Staff Officer.*

[53] Johnson and Buel, *Battles and Leaders of the Civil War.*

[54] Jones, *Life and Letters of Robert Edward Lee.*

[55] Lee, *Recollections and Letters of General Robert E. Lee.*

[56] *ibid.*

[57] Taylor, *General Lee.*

[58] Longstreet, *From Manassas to Appomattox.*

[59] Pendleton, *Southern Magazine.*

[60] U.S. War Department, *The War of the Rebellion.*

[61] Lee, *Recollections and Letters of General Robert E. Lee.*

[62] *ibid.*

The Glorious Summer of Battle

[1] U.S. War Department, *The War of the Rebellion.*

[2] Lee, *Recollections and Letters of General Robert E. Lee.*

[3] Kean, *Inside the Confederate Government.*

[4] Welsh, *Medical Histories of Confederate Generals.*

[5] Freeman, *R. E. Lee.*

[6] Jackson, *Life and Letters of General Thomas J. Jackson.*

[7] Beringer, *Why the South Lost the Civil War.*

[8] Johnson and Buel, *Battles and Leaders of the Civil War.*

[9] Jackson, *Life and Letters of General Thomas J. Jackson.*

[10] Hotchkiss, *Make Me a Map of the Valley.*

[11] Chambers, *Stonewall Jackson.*

[12] Lee, *The Wartime Papers of R. E. Lee.*

[13] Poague, *Gunner with Stonewall.*

[14] Stiles, *Four Years Under Marse Robert.*

[15] U.S. War Department, *The War of the Rebellion.*

[16] Taylor, *Lee's Adjutant.*

[17] Chambers, *Stonewall Jackson.*

[18] U.S. War Department, *The War of the Rebellion.*

[19] Lee, *Recollections and Letters of General Robert E. Lee.*

[20] Jones, *A Rebel War Clerk's Diary.*

[21] Cooke, *Wearing of the Gray.*

[22] Lee, *Recollections and Letters of General Robert E. Lee.*

[23] Kean, *Inside the Confederate Government.*

[24] Evans, *Intrepid Warrior.*

[25] Marshall, *An Aide-de-Camp of Lee.*

[26] McClellan, *The Life and Campaigns of Major-General J. E. B. Stuart.*

[27] Sorrel, *Recollections of a Confederate Staff Officer.*

[28] Fremantle, *Three Months in the Southern States.*

[29] McClure, *The Annals of the War.*

[30] *ibid.*

[31] *ibid.*

[32] *ibid.*

[33] Hood, *Advance and Retreat.*

[34] Fremantle, *Three Months in the Southern States.*

[35] Welsh, *Medical Histories of Confederate Generals.*

[36] McClure, *The Annals of the War.*

[37] Alexander, *Military Memoirs of a Confederate.*

[38] Fremantle, *Three Months in the Southern States.*

[39] *ibid.*

[40] Johnson and Buel, *Battles and Leaders of the Civil War.*

[41] U.S. War Department, *The War of the Rebellion.*

[42] Beringer, *Why the South Lost the Civil War.*

[43] Sorrel, *Recollections of a Confederate Staff Officer.*

[44] Lee, *Recollections and Letters of General Robert E. Lee.*

[45] Lee, *The Wartime Papers of R. E. Lee.*

[46] Davis, *Private Letters.*

[47] Jones, *A Rebel War Clerk's Diary.*

[48] Jones, *Life and Letters of Robert Edward Lee.*

[49] Welsh, *Medical Histories of Confederate Generals.*

[50] Lee, *Recollections and Letters of General Robert E. Lee.*

[51] Welsh, *Medical Histories of Confederate Generals.*

[52] Blackford, *War Years with Jeb Stuart.*

[53] Welsh, *Medical Histories of Confederate Generals.*

[54] Johnson and Buel, *Battles and Leaders of the Civil War.*

[55] Jones, *Life and Letters of Robert Edward Lee.*

[56] Lee, *General Lee.*

A Modern Kind of War

[1] Lee, *The Wartime Papers of R. E. Lee.*

[2] *ibid.*

[3] Chesnut, *Mary Chesnut's Civil War.*

[4] Kean, *Inside the Confederate Government.*

[5] Beringer, *Why the South Lost the Civil War.*

[6] Taylor, *Lee's Adjutant.*

[7] Black, *A Surgeon with Stonewall Jackson.*

[8] Lee, *Lee's Dispatches.*

[9] Donald, *Why the North Won the Civil War.*

[10] Johnson and Buel, *Battles and Leaders of the Civil War.*

[11] McClure, *The Annals of the War.*

[12] Oates, *The War between the Union and the Confederacy.*

[13] Poague, *Gunner with Stonewall.*

[14] Beringer, *Why the South Lost the Civil War.*

[15] Lee, *Recollections and Letters of General Robert E. Lee.*

[16] Lee, *Lee's Dispatches.*

[17] Johnson and Buel, *Battles and Leaders of the Civil War.*

[18] Lee, *Lee's Dispatches.*

[19] Stiles, *Four Years with Marse Robert.*

[20] Robertson, *General A. P. Hill.*

[21] Welsh, *Medical Histories of Confederate Generals.*

[22] Lee, *Lee's Dispatches.*

[23] Johnson and Buel, *Battles and Leaders of the Civil War.*

[24] Lee, *Lee's Dispatches.*

[25] Grimes, *Extracts of Letters of Major-Gen'l Bryan Grimes.*

[26] Lee, *Lee's Dispatches.*

[27] Lee, *Recollections and Letters of General Robert E. Lee.*

[28] Beringer, *Why the South Lost the Civil War.*

[29] Jones, *Life and Letters of Robert Edward Lee.*

30 Taylor, *Lee's Adjutant.*

31 Ruffin, *The Diary of Edmund Ruffin.*

32 Boritt, *Why the Confederacy Lost.*

The Confederacy Unravels

1 Kean, *Inside the Confederate Government.*

2 Gorgas, *The Journals of Josiah Gorgas.*

3 U.S. War Department, *The War of the Rebellion.*

4 Lee, *Lee's Dispatches.*

5 Chesnut, *Mary Chesnut's Civil War.*

6 Ruffin, *The Diary of Edmund Ruffin.*

7 Beringer, *Why the South Lost the Civil War.*

8 Coulter, *The Confederate States of America.*

9 Beringer, *Why the South Lost the Civil War.*

10 Jones, *A Rebel War Clerk's Diary.*

11 Johnston, *Narrative of Military Operations.*

12 Lee, *The Wartime Papers of R. E. Lee.*

13 Gorgas, *The Journals of Josiah Gorgas.*

14 Davis, *The Rise and Fall of the Confederate Government.*

15 Chesnut, *Mary Chesnut's Civil War.*

16 Grimes, *Extracts of Letters of Major-Gen'l Bryan Grimes.*

17 Lee, *Lee's Dispatches.*

18 McClure, *The Annals of the War.*

19 Taylor, *General Lee.*

20 Lee, *The Wartime Papers of R. E. Lee.*

21 Johnson and Buel, *Battles and Leaders of the Civil War.*

22 Wise, *The End of an Era.*

23 Taylor, *General Lee.*

24 U.S. War Department, *The War of the Rebellion.*

25 *ibid.*

26 *ibid.*

27 *ibid.*

28 Chamberlain, *The Passing of the Armies.*

29 Johnson and Buel, *Battles and Leaders of the Civil War.*

30 Poague, *Gunner with Stonewall.*

31 McCarthy, *Detailed Minutiae of Soldier Life in the Army of Northern Virginia.*

32 Grimes, *Extracts of Letters of Major-Gen'l Bryan Grimes.*

33 U.S. War Department, *The War of the Rebellion.*

34 Cooke, *The Wearing of the Gray.*

35 Johnson and Buel, *Battles and Leaders of the Civil War.*

36 U.S. War Department, *The War of the Rebellion.*

37 Blackford, *War Years with Jeb Stuart.*

38 Edmondston, *"Journal of a Secesh Lady."*

39 Chamberlain, *The Passing of the Armies.*

When the War's Over . . .

1 McCarthy, *Detailed Minutiae of Soldier Life in the Army of Northern Virginia.*

2 Johnson and Buel, *Battles and Leaders of the Civil War.*

3 Ruffin, *The Diary of Edmund Ruffin.*

4 McClure, *The Annals of the War.*

5 Lee, *Recollections and Letters of General Robert E. Lee.*

6 Gorgas, *The Journals of Josiah Gorgas.*

7 Taylor, *General Lee.*

8 Lee, *Recollections and Letters of General Robert E. Lee.*

9 *ibid.*

10 Jones, *Life and Letters of Robert Edward Lee.*

11 Boley, *Lexington in Old Virginia.*

12 Lee, *Recollections and Letters of General Robert E. Lee.*

13 *ibid.*

14 Gorgas, *The Journals of Josiah Gorgas.*

15 Jones, *Life and Letters of Robert Edward Lee.*

16 Lee, *Recollections and Letters of General Robert E. Lee.*

17 *ibid.*

18 Early, *Autobiographical Sketch and Narrative of the War between the States.*

19 McClure, *The Annals of the War.*

20 Lee, *Recollections and Letters of General Robert E. Lee.*

21 *ibid.*

22 Fishwick, *General Lee's Photographer.*

23 Davis, *Private Letters.*

24 Lee, *Recollections and Letters of General Robert E. Lee.*

25 Welsh, *Medical Histories of Confederate Generals.*

26 Lee, *Recollections and Letters of General Robert E. Lee.*

27 Gallagher, *Lee the Soldier.*

28 *ibid.*

29 *ibid.*

30 Welsh, *Medical Histories of Confederate Generals.*

31 Lee, *Recollections and Letters of General Robert E. Lee.*

32 *ibid.*

33 *ibid.*

34 *ibid.*

35 Lee, *Memoirs of the War in the Southern Department of the United States.*

36 Lee, *Recollections and Letters of General Robert E. Lee.*

37 Welsh, *Medical Histories of Confederate Generals.*

38 Lee, *Recollections and Letters of General Robert E. Lee.*

39 Welsh, *Medical Histories of Confederate Generals.*

40 *ibid.*

41 Mosby, *The Memoirs of Colonel John S. Mosby.*

42 Welsh, *Medical Histories of Confederate Generals.*

43 Mosby, *The Memoirs of Colonel John S. Mosby.*

44 Welsh, *Medical Histories of Confederate Generals*; Rozear, et al., "R. E. Lee's Stroke."

45 Freeman, *R. E. Lee.*

46 Rozear, et al., "R. E. Lee's Stroke."

47 *ibid.*

Lee, the Lost Cause, and Southern Memory

1 Foster, *Ghosts of the Confederacy.*

2 Gallagher, *Jubal A. Early.*

3 *ibid.*

4 Toplin, *Ken Burns's Civil War.*

5 Connelly and Bellows, *God and General Longstreet.*

6 McPherson, *Battle Cry of Freedom.*

7 Foster, *Ghosts of the Confederacy.*

8 Coulter, *The Confederate States of America.*

9 Connelly and Bellows, *God and General Longstreet.*

10 *ibid.*

11 *ibid.*

12 Jackson, *Life and Letters of General Thomas J. Jackson.*

13 Boley, *Lexington in Old Virginia.*

14 Gallagher, *Lee the Soldier.*

15 Foster, *Ghosts of the Confederacy.*

16 Connelly and Bellows, *God and General Longstreet.*

17 Ropes and Livermore, *The Story of the Civil War.*

18 Donald, *Why the North Won the Civil War.*

19 Glatthaar, *Partners in Command.*

20 McPherson, *Battle Cry of Freedom.*

21 Toplin, *Ken Burns's Civil War.*

22 McPherson, *Drawn with the Sword.*

23 Donald, *Why the North Won the Civil War.*

24 *ibid.*

25 Royster, *Light-Horse Harry Lee.*

26 Connelly and Bellows, *God and General Longstreet.*

27 Donald, *Why the North Won the Civil War.*

28 Connelly and Bellows, *God and General Longstreet.*

29 Foster, *Ghosts of the Confederacy.*

30 Connelly and Bellows, *God and General Longstreet.*

31 *ibid.*

Bibliography

Alexander, Edward Porter. *Fighting for the Confederacy: The Personal Recollections of General Edward Porter Alexander* (ed. Gary W. Gallagher, 664 pp., University of North Carolina Press, Chapel Hill, North Carolina, 1989).

———. *Military Memoirs of a Confederate: A Critical Narrative* (634 pp., Charles Scribner's Sons, New York, 1907).

Andrews, J. Cutler. *The South Reports the Civil War* (611 pp., Princeton University Press, Princeton, New Jersey, 1970).

Beringer, Richard E., Herman Hattaway, Archer Jones, and William N. Still, Jr. *Why the South Lost the Civil War* (582 pp., University of Georgia Press, Athens, Georgia, 1986).

Black, Harvey. *A Surgeon with Stonewall Jackson: The Civil War Letters of Dr. Harvey Black* (ed. Glenn L. McMullen, 249 pp., Butternut and Blue, Baltimore, Maryland, 1995).

Blackford, William W. *War Years With Jeb Stuart* (322 pp., Charles Scribner's Sons, New York, 1945).

Boley, Henry. *Lexington in Old Virginia* (235 pp., Garrett and Massie, Richmond, Virginia, 1936).

Boritt, Gabor S., ed. *Why the Confederacy Lost* (209 pp., Oxford University Press, New York, 1992).

Burt, Nathaniel. *First Families: The Making of an American Aristocracy* (503 pp., Little, Brown and Co., Boston, 1970).

Carmichael, Peter S. *Lee's Young Artillerist: William R. J. Pegram* (209 pp., University Press of Virginia, Charlottesville, Virginia, 1995).

Chamberlain, Joshua Lawrence. *The Passing of the Armies: An Account of the Final Campaign of the Army of the Potomac, Based on Personal Reminiscences of the Fifth Army Corps* (392 pp., G. P. Putnam's Sons, New York, 1915).

Chambers, Lenoir. *Stonewall Jackson* (2 vols., 1133 pp., William Morrow, New York, 1959).

Chesnut, Mary. *Mary Chesnut's Civil War* (ed. C. Vann Woodward, 886 pp., Yale University Press, New Haven, Connecticut, 1981).

Coffman, Edward M. *The Old Army: A Portrait of the American Army in Peacetime, 1784–1898* (514 pp., Oxford University Press, New York, 1986).

Connelly, Thomas L., and Barbara L. Bellows. *God and General Longstreet: The Lost Cause and the Southern Mind* (158 pp., Louisiana State University Press, Baton Rouge, Louisiana, 1982).

Connelly, Thomas Lawrence. *The Marble Man: Robert E. Lee and His Image in American Society* (249 pp., Alfred A. Knopf, New York, 1977).

Cooke, John Esten. *Wearing of the Gray: Being Personal Portraits, Scenes and Adventures of the War* (601 pp., E. B. Treat and Co., Baltimore, Maryland, 1867).

Coulling, Mary P. *The Lee Girls* (242 pp., John F. Blair, Winston-Salem, North Carolina, 1987).

Coulter, E. Merton. *The Confederate States of America, 1861–1865* (644 pp., Louisiana State University Press, Baton Rouge, Louisiana, 1950).

Crute, Joseph H., Jr. *Confederate Staff Officers, 1861–1865* (267 pp., Derwent Books, Powhatan, Virginia, 1982).

Davis, Jefferson Finis. *The Papers of Jefferson Davis* (eds. Haskell M. Monroe, James T. McIntosh, Lynda Lasswell Crist, Mary Seaton Dix, and Kenneth H. Williams, 8 vols., 5116 pp., and continuing, Louisiana State University Press, Baton Rouge, Louisiana, 1971–).

———. *Private Letters, 1823–1889* (ed. Hudson Strode, 580 pp., Harcourt, Brace, and World, New York, 1966).

———. *The Rise and Fall of the Confederate Government* (2 vols., 1515 pp., D. Appleton and Co., New York, 1881).

deButts, Agnes Lee. *Growing Up in the 1850s: The Journal of Agnes Lee* (ed. Mary Custis Lee deButts, 151 pp., University of North Carolina Press, Chapel Hill, North Carolina, 1984).

Donald, David H., ed. *Why the North Won the Civil War* (128 pp., Louisiana State University Press, Baton Rouge, Louisiana, 1960).

Early, Jubal A. *Autobiographical Sketch and Narrative of the War Between the States* (496 pp., J. B. Lippincott and Co., Philadelphia, Pennsylvania, 1912).

Edmondston, Catherine Ann Devereux. *"Journal of a Secesh Lady": The Diary of Catherine Ann Devereux Edmondston* (eds. Beth Gilbert Crabtree and James W. Patton, 850 pp., North Carolina Division of Archives and History, Raleigh, North Carolina, 1979).

Elliott, Charles Winslow. *Winfield Scott: The Soldier and the Man* (817 pp., Macmillan Co., New York, 1937).

Esposito, Vincent J., ed. *The West Point Atlas of American Wars, vol. 1, 1689–1900* (308 pp., Henry Holt, New York, 1995).

Evans, Clement A. *Intrepid Warrior: Clement Anselm Evans* (ed. Robert Grier Stephens, Jr., 598 pp., Morningside Book Shop, Dayton, Ohio, 1992).

Fishwick, Marshall. *General Lee's Photographer: The Life and Work of Michael Miley* (94 pp., Published for the Virginia Historical Society by the University of North Carolina Press, Chapel Hill, North Carolina, 1954).

Flood, Charles Bracelen. *Lee: The Last Years* (308 pp., Houghton-Mifflin Co., Boston, 1981).

Foster, Gaines M. *Ghosts of the Confederacy: Defeat, the Lost Cause, and the Emergence of the New South 1865 to 1913* (306 pp., Oxford University Press, New York, 1987).

Freeman, Douglas Southall. *Lee's Lieutenants: A Study in Command* (3 vols., 2395 pp., Charles Scribner's Sons, New York, 1942–1944).

———. *R. E. Lee: A Biography* (4 vols., 2398 pp., Charles Scribner's Sons, New York, 1934–1935).

Fremantle, Arthur J. L. *Three Months in the Southern States, April–June, 1863* (316 pp., W. Blackwood and Sons, Edinburgh, 1863).

Frey, Jerry. *In the Woods Before Dawn: The Samuel Richey Collection of the Southern Confederacy* (296 pp., Thomas Publications, Gettysburg, Pennsylvania, 1994).

Fuller, John F. C. *Grant and Lee: A Study in Personality and Generalship* (323 pp., Eyre and Spottiswoode, London, 1933).

Gallagher, Gary W. *Jubal A. Early, the Lost Cause, and Civil War History* (50 pp., Marquette University Press, Milwaukee, Wisconsin, 1995).

———., ed. *Lee the Soldier* (620 pp., University of Nebraska Press, Lincoln, Nebraska, 1996).

Geary, John W. *A Politician Goes to War: The Civil War Letters of John White Geary* (ed. William Alan Blair, 259 pp., Pennsylvania State University Press, University Park, Pennsylvania, 1995).

Glatthaar, Joseph T. *Partners in Command: The Relationships Between Leaders in the Civil War* (286 pp., Free Press, New York, 1994).

Goree, Thomas J. *Longstreet's Aide: The Civil War Letters of Major Thomas J. Goree* (ed. Thomas W. Cutrer, 239 pp., University Press of Virginia, Charlottesville, Virginia, 1995).

Gorgas, Josiah. *The Journals of Josiah Gorgas, 1857–1878* (ed. Sarah Woolfolk Wiggins, 305 pp., University of Alabama Press, Tuscaloosa, Alabama, 1995).

Grimes, Bryan. *Extracts of Letters of Major-Gen'l Bryan Grimes to His Wife, Written While in Active Service in the Army of Northern Virginia: Together With Some Personal Recollections of the War, Written by Him After its Close, etc.* (ed. Pulaski Cowper, 137 pp., Edwards, Broughton and Co., Raleigh, North Carolina, 1883).

Hancock, Almira R. *Reminiscences of Winfield Scott Hancock, by His Wife* (340 pp., Charles L. Webster and Co., New York, 1887).

Hardy, Stella Pickett. *Colonial Families of the Southern States of America: A History and Genealogy of Colonial Families Who Settled in the Colonies Prior to the Revolution* (2d ed., 643 pp., Genealogical Publishing Co., Baltimore, Maryland, 1968).

Haskell, Alexander Cheves. *Alexander Cheves Haskell: The Portrait of a Man* (ed. Louise Haskell Daly, 224 pp., Published by the author, Norwood, Massachusetts, 1934).

Heitman, Francis B. *Historical Register and Dictionary of the United States Army, From Its Organization, September 29, 1789, to March 2, 1903* (2 vols., 1695 pp., U.S. Government Printing Office, Washington, D.C., 1903).

Hendrick, Burton J. *The Lees of Virginia: Biography of a Family* (455 pp., Little, Brown and Co., Boston, 1935).

Hitchcock, Ethan Allen. *Fifty Years in Camp and Field: Diary of Major-General Ethan Allen Hitchcock, U.S.A.* (ed. W. A. Croffut, 514 pp., G. P. Putnam's Sons, New York, 1909).

Hood, John Bell. *Advance and Retreat: Personal Experiences in the United States and Confederate States Armies* (358 pp., Hood Orphan Memorial Fund, New Orleans, Louisiana, 1880).

Hotchkiss, Jedediah. *Make Me a Map of the Valley: The Civil War Journal of Stonewall Jackson's Cartographer* (ed. Archie P. McDonald, 352 pp., Southern Methodist University Press, Dallas, Texas, 1973).

Howard, McHenry. *Recollections of a Maryland Confederate Soldier and Staff Officer Under Johnston, Jackson and Lee* (423 pp., Williams and Wilkins Co., Baltimore, Maryland, 1914).

Jackson, Mary Anna. *Life and Letters of General Thomas J. Jackson (Stonewall Jackson)* (479 pp., Harper and Brothers, New York, 1892).

Johnson, Robert Underwood, and Clarence Clough Buel, eds. *Battles and Leaders of the Civil War, Being for the Most Part Contributions by Union and Confederate Officers: Based Upon "The Century" War Series* (4 vols., 3091 pp., Century Co., New York, 1887–1888).

Johnston, Joseph E. *Narrative of Military Operations, Directed, during the Late War Between the States, by Joseph E. Johnston, General, C.S.A.* (602 pp., D. Appleton and Co., New York, 1874).

Jones, J. William. *Christ in the Camp; or, Religion in Lee's Army* (624 pp., B. F. Johnson and Co., Richmond, Virginia, 1887).

———. *Life and Letters of Robert Edward Lee, Soldier and Man* (486 pp., Neale Publishing Co., New York, 1906).

Jones, John B. *A Rebel War Clerk's Diary at the Confederate States Capital* (2 vols., 893 pp. J. B. Lippincott and Co., Philadelphia, Pennsylvania, 1866).

Kean, Robert Garlick Hill. *Inside the Confederate Government: The Diary of Robert Garlick Hill Kean* (ed. Edward Younger, 241 pp., Oxford University Press, New York, 1957).

Lee, Cazenove Gardner, Jr. *Lee Chronicle: Studies of the Early Generations of the Lees of Virginia* (411 pp., New York University Press, New York, 1957).

Lee, Edmund Jennings, Jr. *Lee of Virginia, 1642–1892: Biographical and Genealogical Sketches of the Descendants of Colonel Richard Lee* (586 pp., E. J. Lee, M.D., Philadelphia, Pennsylvania, 1895).

Lee, Elizabeth Blair. *Wartime Washington: The Civil War Letters of Elizabeth Blair Lee* (ed. Virginia Jeans Laas, 552 pp., University of Illinois Press, Urbana, Illinois, 1991).

Lee, Fitzhugh. *General Lee* (433 pp., D. Appleton and Co., New York, 1894).

Lee, Henry. *Memoirs of the War in the Southern Department of the United States* (ed. Robert E. Lee, 620 pp., University Publishing Co., New York, 1870; reprint 1996).

Lee, Robert E. *Lee's Dispatches: Unpublished Letters of General Robert E. Lee, C.S.A., to Jefferson Davis and the War Department of the Confederate States of America 1862–1865, From the Private Collection of Wymberley Jones de Renne, of Wormsloe, Georgia* (ed. Douglas Southall Freeman, 400 pp., G. P. Putnam's Sons, New York, 1915).

———. *The Wartime Papers of R. E. Lee* (ed. Clifford Dowdey and Louis H. Manarin, 994 pp., Little, Brown and Co., Boston, 1961).

Lee, Robert E., Jr. *Recollections and Letters of General Robert E. Lee* (461 pp., Doubleday, Page & Co., New York, 1904).

Long, A. L., and Marcus J. Wright. *Memoirs of Robert E. Lee: His Military and Personal History, Embracing a Large Amount of Information Hitherto Unpublished* (707 pp., J. M. Stoddart and Co., New York, 1886).

Longstreet, Helen D. *Lee and Longstreet at High Tide: Gettysburg in the Light of the Official Records* (346 pp., Published by the author, Gainesville, Georgia, 1904).

Longstreet, James. *From Manassas to Appomattox: Memoirs of the Civil War in America* (690 pp., J. B. Lippincott and Co., Philadelphia, Pennsylvania, 1896).

Malone, Dumas, ed. *Dictionary of American Biography* (Charles Scribner's Sons, New York, 1933).

Marshall, Charles. *An Aide-de-Camp of Lee, Being the Papers of Colonel Charles Marshall, Sometime Aide-de-Camp, Military Secretary, and Assistant Adjutant General on the Staff of Robert E. Lee, 1862–1865* (Frederick Maurice, ed., 287 pp., Little, Brown, and Co., Boston, 1927).

McCarthy, Carlton. *Detailed Minutiae of Soldier Life in the Army of Northern Virginia 1861–1865* (224 pp., C. McCarthy and Co., Richmond, Virginia, 1882).

McClellan, H. B. *The Life and Campaigns of Major-General J. E. B. Stuart, Commander of the Cavalry of the Army of Northern Virginia* (468 pp., Houghton-Mifflin Co., Boston, and J. W. Randolph and English, Richmond, Virginia, 1885).

McClure, Alexander K., ed. *The Annals of the War Written by Leading Participants North and South: Originally Published in the* Philadelphia Weekly Times (800 pp., Times Publishing Co., Philadelphia, Pennsylvania, 1879).

McPherson, James M. *Battle Cry of Freedom: The Civil War Era* (904 pp., Oxford University Press, New York, 1988).

———. *Drawn with the Sword: Reflections on the American Civil War* (258 pp., Oxford University Press, New York, 1996).

Meredith, Roy. *The Face of Robert E. Lee in Life and Legend* (143 pp., Charles Scribner's Sons, New York, 1947).

Morrison, James L., Jr. *"The Best School in the World": West Point, the Pre-Civil War Years, 1833–1866* (255 pp., Kent State University Press, Kent, Ohio, 1986).

Mosby, John S. *The Memoirs of Colonel John S. Mosby* (ed. Charles Wells Russell, 414 pp., Little, Brown and Co., Boston, 1917).

Nagel, Paul C. *The Lees of Virginia: Seven Generations of an American Family* (332 pp., Oxford University Press, New York, 1990).

Neely, Mark E., Jr., Harold Holzer, and Gabor S. Boritt. *The Confederate Image: Prints of the Lost Cause* (257 pp., University of North Carolina Press, Chapel Hill, North Carolina, 1987).

Nisbet, James Cooper. *Four Years on the Firing Line* (445 pp., Imperial Press, Chattanooga, Tennessee, 1914).

Nolan, Alan T. *Lee Considered: General Robert E. Lee and Civil War History* (231 pp., University of North Carolina Press, Chapel Hill, North Carolina, 1991).

Oates, William C. *The War between the Union and the Confederacy, and Its Lost Opportunities: With a History of the 15th Alabama Regiment and the Forty-Eight Battles in Which It Was Engaged: Being an Account of the Author's Experiences in the Greatest Conflict of Modern Times: A Justification of Secession, and Showing That the Confederacy Should Have Succeeded: A Criticism of President Davis, the Confederate Congress and Some of the General Officers of the Confederate and Union Armies: Praise of Line Officers and Soldiers in the Ranks for Their Heroism and Patriotism, and Including the Author's Observations and Experiences as Brigadier-General in the War between the United States and Spain* (808 pp., Neale Publishing Co., New York, 1905).

Pendleton, William N. *Southern Magazine*, 15:620 (1874).

Poague, William Thomas. *Gunner with Stonewall: Reminiscences of William Thomas Poague, a Memoir, Written for His Children in 1903* (ed. Monroe F. Cockrell, 181 pp., McCowat-Mercer Press, Jackson, Tennessee, 1957).

Robertson, James I., Jr. *General A. P. Hill: The Story of a Confederate Warrior* (382 pp., Random House, New York, 1987).

Roland, Charles P. *Reflections on Lee: A Historian's Assessment* (130 pp., Stackpole Books, Mechanicsburg, Pennsylvania, 1995).

Ropes, John Codman, and William Roscoe Livermore. *The Story of the Civil War: A Concise Account of the War in the United States of America between 1861 and 1865* (4 vols., 1270 pp., G. P. Putnam's Sons, New York, 1895–1913).

Royster, Charles. *Light-Horse Harry Lee and the Legacy of the American Revolution* (301 pp., Alfred A. Knopf, New York, 1981).

Rozear, Marvin P., E. Wayne Massey, Jennifer Horner, Erin Foley, and Joseph C. Greenfield, Jr. "R. E. Lee's Stroke," in *The Virginia Magazine of History and Biography*, 98:2 (April 1990), 291–308.

Ruffin, Edmund. *The Diary of Edmund Ruffin* (ed. William K. Scarborough, 3 vols., 2266 pp., Louisiana State University Press, Baton Rouge, Louisiana, 1972–1989).

Scott, Winfield. *Memoirs of Lieut.-Gen. Scott, LL.D. Written by Himself* (2 vols., 653 pp., Sheldon and Co., New York, 1864).

Sorrel, G. Moxley. *Recollections of a Confederate Staff Officer* (315 pp., Neale Publishing Co., New York, 1905).

Stiles, Robert. *Four Years Under Marse Robert* (368 pp., Neale Publishing Co., New York, 1903).

Sumner, Charles. *The Selected Letters of Charles Sumner* (ed. Beverly Wilson Palmer, 1246 pp., Northeastern University Press, Boston, 1990).

Taylor, Walter H. *General Lee, His Campaigns in Virginia, 1861–1865: With Personal Reminiscences* (314 pp., Press of Braunworth & Co., Brooklyn, New York, 1906; reprint 1994).

———. *Lee's Adjutant: The Wartime Letters of Colonel Walter Herron Taylor, 1862–1865* (ed. R. Lockwood Tower, 343 pp., University of South Carolina Press, Columbia, South Carolina, 1995).

Thomas, Emory M. *Bold Dragoon: The Life of J. E. B. Stuart* (354 pp., Harper & Row, New York, 1986).

———. *Robert E. Lee: A Biography* (472 pp., W. W. Norton and Co., New York, 1995).

Toplin, Robert Brent, ed. *Ken Burns's Civil War: Historians Respond* (197 pp., Oxford University Press, New York, 1996).

U.S. War Department. *The War of the Rebellion: A Compilation of the Official Records of the Union and Confederate Armies* (70 vols. in 128 serials, 138,579 pp., U.S. Government Printing Office, Washington, D.C., 1880–1901).

Vandiver, Frank E. *Rebel Brass: The Confederate Command System* (143 pp., Louisiana State University Press, Baton Rouge, Louisiana, 1956).

Virkus, Frederick A. *The Abridged Compendium of American Genealogy* (7 vols., F. A. Virkus, Chicago, 1925–1942; reprint 1987).

Warner, Ezra J. *Generals in Gray: Lives of the Confederate Commanders* (420 pp., Louisiana State University Press, Baton Rouge, Louisiana, 1959).

Welsh, Jack D. *Medical Histories of Confederate Generals* (297 pp., Kent State University Press, Kent, Ohio, 1995).

Wert, Jeffry D. *General James Longstreet, the Confederacy's Most Controversial Soldier: A Biography* (508 pp., Simon and Schuster, New York, 1993).

Wise, John Sergeant. *The End of an Era* (474 pp., Houghton and Mifflin Co., Boston, 1902).

Wolseley, Garnet Joseph, Viscount. *The American Civil War: An English View* (ed. James A. Rawley, 230 pp., A

Index

Note: Page numbers in *italics* indicate illustrations and captions.